HOW ASTOUNDING THE REVELATION

"what manner" - what wonder? Father's love is so unearthly, it's
of this world. It defies human understanding.

OUR PLACE - bestowed upon us - Selected by the Father
LOVE (agape) - undeserved, unselfish, unequaled

OUR PERCEPTION - the world does not know us... it
"to know" - means to know by experience. The
didn't know Christ when He was here
rejects Christians because it has
[ex] See S. Brown notes - Still Smart Alec

OUR PROMISE - "we shall be like Him" - plus
It has told us what we are, and now be
. It will be"
. I PROMISES - I THOUGHT I COULD
backed) all smiling, she
or seen her in a
at Glorieta describing Fa

[ex] Ron Dunn: unanswered prayer

- But didn't God promise to hear our
decisions, lead our lives, show us to
- The Bible is full of such promises
Ps 86:7 - "in the day of my trouble
And you will answer me.
Jer. 29:12 - "call upon me and come
and I will listen to you
Matthew 7:7 - "ask and it will be
seek... we will find
knock, it will be

- Am I the only one, or do you join in
why God didn't make some definitive res
* When we didn't get the clear word
with aging parent with Alzheimer's
* When we

Stop all you are doing and start reading *Son of a Gunn*. Jim henry has been my pastor and friend for many years. His story is compelling and significant.

—Pat Williams
Orlando Magic, Senior Vice President, Author of *Humility*

Jim Henry's story is a testimony of one of the best men and pastors I've known. You will laugh and cry and give thanks to God for this man whose life has touched so many for Christ and His Kingdom. I am so glad my friend Jim has opened his heart to us and shared his lifetime journey with Jesus.

—Dr. Jack Graham
Pastor, Prestonwood Baptist Church

Jim Henry has written an inspiring memoir of his life as a devoted servant of God. It has been my privilege to know him since 1986 when I was coach of The Orlando Renegades in the United States Football League and Jim was a chaplain to the team.

—Lee Corso
ESPN College Football Analyst

I'm glad my friend Jim Henry has written *Son of a Gunn*. In it Jim tells his story well and regales us with wit and wisdom that offer valuable lessons for young preachers, helpful insights for seasoned veterans of the pulpit, and engaging stories for everyone.

—Bob Russell
Retired Senior Minister, Southeast Christian Church

What I love most about *Son of a Gunn* is its realness. Jim Henry reminds us what a life well lived looks like: humble, loyal, and persevering. It's sure to inspire and delight you.

—Dan T. Cathy
Chairman & CEO, Chick-fil-A

You will love the book written by a great man of compassion. As I read it I was reminded of my boyhood days. Like Jim Henry, I grew up beginning in the '30s when America was a God-fearing nation. We were so relaxed during this time, even though we had to endure World War II.

Did you like the books or movies based on *Huckleberry Finn* and *Adventures of Tom Sawyer*? If so, you'll enjoy *Son of a Gunn*. It is written in a way everyone will enjoy it!

—BOBBY BOWDEN
Former Head Football Coach, Florida State University

This book is a remarkable example of what the Lord did for a young Tennessean boy: blessing him with limitless scope of influence and the opportunity to change innumerable hearts. I consider it a privilege to call Jim my friend for over thirty-five years.

—DON DIZNEY
Chairman/CEO, United Medical Group

A powerful, must-read story! Recounting his humble beginnings, Jim Henry chronicles his life with laughs, tears, and much humility...as he served as the senior pastor of one of America's mega churches, president of the Southern Baptist Convention, and continued more than a decade of service after what many would consider retirement.

—JOHN BOZARD
President, Orlando Health, Inc.

Jim Henry is known as a minister's minister. He has a grasp of the truth he preaches without reservation. His life is a reflection of the Jesus he serves. I am privileged to commend his new book to you. Well done, Jim, and may the Gospel you speak of go to the four corners of the earth.

—J.C. WATTS, JR.
President & CEO, Feed The Children

SON OF A
GUNN

SON OF A GUNN

GUNN

WHERE A JOURNEY OF FAITH CAN LEAD

JIM HENRY

Son of a Gunn—Where a Journey of Faith Can Lead
by Jim Henry

Published by HigherLife Development Services, Inc.
PO Box 623307
Oviedo, Florida 32762
(407) 563-4806
www.ahigherlife.com

Unless otherwise noted, Scripture quotations are from the Holy Bible, New International Version, copyright © 2011 by Zondervan Publishing Company.

ISBN 13: 978-1939183927
ISBN-10: 1939183928

Cover Design: Dee DeLoy

First Edition
10 11 12 13 — 9 8 7 6 5 4 3 2 1
Printed in the United States of America

This book is dedicated to my Lord Jesus Christ,

who, by His grace and sacrifice,

made this son of a Gunn into a son of God.

CONTENTS

Foreword xi

Preface with Acknowledgments xiii

Chapter 1   Son of a Gunn 1

Chapter 2   A Little Boy and a Big War 13

Chapter 3   The Sawdust Trail 23

Chapter 4   The Worst Butterfinger I Ever Ate 33

Chapter 5   Mr. Foster Wants to See You 37

Chapter 6   Belle of the Blue 47

Chapter 7   School Bells, Wedding Bells, and Church Bells 53

Chapter 8   I Move We Fire the Preacher 65

Chapter 9   We're Going to Hollywood 77

Chapter 10   Music City, Here We Come 85

Chapter 11   Buckle Your Seat Belt 93

Chapter 12   We're Going to Disney 109

Chapter 13   The Better Plan 117

Chapter 14   No One Else Believes It Either 129

Chapter 15   White House Calling 145

Chapter 16   Standing, Sitting, Praying... In History 155

Chapter 17   Air Force Two 173

Chapter 18   When All of Israel Was Silent 183

Chapter 19   A Dallas Parade and "Bush 43" 191

Chapter 20:   Al Gore and the Burning of Black Churches 197

Chapter 21   Madeleine Albright and Religious Persecution 203

Chapter 22   Born-Again Peanut Farmer and Peacemaker 211

Chapter 23   We're Not Going to Disney 219

Chapter 24   When Tiger Came to Church 225

Chapter 25   Backroom Politics, Rose Garden, and
National Treasure 245

Chapter 26   Next 245

Chapter 27   I Forgot to Remember 255

Chapter 28   The Best Is Yet 267

FOREWORD

Jim Henry is truly one of the most loveable men of God I have ever known! From the first time we met in a classroom at New Orleans Baptist Theological Seminary in 1960 until today, he has remained one of my dearest and closest friends.

I have had the joy of conducting revival meetings in every church he has pastored—as a matter of fact, so many times I have now lost count. And on every occasion my admiration and respect for him was only strengthened.

When I think of Jim, I am reminded of what C. I. Schofield said in evaluating the ministry of the powerfully used evangelist, D. L. Moody. He pointed out that Moody passed the two tests many preachers so often face: the discouragement of obscurity and the danger of prominence. He wisely observed that Moody was faithful to God as a shoe salesman when very few knew him; and he was also true to God after he became a renowned evangelist and thousands knew him.

With great joy I have watched that same scenario unfold in the life and ministry of Jim Henry. When he began his ministry in obscurity, serving a small church in rural Mississippi, I never saw him whine or heard him complain. Many years later when he walked across the platform as the newly elected president of the Southern Baptist Convention, I never saw him strut nor heard him brag!

To those of us who know and love him, he has just always remained "Brother Jim"—a man greatly used of God, but who has been wise enough never to have boasted about it!

For the hundreds of friends who admire and respect him, this book will be a treasured keepsake. For those who may not have had the privilege of knowing him, it will be a close and encouraging inside look at a truly unique and gifted servant of God.

And in keeping with the clever title he has chosen for these memoirs, about all I know to say in conclusion is this: *"That Son of a Gunn"* sure has written a delightful book!

Evangelist Junior Hill
Hartselle, Alabama

PREFACE WITH ACKNOWLEDGMENTS

READ THAT C.S. LEWIS reported that he came into the Kingdom of God kicking and screaming. That's how I was about writing my life story. I was reluctant for a number of reasons. I struggled with the thoughts: *Who would be interested? When would I find the time to write a book? Would writing my memoirs seem self-serving? Did I want to dig through the volumes of journals and memorabilia to pull out the information? Who and what would I include? Could I handle the gauntlet of emotions I knew I would resurrect as I recounted the joyful, the sorrowful, the bitter, and the sweet moments of my life journey?*

So, I put the writing of my story on hold for at least twenty years. However, during that time, I had three people who kept prodding me to do it. My mother often said to me, "You ought to do it for the family's sake, if for no other reason. If you don't, they will not be able to trace the footsteps of your life. You've had some interesting opportunities and experiences." (Sounds like a mom, doesn't it?) The second person who encouraged me to get this project done was Georgia Long—long-time friend, church member, owner of a wonderful Christian bookstore in Orlando, encourager to pastors, and a generous being to a fault. She has given me hundreds of books over the years. Nearly every time I saw her, Georgia asked, "When are you going to write this book? Don't wait until you're too old." The third person who greatly encouraged me to write my story was Junior Hill—friend since seminary days, pastor, evangelist, and author. Having gone through the process of writing his own memoir, Junior told me it would be worth all that it would take to tackle this project, if only on a personal level as I would see the hand of God in my life. It would increase my love and gratitude for my Lord Jesus. He was right. I have laughed, teared up, shouted praises, prayed gratefully, and looked over my shoulder: awed at the grace and goodness of my Father.

One of my greatest concerns is that I did not want my writing this book to be seen in any way as my being proud or boastful. By the Lord's providence and sovereignty, He put me in situations—some in an historical context—that included national and international leaders and personalities, as well as world-shaping events—that gave me an inside view that I never dreamed I would have. Being a history major in college and having regularly journaled for fifty years, I had made notes from observations—some large and some small—that I think will be interesting to the reader.

It was also a concern of mine that I not be hurtful to anyone. I have sought to be honest in my reporting. I felt some apprehension that my writing about some events, people, or institutions might come across in an unfavorable way. My intention is not to do that. I pray that I have succeeded. For those reasons, I have left out some of the things I saw, heard, and journaled.

Another concern was leaving out people and events that have shaped my life. I have tried to include many; however, there are countless others that merited inclusion. I just ran out of space. Even as I wrapped up my work, another person or experience would pop up. As I recalled these individuals or events I would murmur to myself, "Why didn't I get them or that worked into my story?" So, if you read this book and do not find your name, know that you are written in the Lord's Book of Remembrance (see Malachi 3:16) and I am eternally grateful for the positive example, prayers, and love you have poured into my life.

It is my fervent prayer that our treasured children—Kitty, Betsy, and Jimmy; our wonderful sons-in-law—Danny and Stan; my superb daughter-in-law, Tammy; our cherished grandchildren—Caleb, Seth, Trey, Will, and Asa; our great-grandson, Shiloh; and our great-granddaughter, Belle, will be encouraged to love Jesus and be faithful to Him all their days. We deeply love you. There is no way on this side of eternity you can begin to know the great joy each of you have brought into our lives.

To the Friday morning 6:30 a.m. "band of brothers" from Two Rivers and First Baptist Orlando who counseled, corrected, cajoled, occasionally complained, and comforted me for nearly fifty years: You are unforgettably appreciated, loved, and cherished.

To my Jeanette—beautiful wife; wise, godly life partner for fifty-six years: thank you. Your quiet strength, sanctified common sense, unselfish love, and deep faith have been a constant source of joy. I love you forever.

To those who have walked with me and come behind me—pastors, staff, men and women of faith: may your life be strengthened in your faith journey. People like you have powerfully touched my life.

To ministry teammates, deacons, lay leaders, and assistants—Ann, Dot, Marty, Sandra, Sandi, and Suzie: thanks for your patience, perseverance, and protection of my time and study.

To Laura; Lou and Marion Daniele; Kathy Siegel; and Dawn Harris, whose compassion, care, and commitment to Jeanette are magnificent displays of the heart of God: thank you for enabling me to keep on keeping on at home and beyond.

To Kris and Robin DenBensten, who have blessed so many through their faithful living and consistent witness for our Lord—as individuals and as a family—through times of crisis, trials, and blessing: thank you for your gracious encouragement and magnanimous help with this project.

To our talented cover designer, Dee DeLoy, thank you for your excellent work on this project. I am so appreciative of your going above and beyond!

To Marilyn Jeffcoat—who has written, edited, and encouraged my writing experiences for over twenty years; and without whose expertise my experiences, preaching, and dreams would have never come to life: thanks!

Jason Allen, the President of Midwestern Baptist Theological Seminary in Kansas City, Missouri, is a lover of biographies. He said that a great biography has at least four ingredients: a celebrated person, a colorful personality, consequential times, and clear writing. As I reflect on his criteria, I know it passes the test of "consequential times." I pray it is "clearly written." I am not a "celebrated person" or "colorful personality," just an ordinary guy who has experienced what God can do when he places his life in the hands of his gracious and sovereign Savior. I pray that as you peruse these words and pictures, they will point you to my magnificent Lord and Savior, Jesus Christ, who took this kid who had little to offer Him and gave him a life he could never dreamed possible in his wildest imagination. Throughout the years of my life and ministry, my Almighty God has proved His Word: *"To Him who is able to do immeasurably more than all we ask or imagine, according to His power that is at work within us, to Him be glory in the church and in Christ Jesus throughout all generations, forever and ever!"* (Ephesians 3:20-21).

As King David reflected on his life and God's goodness and faithfulness, he said, *"Who am I, O Sovereign Lord, and what is my family, that You have brought me this far?"* (2 Samuel 7:18b). I am no king. I am no David. However, David, son of Jesse, and I, son of Gunn, share mutual heartbeats of awe, wonder, and gratitude for our great Lord who chose to write His" glory story" in our hearts and lives.

CHAPTER ONE

SON OF A GUNN

TWO SISTERS—BOTH NEVER MARRIED and retired school teachers— lived two doors down from our little duplex in Nashville.[1] Sometimes they were unhappy about the noise we neighborhood boys made with our shouting and lively play. Often they would stare out the door and eventually scold us. My brother, Joe, and I finally decided that there had to be some kind of retaliation from us—the innocents—for such personal attacks.

Filling up a couple of buckets with dirt and then properly mixing the dirt with just the right amount of water allowed us to make awesome and cohesive projectiles. We waited and watched for them to leave their home. When they puttered away in their little car on a shopping trip, we took up our battle stations at the side of their clean, white-side-walled house and began our aerial assault. We howled with delight as we bombarded their home and watched as our mud balls splattered and burst... some sticking to the walls and others slowly oozing down to the ground. Soon their formerly tidy house looked like a kid covered in brown freckles.

---

[1] That duplex is now a part of the Vanderbilt University campus.

With our fearless, stealth attack behind us, Joe and I went about our business. Soon thereafter, we seemingly innocent boys watched the two sisters survey our effective bombardment. They must have had assistance from the F.B.I. or the C.I.A. as they quickly tracked us down, the culprits of this supposedly covert mission.

Quickly summoned by an irate mother and two ruffled, very upset school teachers, my brother and I were forced to cough up a confession. Of course, our apparel—muddy shoes and clothing—was a dead give-away of our dastardly deed! We were immediately ordered to pay the penalty of our crime: clean it up and apologize. This we agreed to do, as we well knew that if we refused, there would be far greater retribution for us to pay.

As those little ladies marched off in smug indignation, I thought I heard one of them remark, "That serves them right, those little sons of a gun!" And, they were right about that! My brother and I are the sons of a Gunn. My paternal grandmother was Ruth Yates Gunn, a descendant of a well-known, middle-Tennessee family, who were immigrants from Scotland. Hence, I have always taken quiet pride in being "a son of a Gunn."

We have been able to trace our family's history back to James Gunn, who settled in an area of beautiful farmland near the town of Springfield, in Robertson County, Tennessee, in 1811. Springfield is located less than an hour's drive from Nashville, the state capital. The Red River[2] graces that part of the state. The following spring—in 1812—his brother, Thomas, followed. No time was lost in building a meetinghouse, a gospel-preaching station, near his dwelling. Shortly afterwards, a camp meeting was held. Camp meetings were a staple of that era. They were the

---

[2] I grew up enjoying fishing and swimming in that river, as well as watching my Uncle Bascom reach under its slow-moving waters to grab a catfish with his hand!

forerunners of the revival meetings of more recent decades. These camp meetings originated in England and Scotland, and were distinguished by fervent, evangelistic preaching. In *History of Methodism in Tennessee* it says that "great good was done and the cause of Christ was advanced"[3] through the ministry of the Gunn brothers.

In their fervor to spread the Good News of Jesus Christ, the Gunn brothers regularly traveled from twenty to fifty miles in a day, in every direction—frequently going twenty miles and back the same day and night. In their commitment to reach as many as possible with the gospel message, this pair of itinerant, frontier preachers wore out horses and saddles—and did so without any compensation or travel expenses. I have no doubt that not only hundreds, but thousands, were brought to a knowledge of the truth through their impassioned ministry. They traveled throughout Tennessee—into Sumner, Davidson, Dixon, Montgomery counties, and in every neighborhood in my ancestral home county, Robertson County—as well as into Simpson, Logan, Todd and Christian counties in Kentucky.

The Brothers Gunn used the team approach in revivals. Thomas generally led off. It is written of Thomas that "he was well versed in Scripture, apt to reprove any misconduct, and always spoke in boldness. He suffered no false doctrine to go unnoticed and was ready in debate. He was death upon whiskey, drinking, tobacco chewing, and coffee drinking."[4] In his account of Thomas's preaching, John McFerrin wrote: "He was one of the most powerful men I ever heard. When he no longer could stand to preach, he

---

[3] McFerrin, John B. *History of Methodism in Tennessee.* Nashville: Pub. House of the M.E. Church, South, 1886.

[4] Ibid.

would sit and preach for an hour or more, with zeal and energy, and his voice as clear as a new bell. He might be heard one mile in distance."[5]

James was described as "soft, mild, deliberate, and spoke with tenderness and great affection, and at all revival meetings would get hold of the feelings of his hearers. Thomas, having laid the foundation, James with affection, invited all to come to Jesus. Such was his pathos, that none but the hardest sinner could resist. At the great meetings, Thomas led off and James followed, to heal the wounds that Thomas had inflicted."[6]

James continued preaching until September, 1848. Confined to bed before his death, he called for a fellow pastor to come to see him. He was asked, "You are not afraid to die, are you?"

"No, no, that is not the reason. But I love my family. I am glad when my children and my friends come to see me. But if it be God's will, I shall go. I have not a fear or doubt. My sky is clear. My soul is happy at the thought I am to be free from sickness and suffering."

Two weeks later James lost his speech and became motionless, yet sensible. When his brother, Thomas, would come in and ask him if he was happy, James's countenance would provide the answer. The evening he went to be with the Lord, his brother took him by the hand and pointed upward. With his countenance beaming with joy, James feebly responded, "Yes, yes!" He then gradually slipped away into the arms of Jesus.[7]

When I was introduced to some of my family history through *The History of Methodism in Tennessee* by John B. McFerrin, I discovered that both of those preachers were six feet tall or taller, muscular, and well-proportioned.

---

[5] Ibid.

[6] Ibid.

[7] Ibid.

While I missed out on that part, I was called by the same Lord who called them to preach.

Looking deeper into my lineage, I found records of a Henry serving with General George Washington. Another relative, Sterling Gunn, assisted in placing and firing the first gun upon the British at Yorktown.

The Henry and Gunn families were part of the Robertson County Mounted Volunteers in the Second Seminole War (1836). According to the newspaper *National Banner*, "Their heroic blood was roused at the sufferings of our neighbors; the need of the presence of our gallant Tennesseans to protect the women and children, farms and towns of their own country from the tomahawk, the scalping knife, and the fire brand of the merciless savage."[8]

In my reading about the Gunn clan of Scotland, I found out they were a small clan that was noted for their fighting ways. No wonder that when the Civil War broke out, they were among some of the first to sign up. One of the Gunns, Private John Gunn of the E. Company, Tennessee Confederate Volunteers, was captured by General Ulysses Grant's army at Fort Donelson, Tennessee, in February, 1862. He died in a Union prison camp. At the site where he was imprisoned—now Oak Woods Cemetery in Chicago, Illinois—John Gunn's name is inscribed on the Confederate Mound Monument, which commemorates the four thousand who died at that prison.

Private Miles Gunn of the 11th Tennessee Confederate Infantry was captured at the fierce battle of Franklin, Tennessee, on December 17, 1864. He died in May of 1865 in Richmond, Virginia, as the terrible conflict drew to a close. The sad conflict left a scar on the nation in many ways. In fact, on the family farm in Robertson County, a spike is firmly embedded in a

---

[8] *National Banner. Nashville, 1836.*

huge tree. According to family lore, that spike was used by Confederates to climb and spy out any invading Union trooper. The spike remains as a visible memorial of the war that came through our backyard.

On the paternal side, I have not done as much research, though I know we can trace back to Patrick Henry and Virginia roots. Both sides of my father's family are immigrants from Scotland and England and on my mother's side from Holland.

Most of my earlier memories tend to be rural, though I was born in the city of Nashville. I have read, as well as listened with fascination, of family legends, tales, and probably, some myths. My great-great-grandfather on the Gunn side of the family was John L. Yates, who built the first bridge in Robertson County, Tennessee, to assist in hauling tobacco to market. The foundations of that bridge remain and can be seen today. He is also remembered for riding a white horse and carrying a pistol at his side. Apparently, he carried large sums of money on his person. On his deathbed, he was visited by a lady neighbor, who was wearing a large dress. He died shortly after her visit. When the family looked for his money, which he kept by his pillow, it had disappeared. This led to the suspicion that the lady visitor had made a visit that "paid off" for her!

My mother, Kathryn, is the older of two children born to Marshall and Hazel (Pope) Fisher, who were farmers. On their fertile fifty-acre farm, I saw the fruit of their hard work: apple, pear, peach, and cherry trees. The garden was filled with an abundance of tomatoes, potatoes, green beans, lettuce, beets, and turnip greens.

Tobacco was the main source of their income. Visits to the family farm would mean working in the fields, sometimes picking off ugly, green tobacco worms that I enjoyed throwing at my brother, and vice versa. Getting twenty-five cents for each quart we picked, my brother and I also picked strawberries. Picking was sometimes interrupted when an overly ripe berry became a missile hurled at my innocent and unsuspecting brother.

I have watched my grandmother churn butter in a wooden churn, as well as fix a table full of country-fresh, soul food to feed the neighbors when they came to assist in hog-killing time in November. Momee, as we affectionately called her, cooked on a wood-burning stove, drew water from the well or barrels that caught the rain water. I can still taste her rhubarb and sweet potato pies.

Granddaddy Fisher was a quiet, gentle man with a great sense of humor—a trait both granddads carried. Sometimes, he would sleep in the attic with my brother and me. He would pretend to snore and occasionally make the sound of passing gas that always caused an eruption of giggles from us. When it rained, the patter of raindrops on the tin roof became a rhapsody that soon lulled us to sleep.

Indoor plumbing was nonexistent on my grandparents' farm. Therefore, the outhouse was a familiar place of relief for us. Toilet paper was a rarity, so catalogs from Sears-Roebuck or Montgomery Ward, as well as newspapers, corncobs, and leaves. One of my favorite ways to pick on my little brother was to catch him in the outhouse, take a long tobacco stick, slip in the back of the two-seater, and prod him on his bottom. Of course, this produced howls of protests from my brother followed by his quick exit to tell Momee of the cruel deed, and my prompt denial of such ridiculous behavior.

We were exposed to mules, horses, pigs, sheep, goats, and chickens. Meat was provided from smokehouses where bacon, ham, and other meats were cured and fetched whenever needed. Dogs and cats were also a part of farm life. We experienced our first touches with death when a favorite pet disappeared or was hit by a passing automobile. I can still recall my Momee catching a chicken, wringing its neck, and watching it flop around until dead. That became dinner and the delicious smell of fried chicken quelled any remorse of the untimely and uncomely death of this provision.

Church was a normal part of my grandparents' lifestyle, especially on the Fisher side of my family. We prepared for church. Clothes were washed and ironed. Filled with scalding hot water heated on the woodstove and cooled enough to step into, a big tub was where we were scrubbed clean. Neither grandparents owned a car, so we walked or were picked up by kind neighbors.

Momee Fisher was an excellent and much beloved teacher of the Bible, who taught generations of girls and women. When I preached in Tennessee or even other places, it was not uncommon to have ladies approach me and say, "Mrs. Hazel was my teacher at Hopewell."

When we had to walk to church, we had to cross a small creek. Momee always dressed up for church, and this included wearing stockings. When we got to the creek, she would take off her shoes and stockings, wade across, dry off with a towel, don her stockings and shoes, then continue the trek to church.

While I loved all my grandparents, Momee had the greatest spiritual impact on my life. The following letter that underscores her wisdom and godliness was passed on to me by my mother. It was a letter written to Gladys and Dick Pope and dated November 9, 1953:

> *You said one thing that has stayed with me, and I have thought of it each day. And that was your pastor couldn't preach so well, and you didn't guess you would go so much. Now I know how to sympathize with you. We have had one just like that. But he was a good man, a good pastor, but not so good preacher. But we loved him, and he was wonderful when Papa went away. No pastor could have done more unless he preached a better funeral, and I was pleased with it; thought it was good. So don't stay away from church, but go and support him all you can, especially*

pray for him. After all, he needs your cooperation more than a stronger preacher, and you know the Lord doesn't always call eloquent speakers to speak for Him. Moses was a good example. His excuse was, he couldn't talk and the Lord asked him, "Who made man's mouth?" (Exodus 4:10-11), and he did not excuse him. And, too, the Lord said, "Blessed are they that the Lord finds being faithful when he comes." And by going, you will help somebody else to go; maybe your children and grandchildren. Our young people and children can't be kept in services too much, for the devil is bidding so high for their souls. They have a hard road to travel to keep from yielding to his temptations. Thanks be to God, he has promised if "we will train them up in the way they should go when they are older they will not depart." Proverbs 22:6. So, go to church every time it is possible and you will get a blessing.

Lots of love,

Hazel and Mart

Momee was stricken with cancer the year I got married. She was very excited about our big day, and had picked out the dress she planned to wear. However, because of her weakening condition, she was unable to attend our wedding. I wish that godly woman, who so powerfully had influenced me, could have shared that milestone with us, but it was not to be. Eight months later, in August, 1960, she died at home, and went to be with Jesus. By her bed, they found her Bible with a tissue inserted to mark John 14:1: *"In my Father's house are many mansions. I have gone to prepare a place for you...."* All the money in the world could not purchase such a blessed spiritual heritage!

My mother was born April 3, 1918. She was named Catherine, but one day in grade school she decided she did not like the spelling of her name and changed it to Kathryn, which it remains to this day. Mom was (and is) a beauty. I just recently found out she was runner-up in the Robertson County beauty contest. Of that, Mom explains that she was the only country girl in the contest, the rest of them being from the county seat of Springfield: "I may have won, except there could have been some politics involved. You couldn't let a county girl defeat all the city beauties." She laughed when she told me. However, knowing people as I know people, I am guessing she may have been right.

Her parents paid a county school bus driver extra money to drive out of his way to pick up Mom as their farm was beyond his route. It paid off. There in Orlinda High School she met those who became lifetime, cherished friends, including a certain wavy, black-haired, young man named James William Henry. She saw him on the football field and learned more about him. She decided she did not want to date him. However, my dad persisted and finally persuaded her to give him a chance. She did. The Henry magic worked! Two years later they became one. Mom and Dad were married in the home of Pastor Tommy Meador.

The newlyweds set up housekeeping in Nashville, Tennessee, where Dad worked at H. G. Hill grocery store. Dad's oldest brother, Bascom (from whom I got my middle name), was also employed there. Dad made $12.00 a week. When I was born, he laughingly shared his recollection of his manager's calling him in to congratulate him and saying, "Since you now have added financial responsibilities with that son, I'm going to give you a raise: 50 cents a week." I am amused to think that on October 1, 1937, at Baptist Hospital in Nashville, Tennessee, my life began, and I was worth fifty cents!

With All My Heart

To My Family:

This book's for you. Each of you have made my life immeasurably richer—not so much in terms of that which is material, but in the very substantial measures of the sheer joy of finding and living the abundant life that each of you has brought to my life and our entire family. The memories we share are priceless. As you know me to the core, the fact that I am sharing with others that I am truly a "Son of a Gunn" won't surprise any of you! There are no words to adequately express my deep love for each of you that is grounded in God's great, unconditional love for us as His Family.

CHAPTER TWO

A LITTLE BOY AND A BIG WAR

NOT LONG AFTER I came into the world, World War II began. Our family moved into a housing project called Vine Hill. Dad worked at the Vultee, which produced fighter planes for the war effort. He often rode the bus to work. While doing so, he became friends with a young man named Frank Clement. Dad told me that this young man would shake hands with passengers and say, "I'm Frank Clement. I will run for governor someday. Please, remember me, and vote for me."

At age of 32—the youngest person to be elected governor in state history—Frank Clement became governor of Tennessee in 1952. My family campaigned vigorously for him. I wore "Frank Clement for Governor" T-shirts; handed out bumper stickers and pamphlets; and attended campaign rallies. On election night, our family went to the Hermitage Hotel in downtown Nashville to watch the returns roll in and joined the growing excitement as his election became apparent.

While I was a student at Georgetown College, Governor Clement addressed the school in chapel. Afterward, he invited me to fly to Nashville with him. I threw some things in my battered suitcase with a big "G" on the side of it. Off I went to experience my first flight. My mom was embarrassed that I had flown with the governor with that beat-up suitcase; however, she quickly forgave me!

A couple of years earlier, I had another unforgettable experience with Governor Clement. My cousin, Jimmy Hendley, and I were hitchhiking to Hopewell Baptist Church for their 100th anniversary celebration. We had stayed in Nashville through Saturday to attend a high school function, and prevailed upon our parents to let us wait until Sunday morning to go to Hopewell. My parents and younger brother had gone out a day earlier. Jimmy's dad took us to the city limits and dropped us off on the highway to Springfield. Praying for a kind driver to pick us up as we did not want to miss the big day at the celebration and dinner on the grounds, the two of us stuck out our thumbs.

Traffic was sparse that early morning when suddenly we spotted a big black Oldsmobile barreling down the road. We put on our biggest smiles, stood straight and tall, and hoped for the best. Then we spotted something different about the car: It had antennas jutting up from its rear fenders. About the time it came by us, we saw the big hat of a Tennessee State Highway trooper driving the new Olds with a passenger in the back seat. Scared we could be given a ticket for hitchhiking, my cousin and I got nervous.

Our anxiety was heightened when the car brakes began to squeal as the trooper braked to a complete stop. Putting our fear aside, we ran toward the car. As we approached, I saw a big number "1" on the license plate. I thought this guy must have stood in line all night to get the prestige of having that number "1" on his license plate! Rolling down the window, the trooper asked, "Where are you boys headed?"

"We're going to church near Springfield," I replied. "We are trying to get there for the hundredth anniversary of our church." (I thought that might spark compassion on the trooper's part, and he would let us off the hook.)

The voice in the back of the Olds spoke up, "Get in, boys! I happen to be going there myself."

We did not hesitate as we piled in the back seat. Lo and behold, there was my governor and friend, Frank G. Clement! He shook our hands, welcomed us aboard, and informed us he was the preacher at Hopewell that day. (The governor and his family also had roots in that area.) We were running late, so the trooper put the hammer down on that black Oldsmobile. Off we roared toward the church. As we rounded the curves on the gravel road, it dawned on me that my parents, grandparents, family, and friends would be there when we drove up. The sheer joy of the anticipation at their shock was more than I could contain.

Our delegation arrived in a cloud of dust and gravel, as our impressive ride screeched to a halt. Whisking back and forth like a fish frantically trying to get off the hook, the long attachment of the governor's communication apparatus seemed to summon the large crowd that had gathered outside. Everyone wanted to see the arrival of their special guest, who by now was a rising star in national politics. As soon as I could, I stepped out, just in time to see the awe and shock of my brother, family, and friends; and said, "Thank you, Governor. Sure appreciated the lift." (This unbelievable event propelled me to immediate hero status to my buddies who followed me around and wanted to know how I managed such a feat.)[9]

The World War II years brought memories of paper drives and collection of metal that we brought to school to assist the war effort. I remember air raid drills in which all lights were turned off, blinds were closed, curtains drawn, and candles lit. Men in military uniforms were everywhere. It was not unusual to see military convoys rumbling through the streets. I clearly remember one day in particular: I came in from playing and saw my mother, who was standing at the ironing board, weeping. "Momma, what's wrong?" I asked.

"President Roosevelt just died," she replied somberly.

The war affected us in other ways. My mother's brother, Jack, went into the Navy. He was aboard a ship that was engaged in the middle of the struggle with the Japanese for control of the Pacific. Uncle Jack never talked about it until recently. One day over lunch, I was able to get him to open up. He was a mere seventeen-year-old watching the horrors of war unfold before him: kamikaze planes just missing his ship and coming so close he could see the faces of the doomed pilots; bodies floating in the water and ships on fire; guns firing in an incessant staccato; the shouting of orders; working eight hours, sleeping four. When most boys at seventeen were playing ball, dating, dancing and driving, he and the "greatest generation" were fighting

---

[9] In later years, Governor Clement's son, Bob, became a U.S. Congressman representing Tennessee 5th District for fifteen years (1988-2003). I was greatly privileged when Bob hosted a reception in Washington, D.C., in my honor after I became the president of the Southern Baptist Convention. There I met many U.S. representatives and several senators. Later in that evening, we attended a Johnny Cash concert. While there, I had the privilege of meeting and praying with this music legend, who was fighting a cold. Singing some of his great hits and closing with a clear-cut testimony for Christ followed by a song he had written about the blood of Christ, he performed to a packed house.

for liberty and freedom. Uncle Jack and those valiant men and women are real heroes. I call him on Memorial Day and Veteran's Day to say thanks, which is so little to do for any of those who gave so much.

In 1944, Dad was transferred to Allentown, Pennsylvania, to build war planes at plants there. We took the train to our new hometown that was filled with men in Army uniforms. (I recall their whistling at my beautiful mother.) The people talked differently in that part of the country. I remember wondering if they might be the Germans. Along those lines, I was put in the "slow class" at my new school, Woodrow Wilson Elementary School, because I was from the South. Talk about bias and profiling! This was rectified later when they moved me up to the appropriate grade level.

The draft notice came for my father to report for induction into the military. The long war had reduced the pool of resources. However, before Dad left us, President Harry Truman had the courage to decide to drop the secret weapon—the atomic bomb—on Hiroshima and Nagasaki which ended the war and the bloodletting.

We returned to Tennessee, but housing was unavailable because of the thousands of returning veterans. Living with my grandparents, I attended Orlinda Elementary School for a brief time. My class had two classes in the same room.

In my class two cute girls—Kay and Mary Eleanor—caught my eye. As Valentine's Day approached I asked my grandmother Fisher to help me make cards for my friends and something special for Mary Eleanor. My always resourceful grandmother made some divinity candy, found a heart-shaped box in which to place the delicacies, and tied a nice bow on top. My dad asked me who it was for, and I told him. Dad said, "When you hand it to her say, 'Why don't you give me a big kiss?'"

The next day I told the teacher I had a special gift to deliver and wanted to do it when all the cards had been handed out. I called Mary Eleanor to the front of the room, gave her the candy, and repeated Dad's words verbatim. I don't know who was the most shocked: the teacher or Mary Eleanor! The rest of the story escapes my recollection. However, I don't think I collected on my request.

Life in those days consisted of having foot races with my beloved cousin, Phil, to see who would collect the quarter from my granddaddy Pap, and listening to the old, stand-up radio, which was housed in a huge cabinet. Many afternoons and evenings found us tuned in to *Superman, The Shadow, Suspense Theater, Inner Sanctum, The Great Gildersleeve,* and *Amos and Andy.* Another memorable part of my boyhood was going to Springfield on Saturdays with my Dad, Uncle Lem, Grandad Pap, and cousins to catch the westerns with Roy Rogers, Gene Autry, Lash LaRue, the Lone Ranger, Johnny Mack Brown; cartoons; and serials… all while munching on popcorn and cheering our heroes as they fought against the bad guys.

Sometimes I rode shotgun to deliver mail with my Uncle Marion, who was nicknamed Pharo. He was given that nickname when, in his younger days while in Sunday School class and not paying attention to the teacher's earnest efforts to impart biblical knowledge to a room full of high energy boys, she asked the class, "Who wrote the Ten Commandments?"

One of his buddies nudged the inattentive Marion and whispered, "Pharaoh," which he proudly repeated. From that point on, he was "Pharo," (kids' spelling of Pharaoh).

I have fond recollections that revolve around food. A favorite thing was stopping at country stores for bologna; crackers and cheese (sliced in front of you); and Cokes with peanuts stuffed in to make them fizz. Christmas and Thanksgiving were family reunion times, when we feasted on Mama Ruth's coconut, jam, and caramel cakes, as well as her boiled custard. The big table was laden with every kind of food imaginable. The men ate first, then the children and women. Our prayer was that the men would not eat all the white meat and save a "pulley bone" (the wishbone) for us. Come nightfall, Roman candles, sparklers, and fireworks lit up the night sky. We were left full and happy on those special occasions.

I enjoyed living with my grandparents, yet all too soon a duplex in Nashville opened up in a neighborhood near Vanderbilt University. It consisted of a kitchen, one bedroom, and a living room. There was one bathroom between us and the apartment dwellers on the other side. We learned to knock on the door before barging in. If it was a child our age in the bathroom, and if we knew it, we would knock on the door and say, "Hurry up!" (So much for privacy.)

While living in our new home, I attended Eakin Elementary School, where I listened to the Lord's Prayer played on a Victrola, recited the Pledge of Allegiance, and received a healthy dose of faith and patriotism, (sadly missing in our current America). I enjoyed school, made fairly good grades, and lived in reverent fear and respect of our principal, whom some of the boys called Black Maria[10] when she was out of earshot.

One of my best friends was Buddy Parsons, who by strength and size would double me. We had great times growing up together. Frequently, he would "double-ride" me on his bike as my transportation to school. Buddy grew into a star basketball player at West High School and played on a team that won the state championship, even though the team was most often outsized. Their win to the championship is one of those legendary feats in

---

[10] The origin of this non-racial slur is unknown to me. It predated (by decades) the Marvel Comics fictional villain. It may have been tied to the old slang term for a police paddy wagon used to transport prisoners.

Nashville sports annals. Buddy and I later worked on staff at Ridgecrest Baptist Assembly in North Carolina.[11] He remains a cherished friend and brother in Christ.

Life became a mixture of work and play. I carried paper routes with Walter Biffle, a college student, who later became an executive with Sears-Roebuck. We delivered twice a day. I learned to roll and throw papers on porches with David-like, slingshot ability. I sold Christmas cards to neighbors and employees at the Baptist Sunday School Board (now LifeWay). I also delivered milk, and was paid with all the cottage cheese and chocolate milk I could eat and drink.

Since Vanderbilt University was nearby, I raced to their baseball diamond as soon as the school bell rang. The reason I ran was that the first one there was chosen as the batboy for the visiting team. Payday was a splintered bat or scuffed-up ball, and it opened other doors too: I got a job selling programs, popcorn, and Cokes at Vandy's home games. This guaranteed entrance to the game and some pocket money. This also carried over to my college and seminary days. When Vandy was in town, Scoop Hudgins, who later worked in the SEC Commissioner's office, would get me in to the games to serve as a spotter or work at some other task. He offered to help me get in Vanderbilt when I graduated from high school to work as a manager or assist in the athletic office; however, a deficiency in math and God's other plans, kept me from getting a degree from that great school, but I continue to follow it with an embedded loyalty to this day.

Sometimes we parked cars in our backyard when big games like Alabama, Ole Miss, or Tennessee were played. I would stand on the Natchez Trace[12]

---

[11] Now called Ridgecrest Conference Center.

[12] Reference to an avenue in Nashville.

and shout, "Park here! Park here!" I think we charged one or two dollars for the privilege. This was a pretty good gig, until one Saturday it poured rain and our backyard became a quagmire. My brother, Joe, and I disappeared either to the game or a movie. When we returned, we found our mud-splattered Dad, who had been pushing cars out of their muddy traps. To put it mildly, he was not too happy.

My youth is full of memories of watching Christmas parades with my family; eating Krystal's hamburgers, Varallo's chili, and Charlie Nicken's barbeque (uniquely enjoyed between two corncakes instead of buns); learning to swim at the YMCA; getting vaccinations at the Nashville Public Health Building; surviving the epic "Blizzard of 1951," when the city of Nashville was shut down for days by ice and snow, which we survived by warming food on our gas-fed heater; catching the bus to First Baptist Nashville for Sunday school or being given a ride by the McDowells who owned a big Fraser auto, which was known for its width and big seats.

Dogs have always been a part of our family journey. We adopted a mongrel that wandered into our yard, and gave her the dignified name of Poochie. She was our buddy, on whom we lavished our love and attention. One weekend we went to visit our grandparents in Robertson County. Mom and Dad did not go with us. At the end of our weekend stay, Dad and a neighbor came to bring us home. During the return trip, Dad said, "I've got some bad news for you. Poochie died."

"Where did you bury her?"

"In the backyard," he somberly replied.

I couldn't believe it. I held back the tears. As soon as the car stopped, I raced for the backyard. Sure enough, there was a little mound of dirt, and, I think, a miniature cross made up of small sticks had been placed there by my dad. I began to cry uncontrollably, and ran into the house. My mom was sitting in a big chair in our living room and opened up her arms. She held me, comforted me, stroked my shoulders, and whispered encouragement to me. Though I was getting some size on me and really too big for my mother's lap, I was a little boy with a broken heart who needed Mom's comforting. Mom's love and care well reflected the compassion of my Lord Jesus, who, I found out as life moved on, would be the Eternal Comforter, who *"comforts us in all our troubles"* (2 Corinthians 1:4).

Against cries of protest and pain from being uprooted, the moving van came to our home again when we moved across town to a house that we could call our own—one without an outhouse or shared bathroom! Luxury comes shaped in different packages; and I felt we had moved into the Hyatt Regency.

With All My Heart

To All Military Veterans:

Though you may not be able to comprehend the world events that swirl around you—from local to international—they have a way of shaping your life, both philosophically and practically. Military people became my heroes because early on in life I saw them as protectors. In my childhood, living frugally was a lifestyle—the rationing of food, gas, and other things we take for granted today. These early experiences impact my life to this day. War is a terrible thing, yet sometimes necessary, to thwart oppression and insure freedom. I have found that even in the worst of times, we glean good lessons that benefit us in the long haul. My deep thanks to all who gave some, and to the some who gave all.

CHAPTER THREE

THE SAWDUST TRAIL

AM NOT SURE WHERE our family's old illustrated Bible storybook came from, but it made an indelible impression on my mind. The stories of Daniel in the lion's den; David and Goliath; and Jesus hanging on the cross gripped me. I read and reread them.

My spiritual legacy tree was like many in those days. My mother, as a young girl, had been saved and baptized with her dad at Hopewell Baptist Church. Mom's mother, my grandmother Hazel, was a godly, Spirit-filled Bible teacher. Her mother, my great-grandmother Pope was also a woman of faith. I vaguely remember her. My most memorable time with her was on her deathbed. I stood by her bed and recited Psalm 23, which I had memorized. Because of my young age and short stature, I stood even with the bed on which she was lying. This was my first encounter with the death of a person and I shall never forget it. Looking back, I do not recall seeing evidence of my great-grandfather's being a believer. Tragically, he took a gun and killed himself in the den of my grandmother's home after my great-grandmother's death.

On my father's side, the family had long roots in the Methodist tradition as previously mentioned. They belonged to the local Methodist church in

Orlinda, Tennessee, and are buried in the cemetery by this historic church. I do not recall their being active in the church. Perhaps, they were at an earlier age. My dad and his three older brothers attended the Baptist church. Dad's oldest brother, Bascom, was a godly man, who served many years as the preschool director in the Judson Baptist Church in Nashville. Marion ("Pharo") had a beautiful voice; sang in the choir, as well as at numerous weddings and funerals; and was a faithful member of the Orlinda Baptist Church all of his life. Lem, the next youngest to Dad, was a deacon and a pillar in the Williams Chapel Baptist Church near Orlinda.

My Uncle Lem was married for fifty-six years and never spent one night away from his wife, Wilma. Also, he shared an interesting dream he had with my dad. In it, he dreamed the order of death of the four Henry boys: first, Pharo; then, Bascom; then, Dad; and lastly; Lem. And this is the exact order in which they went to heaven!

Dad, who made a profession of faith as a young man, attended church with us at times. Mom was the rock. I never heard my Dad pray publically or saw him reading the Bible in my growing-up years. I sorely missed having that spiritual mentoring and modeling. My father had his demons to fight, especially alcohol. He stayed sober for weeks, then went on a binge. This proved to be unsettling and embarrassing for us. Not knowing in what condition I would find Dad, I was careful about bringing friends home. I never knew if he would have an accident while driving, or if he would show up at events in which I was participating, or, if he did, what shape he would be in when he arrived.

One day, after he was sobering up from a tough bout with his old adversary, alcohol, I sat down with Dad for what turned into a long talk. At that point in my life, I had been a pastor for nearly a decade and was currently serving as the senior pastor at Two Rivers Baptist Church in Nashville. As I had done so many times with others, I shared the gospel with Dad and asked him if he would like to nail down his relationship with Jesus. He said he did, and then prayed with me. The results? The following is an article I wrote in our church newsletter that spells it out:

With All My Heart

To some people, I'm sure he is a rather ordinary looking man. To see him, you would suppose he was a plain, average, Mr. American citizen (if there's anybody like that anymore). He is average in size; his hair has an attractive salt-and-pepper appearance; and, by nature, he is affable and amiable. He's the kind of man that you see at the ball games, the voting booths, and the local veterinarian's office (as he loves animals). But, the kind face that greets you has experienced some hard knocks in "The University of Life."

He grew up in the country, as the youngest of four boys. He moved to the city with his young bride; went to work for H.G. Hill grocery store for $12.00 per week; and received a fifty-cent raise when his first son was born. He later went to work for a major firm, building airplanes to help win WWII. When the war was over, he moved his family and began working for the state government. Good times brought more income; and materially things were really looking up.

Then, a heart attack… and another one. And a very rare illness involving a streptococcus organism that went into his blood stream and pushed him to the very brink of eternity before the healing hand of God intervened, and the fever and raging illness subsided. Some more years passed, and then a tightening in the throat and a doctor's diagnosis showed cancer of the throat. Surgery followed, and he lost some things; but gratefully, his vocal cords remained intact. He could still communicate with his wife, children, grandchildren, employees, umpires, and referees.

There were other valleys. Dark, ominous, fearful, numbing, bewildering walks down pathways of hurt. But then, the light really broke through one evening. The peace, the love, the understanding came pouring in like a spiritual Niagara Falls. And then there was peace in the valley. For the Living Lord of all the ages had spoken in new terms to His child.

So, the rather ordinary looking man you saw walking down the aisle of our church last Sunday to publicly declare his real commitment to the saviorhood and lordship of Jesus Christ is a rather extraordinary man in my life—that's my dad!

Trusting Him for AD 1971—

Pastor

Dad's life was truly transformed. He read his Bible. He was faithful in Bible class and worship. He was a tither. He gave the blessing before meals. He told me he loved me and kissed me—things he rarely did in my younger years.[13] The Lord, indeed, redeemed the years the locusts had eaten. In April of 1994, Dad collapsed with a heart attack in his Nashville home. Somehow, Mom got him in the car and raced him to the nearby Memorial Hospital, where he struggled to overcome the attack and emphysema. The doctors decided to do surgery. I flew to Nashville to be with him and Mom.

On his way to the operating room, I walked beside the gurney. I asked the nurses if we could pray just before they rolled him to surgery. I held his hand and prayed. When I finished, he announced to all the nurses, attendants,

---

[13] Years later, after reading Gary Smalley's book *The Blessing, I wanted Dad to give me the blessing of a father to a son. He said he would be glad to do so. I knelt down in front of him. He put both hands on my shoulders and said, "I have always loved Jimmy. I know he is a servant and a man of God. Bless him and use Jim for helping lead souls to the Lord…" It was so special. He then gave me a big hug. I would not trade that moment for all the world.*

and family: "This is my son, Jimmy. He is president of the Southern Baptist Convention." Only problem: I wasn't! I had announced my intention to be nominated earlier in the year; however, my good friend, Fred Wolfe, had also announced. I had no idea I would be chosen, but in God's providence, I was. Maybe the Holy Spirit gave Dad a glimpse into tomorrow, because he died on May 22, 1994, a month before I became president of the Southern Baptist Convention.

Dad fought for life; and we did everything to give him a fighting chance. Following a bedside visit, I returned to Orlando. As I was preparing to preach on Sunday, Roxie Mathison, a family friend, was with Mom and Dad as they were preparing to move Dad to another facility for treatment of his failing kidneys. Roxie called me on the phone and said, "Here's your Dad." With a raspy, weak voice, my dad spoke his last earthly words to me: "Jimmy, I love you." Until we reunite in heaven, I will treasure those words.

Attending church "every time the doors were open" was fundamental to the way I was raised. We attended First Baptist Church of Nashville, as well as Hopewell and Orlinda Baptist churches when we lived or visited in the country. God always provided the transportation we needed to get to church every week. As our family did not own a car until my junior year of high school, we would ride the city bus or accept the kindness of church members to get us to church each week.

Through regular church attendance, I did a lot of hymn singing in all of our church meetings. I came to love the great hymns of our faith. While I never intentionally tried to memorize them, their lyrics became ingrained in my heart and mind. To this day, I can sing most by memory, including most of the stanzas... except for the next-to-the-last stanza, which Baptists tend to leave out for some reason. (Maybe to beat the Presbyterians to the restaurants after getting out of church!)

One of my lifetime favorites is "The Old Rugged Cross." I clearly remember listening to my mother play that powerful hymn on the piano in the parlor of her parents' home. It was the only time I ever saw her play the piano; however, it was significant to me as that hymn etched itself into my soul. To this day, it is one of my favorites.

An old-fashioned tent revival—complete with sawdust,[14] fans, and benches—was pivotal in my life. While I was attending one I came under conviction. I asked Mom some questions about what I was feeling and battling inside. I wanted to come to Jesus, but there was a fear in my heart. The process of my surrendering my heart to Christ was coming to its forever life-altering climax.

Soon after on a hot August morning at the Hopewell Baptist Church, as I was sitting next to the aisle, my heart beat so loudly I felt it would jump out of my shirt. On the first verse of the closing hymn of invitation, I walked the aisle and was greeted by Pastor Oscar Lumpkin. (Years later, in Orlando, I had the joy of pastoring him, wife Lorene, and daughter Cindy.) I did not pray "The Sinner's Prayer," or comprehend the Trinity or the virgin birth. Yet, I made the great exchange that morning. My heart was filled with joy. It seemed a heavy load had been lifted off my young heart and mind. I rushed home to my grandmother Momee to tell her what happened.

My desire was to be baptized in the old, concrete baptistry outside the front of the Hopewell Church. I had seen others baptized there in the cold

---

[14] This chapter is entitled "The Sawdust Trail" as it refers to the path of my salvation, as well as others in my family. The sawdust trail was a term from days gone by to refer to the sawdust that covered the floors of the temporary buildings or tents used by itinerant ministers for revival meetings. The sawdust would help hold down and improve the smell of the dust on the dirt floors of these structures. Coming forward during the invitation became known as "hitting the sawdust trail."

water that was pumped from a nearby source. My mom wanted me baptized at First Baptist Nashville. So, on a cold, February night in 1947, my beloved pastor, Dr. W. F. Powell, immersed me in the baptistry in that historic church. Dr. Powell gave me my first big Bible, which he autographed (and which I still own and cherish). I cut a picture of him from the church newsletter, and pasted it beside his name and the Scripture he had given me: *Do your best to present yourself to God as one approved, a workman who does not need to be ashamed, who correctly handles the word of truth* (2 Timothy 2:15). Dr. Powell told me to memorize this verse, which I did. It has been a constant companion—a reminder of the sacred trust I had been given.

First Baptist provided me with a wealth of godly teachers and examples of those living sold-out to Christ: Hardy Bass, Mrs. B.B. McKinney, Dr. Roy Ackland, Mrs. Curtis Bell, Cecile Smith, and Helen Conger. God used Florida Waite—the librarian who stood at the door of the library, invited me in every week, and introduced me to some new books I must read—to open my mind to a world of new horizons and whet my appetite for reading. During those formative years, I learned the books of the Bible; memorized Scripture; became a Royal Ambassador; and acquired the ability to stand and talk on my feet, an invaluable gift later in my life. I also developed a passion for going to the Nashville Rescue Mission that was located near the church. There I saw the brokenness of humanity, hunger, and homelessness—all of which deeply touched me.

Eventually, our family left First Baptist and joined Eastland Baptist, which was near our new home in East Nashville. The church established a mission in a growing suburb named Dalewood. We joined there. My mom became their church secretary and served at Dalewood for twelve years. Again, the Lord put great Christians in my life: the Fred Wrights, Charlie Wheelers, E.K. Walkers, James Smarts, and Richard (Dick) Kornmeyers. (Dick gave my name to the pulpit committee at Two Rivers ten years later). May those who serve the Lord in whatever capacity or through whatever means not think they have little influence because God truly uses their service for eternal impact!

Shortly after seminary, the genuineness of my faith was challenged and my soul aroused through something a preacher said at a revival service. I was compelled by the Holy Spirit to examine my heart and ask myself the hard questions: *Had I made a genuine confession of faith? Was I committed on my mother's faith? Did I understand what I was doing?* I knew well the mandate found in God's Wor*d: "Examine yourselves to see whether you are in the faith; test yourself"* (2 Corinthians 13:5). So, this I did in earnest. I read. I prayed. I sought the face of God. I looked to 1 John[15] for the assurance I could find in the Scriptures. I needed to know that I was certain about my relationship and commitment to the Lord.

All this soul-searching exposed a major problem in me: pride! I felt sure I should be pastoring a larger church. After all, I had a college degree and three years of seminary. On a visit to Nashville, I made an appointment with Dr. H. Franklin Paschall[16] and urged him to find a place on his staff—like associate pastor—for me! He was most gracious, but told me nothing was available. That prideful attitude was exposed as I dealt with the Lord. This led to a brokenness and repentance that I deeply needed. In turn, my heart's

---

[15] *If we confess our sins, He is faithful and just and will forgive our sins and purify us from all unrighteousness (1 John 1:9).*

[16] Later, as pastor of Two Rivers, I was invited to speak at an adult Valentine's banquet at First Baptist, Nashville. Dr. and Mrs. Paschall were our hosts. He never mentioned my earlier visit. Over time, we became good friends. He was one of those who strongly encouraged me to be a candidate for president of the Southern Baptist Convention. When Dr. Paschall went to be with Jesus, I was highly honored to give a eulogy, along with Ed Young of Second Baptist Houston, at his memorial service.

desires to know Him intimately and serve Him faithfully became more fully entrenched in my soul. If remaining humble before God and others meant my serving in a rural church all of my life, I did not care.

The second thing that sealed my relationship to Jesus occurred in my study one morning at Two Rivers. While listening to music from *Celebrate Life*, I was overwhelmed by the love and grace of God. Words are inadequate to record what transpired. On my knees, I poured out my heart afresh in repentance, faith, and love for Jesus. It was a time when God said, "Jimmy, I love you." I knew I trusted in Jesus alone and His promise: "*I write these things to you who believe in the Son of God so that you may know that you have eternal life*" (1 John 5:13).

I can relate to the words of the old hymn: "Nothing to the cross I bring, simply to the cross I cling;"[17] I also connect with the words penned by John Newton, who wrote the text of the hymn *Amazing Grace*, "Although my memory's fading, I remember two things very clearly: I am a great sinner and Christ is a great Savior." In my heart and mind, I was shouting, "Me, too!" My great Savior was with me that day in my study as He had been with me through all days and stages of my life.

With All My Heart

To All Concerning the Most Important Commitment in Your Life:

The spiritual dimension of our life is the only one that lasts forever. Where we spend it and with whom we spend it outweighs everything else. To trust Jesus Christ as your Lord and Savior yields the greatest

---

[17] Augustus M. Toplady (1740-1778), *Rock of Ages.*

reward: the assurance of spending eternity with the One who loves us and died for us as His provision for our sin. It is all about relationship. He wants us forever with Him. I have never met anyone who regretted being a Christian. I have not. Not for one moment.

CHAPTER FOUR

THE WORST BUTTERFINGER I EVER ATE

WAS NOT TOO HAPPY about moving away from my friends at Cavert Junior High School and going across town to begin school at Bailey Junior High School. But, I soon found new friends in the neighborhood and the school. Being small of stature, I chose to pursue finding a way to play basketball. Charlie Malin, my former coach at Cavert, had encouraged me greatly. Bailey had a good coach in Frank Rutherford. I tried out for the team and waited nervously to see if I made the final cut of twelve players. I was on the posted list!

My jersey number was 22. We had a good team with players like Glenn Lawrence, Harold Pickle, Jerry Vandenberg, and Hugh Womack. Many of my teammates went on to excel in high school and college ball. My playing time was somewhat limited because of the better players in front of me. They could have called me "Judge," because I sat on the bench a lot! My prayer life was strengthened because I prayed earnestly we would have such a large lead that Coach could put me in.

We managed to get to the finals of the Junior High City Championships. Guess who our opponents were in the game? My old school and buddies at Cavert! It was a good game; however, they pulled away from us in the second half. In an act of grace, Coach Rutherford inserted me in the game near its end. With a few seconds to go, I got the ball in the corner. I so badly wanted to score against my old buddies. I literally threw up a prayer as I shot the basketball. The ball hit the edge of the backboard, bounced high, and then, somehow, caromed into the bucket. While it did not win the game, it provided me some small consolation in our defeat.

Our junior high school did not have soccer, football, or many of the other sports or athletic opportunities that schools provide today. We did have a track team; however, I was not fast or strong enough to compete in most events. But I found a way to compete in another racing event: a sack race. It fit me perfectly. A participant could run in the sack as an individual or with a teammate. The event was simple. We were given a large gunny sack into which we stepped and then gathered around the waist. We held it with one hand as off we ran. In a sense, we were running on tiptoes in a sack! I got pretty good at it, and won or placed several times during my junior high years.

School was a blast. I was involved in as many groups and activities as I possibly could. We had a mock presidential election to mimic the primaries and general national elections. For some reason I chose to be Senator Richard Russell of Georgia. Unfortunately, neither of us won on the local or national level! By God's grace, I was elected president of our ninth grade class. That gave me an undue amount of pride that spilled over in a classroom situation.

One of my teachers was a young lady whose name was Elizabeth. All teachers were to be properly addressed as Mr. or Mrs. as a matter of respect, and rightly so. One day I decided to call her "Elizabeth" in a classroom setting. She corrected me and strongly advised me to address her in the proper manner. I refused. She told me I could just sit in my chair until I addressed her appropriately. I just sat there.

School was out; the halls grew quiet; and Elizabeth and I just sat there, glaring at each other. As the afternoon wore on, I realized I had to make a decision because my folks would be expecting me home. How could I explain my situation without receiving further wrath at home? Grudgingly, I finally said, "Mrs. Elliott," and walked out the door past her not-too-happy face!

Another unforgettable transgression occurred one afternoon after school. The local pharmacy was on my route home. It was tended by a genial, white-haired patriarch called Dr. Morgan. Usually, I was with a group of my friends who stopped for chatter, milkshakes, cake, and candy. On one particular day when everyone else was buying and eating, I found myself with no money to buy a snack. As I walked past the candy display, my eyes fell on one of my favorite foods: a Butterfinger. Glancing around, I saw no one near me, and Doc had his back to me. I succumbed to temptation and quickly grabbed the delicacy. I joined my friends, unwrapped my stolen trophy, and began to eat. It suddenly lost its appeal and taste. I ate quickly trying to destroy the evidence of my theft.

When I got home, guilt lay heavy on my heart. The Lord deeply convicted me of my transgression. I felt so guilty that when I heard a police siren up the street, I thought the police must be coming to arrest me! As soon as I could accumulate the money, I headed back to the store to see Dr. Morgan. Finding a time when no one else was near, I asked to speak to him. I related my experience, asked his forgiveness, and placed the Butterfinger money in his hands. Not knowing if he would report me to my parents or the police, I was so relieved and grateful when Doc placed his hand on my shoulder and told me, "I forgive you. Don't do it again."

I left that pharmacy with a much lighter heart. In reflection, I see his action was much like my Lord Jesus: grace, forgiveness, and "go and sin no more."

With All My Heart

To All Who Did Something Wrong and Are in Need of Forgiveness:

There is no good sin and no good wrong. When we do mess up (and we all do), something happens inside us: a thing called guilt kicks in. Guilt that leads to confession is good. When confession is made and forgiveness is given, it reminds me of what a young man told me when he became a Christian: "It's like you are on a long, exhausting hike with a backpack. Finally, your scoutmaster says, 'Take a break, and take off your backpack.' That feels so good. So does the grace and mercy of the Lord. It feels good!" So, just do it. Keep short sin accounts with God and others. It feels good!

CHAPTER FIVE

MR. FOSTER WANTS TO SEE YOU

ALL MY BUDDIES WERE going to East High School. Being within walking distance and familiar terrain, it was the logical choice for me. However, Mom had other ideas. Litton was the other high school option for me. It was in our county, had an outstanding academic reputation, and an excellent athletic program. Mom ruled. Off to Litton I went. In the long run, her wisdom proved best. As we did not have a car, I had to hitchhike to school. Sometimes, I got a lift all the way to school. Other times, I only got far enough to catch the school bus that ran to the county line. To the best of my memory, I was never late for school in those three years.

I threw myself into the new school with all my heart. It was my goal to know everybody by, at least, their first name. Although our school was one of the largest in Tennessee, I think I succeeded at my task. This proved to be of great value when, in my junior year, I was chosen president of the student body.

High school days put me in touch with great teachers and coaches. Miss Moss gave me a growing love for history. Coaches Fentress, Moore, Webb and Harris taught and coached me. Looking back, I see the positive impact of many excellent public school educators on my life... that is, with the exception of one. My junior high math teacher rarely answered any of my questions about algebra. If she did, she did so with such a glowering scowl on her face that it made me reluctant to ask again. Her insensitivity and unkindness marked my math progress and left me handicapped forever. Encouraging and helping students is so important. That example aside, most of my teachers and coaches were Christians who were highly concerned about their students and grossly underpaid.

Litton High School was a state power in athletics—especially in football—which produced numerous championships, as well as many college and professional players. Since I weighed all of 120 pounds, my playing on the football team was out of the question. Desiring to soak in some of the excitement and mystique that surrounded that exceptional football program, I took the initiative my senior year and asked Coach Bill Harris if I could be a manager. Coach "Thunder and Tarnation" (closest I ever heard him to uttering an expletive) Harris agreed.

Two fellow seniors, Ted Ridings and Stewart Jackson, were fellow managers. We decided we would be the best and fastest managers to be found. We thrived when we performed our duties before the big game crowds, as we listened to the familiar "Marching 100 Band" that marched in the Rose Parade and Macy's Thanksgiving parades, and when we celebrated at post-game "sock hops" in the school gymnasium. Those friendships continue to this day.

I asked that we have prayer before the ballgames in the stadium. Our principal, Mr. Foster, gave the permission for us to do so. These pregame prayers created a positive environment for the fans and the players. It was often my privilege to lead those prayers.

Pep rallies on Fridays before a game were much enjoyed by our student body. 1,200 of us packed the gym. The pep band and cheerleaders kept us roaring. Our fight song, "Litton High Forever," was sung at the top of our voices. Seniors had the privileged section of the middle part of the balcony in the gym. Sometimes, football players chose some hapless victim to toss around like a volleyball from section to section.

One day, in the midst of our shenanigans, Mr. Foster strode to the microphone and, with a tint of anger in his voice, abruptly dismissed the pep meeting halfway through. We immediately returned to our class schedule. We had hardly settled in when an office "runner" appeared at our door, whispered to the teacher, who then said, "Jimmy, Mr. Foster wants to see you in his office."

For what? Trips to the inner sanctum of that office were not usually occasions for tea and cookies. Mr. Foster had me sit down and said, "Aren't you the president of the student body?"

"Yes, sir," I replied.

"Did you see that mess going on with students being thrown around—a dangerous thing, and not what we're about?"

I think I managed to meekly say something like, "I was in the vicinity."

In no uncertain terms, he told me that the student body would be reassembled and I would proceed to announce that beach ball antics with human beings were not tolerated and would never happen again. I did as I was told. That was the last of the human volleyball activities at the pep rallies. And I learned a huge life lesson about accountability!

I dabbled in many things those wonderful three years of high school. Running the mile and half-mile, I managed to letter in track. Even though I had short legs, I had good stamina that allowed me to win or place in most of the track meets. My senior year, I was able to qualify for the regional semi-final. There I found myself in the same heat as Tandy Rice, who, at that time, was the human equivalent of Triple Crown winner American Pharoah. Tandy took off. I chased him as hard as I could, but to no avail. All I could see was his silky, smooth stride vanishing in the widening distance between us. Tandy went on to be a very successful businessman, as successful in that world as he was in track.

My senior year of high school I managed to make the varsity basketball team; however, I chose not to play on the team. Because my playing time was going to be limited, I quit. That's the only thing I think I ever gave up on. If I undertook an assignment or made a commitment, I tried to stay by it. Now, if life gave mulligans[18] and I had another shot, I would have stayed on the team for the camaraderie of teamwork and the discipline the sport provided. God used this experience as a life lesson to help motivate me to keep from giving up on some more important matters in my future.

Another venue for my energy was forensics. In one of these "momma-made-me-do-it" experiences, Mom decided I should take speech lessons. The teacher was the renowned Mrs. Jordan, who met with her students in an old building in downtown Nashville. She had coached many successful students and adults in the proper technique of communication.

Mom had gone back to school and taken secretarial classes at a business school to better prepare her to garner some family income. Later she worked on the staff of Belmont University; several churches—First Baptist Nashville, Eastland Baptist, and Dalewood Baptist; as well as stints in the

---

[18] For you non-golfers out there, a mulligan is a golfing term for a second try. The number of mulligans used in a game is agreed upon before the game begins. A golfer can redo a shot by taking one of his mulligans.

business world. My speech lessons were one of the things she sacrificed to make happen. Mrs. Jordan was a taskmaster. She drilled me, gave me things to memorize, made me repeat phrases, and hammered at my pronunciation. Under her tutelage, I competed on the local, regional, and state levels.

My senior year of high school I was successful in winning my way to the finals with a humorous rendition of *Little David*, a monologue depicting the biblical hero David—his shepherd-boy life and epic encounter with Goliath. We had four rounds in which to compete and win in order to progress to the finals. We were graded by judges with the results posted for all to see. I prayed before each round and found myself in the top division the first two rounds. By the third round, I was confident and felt pretty self-sufficient. So, I did not pray. When the results were posted, I had fallen into the losers' bracket. While it did not disqualify me, it made the possibility of winning very difficult.

I went into the men's restroom and found a quiet place. There I repented of my pride and self-assurance. I asked the Lord to help me do my best in the last round—win or lose. When the judges posted final results, somehow I had managed to come out as the state champion. I knew immediately Who had seen me through. With a humbled heart full of gratitude, I quietly thanked and praised Him. Life lesson learned: "*Whatever you do, work at it with all your heart, as working for the Lord, not for men*" (Colossians 3:23).

As teenagers, my friends and I spent lots of time driving around together in our families' cars. My family finally got a 1954 two-door, green and white Chevy with power glide transmission. My brother and I dubbed our car "Power Slide." I can remember buying gas for as little as 12½ cents a gallon. A friend of mine had a vintage Model-T Ford with a rumble seat. With girl-friends by our sides, we drove around our favorite drive-ins and hang outs, like the Krystal. Most of our dates were double dates, which worked out well for me as I was often dependent on my buddies for transportation.

One of the biggest challenges for me, as a teenager, was the process of getting a date, especially for major events like the prom. To get on the phone, dial the number, make some general conversation, and then move to the climactic moment of asking, "Will you go with me to… the movie… the sock hop… the prom," were the mental and emotional equivalents of bungee jumping off the Golden Gate Bridge. Somehow, I was able to find female accomplices who were full of grace and mercy!

On the spiritual and church front, I kept busy. Our church at Dalewood had youth week, where students substituted for the adults as the preacher, ushers, teachers, and so forth. I had the privilege of being the pastor a couple of times. It greatly pleased me to look out and see my high school friends there to encourage me.

Billy Graham came to Vanderbilt University Stadium for a crusade my senior year. The last night of the crusade the stadium overflowed, and people sat on the field. I sat under the goal post where only a short time ago—on a cold Thanksgiving Day—our school had fought the powerhouse Montgomery Bell Academy in Nashville, which ended in a 20-20 tie, in the play-off for local high school football supremacy. Sitting there that special night, I would have never thought that, in 1983, at the Orlando Citrus Bowl, I would have the joy of introducing Billy Graham at the Central Florida Billy Graham Crusade.[19]

Three wonderful summers—1952, 1953, and 1954—I served on the staff at Ridgecrest Baptist Assembly in North Carolina. For the first time, I was

---

[19] It was my privilege to serve with my colleague, Dr. Howard Eddington, senior pastor of First Presbyterian Church, Orlando, as cochairman of that historic, life-changing event.

exposed to preachers like Dr. W.A. Criswell of First Baptist Dallas and Dr. Baker James Cauthen, the passionate voice of missions as president of the Foreign Mission Board.[20] I met godly college students and staff members.

While at Ridgecrest, I had my first serious girlfriend—a lovely, young lady from Louisiana. We corresponded fairly regularly. She was a freshmen at Baylor University; I was a senior in high school. Letters were less frequent. In December, I received a letter that I did not open until I got to my locker at school. We were playing the championship game for school intramurals. I dressed out for the game before opening the letter for my pregame inspiration. To my dismay, it was a "Dear John" (or "Dear Jim") letter, which effectively ended our long-distance relationship. At first I was sad; then I was mad. I took it out on the basketball court and scored the most points I had ever knocked down before or after![21]

A highlight to staff life was weekly gatherings. Mr. and Mrs. Willard Weeks—affectionately dubbed "Mom and Dad Weeks," as they served as stand-in parents and grandparents for most of us—led the meeting. Dad Weeks always read 1 Corinthians 13 in different translations, or had someone fluent in another language recite that passage. That Scripture, along with Psalm 121:1—"*I will lift up my eyes to the hills,*" which graced the entrance to the boys' camp—became, and remain favorites to this day.

Spiritual highlights were many; however, one became a lifetime reminder of God's love and His control over my life. The summer of 1952 was my

---

[20] Now called the International Mission Board.

[21] Preaching in Louisiana years later, I saw my Ridgecrest girlfriend. She introduced me to her husband to whom she was happily married. We—both happy in our unions and she long-time forgiven—exchanged a few minutes of catching up as old friends—now brother and sister in Christ.

first summer to work at Ridgecrest.[22] I was officially employed by the Baptist Sunday School Board to work in visual aids (now media) to assist with audio and visual equipment. One day I began to experience pains on my right side. A visit to the doctor and subsequent tests confirmed a problematic appendix. I needed surgery.

Taken to a hospital in Asheville, I was three hundred miles from home and family. My wonderful boss, Richard Kornmeyer, and his wife, Josephine, were there with me. They were the closest thing to family I had at my summer home. The hospital staff took me into a darkened room to prep me for surgery. Alone and somewhat afraid, I asked an orderly for a Bible, which he brought. I prayed before I opened it that the Lord would see me through this health crisis, and show me a word of comfort from His Word. I stuck my thumb into the pages and opened it to Romans 8:31: *"If God is for us, who can be against us."* Another passage—Romans 8:28—also caught my eye: *"In all things God works for the good of those who love Him, who have been called*

---

[22] Ridgecrest has been and is one of the key components of my life. Our three children, five grandsons, son-in-law, and countless others have benefited from its hallowed ministry. It has been my honored privilege to have preached or taught there in every decade from the 1960s until the 2010s. Working as cochair with Glenn Wilcox, I served with a host of others to launch a financial campaign to enlarge and beautify Ridgecrest's facilities and grounds. When I redeployed (retired) as pastor of First Baptist Orlando in 2006, one of the gifts our generous people lavished on us was to collect the funds to name one of the beautiful auditoriums "The Jim Henry Auditorium" on the Ridgecrest campus, which was a total surprise to me. In the fall of 2006, a large group from our church came to Ridgecrest to dedicate that place and facility to the glory of God. When I am on the campus, I slip into that quiet place and reflect on the goodness of God: *Why me when so many more are far more worthy and deserving?* I am continually overwhelmed and humbled by it all.

according to His purpose." Instantly, I was set at ease. I am glad I did not turn to a passage that said, *"And he died"!*[23]

The surgeon walked into the operating room and told me the anesthesiologist was going to give me sodium pentothal to induce sleep. I was instructed to count to ten, and assured I would be playing basketball a week later. Then the surgeon said, "I am going to pray if you don't mind." This godly doctor verbalized a prayer to our Lord for assistance for himself, the surgery team, and me. By the time he said, "Amen," and I got to three, I was in dream world.

To his word, a week later I was playing basketball. When I get to heaven, I want to see him and thank him for being God's agent to a teenage boy. The reality of God's presence that night has been a leaning post all of my days. Three Scriptures—*"I am with you always"* (Matthew 28:20); *"Never will I leave you, never will I forsake you"* (Hebrews 13:5); and *"My Presence will go with you, and I will give you rest"* (Exodus 33:14)—have remained soft pillows for my fearful heart.

With All My Heart

To All Who Are in Positions of Responsibility, Trust, and Influence:

I recall a childhood song we often sung: "Oh, be careful little eyes what you see… Oh, be careful little ears what you hear… Oh, be careful little hands what you do…" Why? "Because the Father up above is looking down with love." We are not just accountable to God for our actions. We all have others who are watching us. Responsible

---

[23] Genesis 5:27 reference to Methuselah.

leadership—whether at home, school, workplace, church, or in the community—is a weighty matter. Even when not realizing it, we can make responsible choices that will make a huge difference in our sphere of influence.

CHAPTER SIX

BELLE OF THE BLUE

T HE "POWER SLIDE" CHEVROLET drove off and left me, with my two suitcases in hand, in front of Professor Fields' home. This is where Mom and Dad dropped me off to begin my college days at Georgetown College. I ended up at Georgetown, because I had met several Georgetonians while working at Ridgecrest. I was impressed with the spirit of those guys—John Parker, Don Fields, and Tom Grissom. They urged me to check out the school before I made a final college choice.

In God's timing, Dr. H. Leo Eddleman, president of the college, was preaching at a Nashville church. Mom and I went to hear and meet him. Dr. Eddleman—a brilliant scholar, missionary to Israel, fluent in Hebrew— greeted us with warmth and enthusiasm. On the spot, he offered me a scholarship to help defray the cost if I decided on Georgetown. That was the tipping point. Off to Georgetown College, located in the heart of beautiful bluegrass country, we went.

There was no campus housing available, so they placed me in the Lambda Chi Alpha fraternity house. My first roommate was Richard Stephens, son of a Baptist pastor. We became lifelong friends. Together Rich and I joined the U. S. Army Reserve. We often mused that if the Russians had seen the two of us as 120-pound privates hauling rifles and backpacks, they would have felt confident they could win the Cold War! Rich was one of the godliest men I've ever known. After college, Rich went on to become a pastor and Army chaplain. He and his future wife, Nancy, whom he met at Georgetown, impacted thousands of lives, including ours.

College days were busy. I participated in intramural sports, worked on the college newspaper staff, ran for class office (unsuccessfully), and was active in the fraternity. To help pay my way through school, I washed dishes in the school cafeteria and worked at different jobs at the president's house. Days and nights were filled with homecomings; announcing Tiger basketball games; late night ping-pong games; trips to the local greasy spoons and truck stops for hamburgers and chili at midnight; attending athletic events; and, for my first two years, not much study. By my junior year, I got more serious about my studies and my future. Three events occurred that altered my heart and mind, and became life-changing experiences.

The first was in a worship service. The Georgetown Baptist Church was student friendly. Periodically, they would ask fraternities, sororities, and other campus entities to be in charge of the Wednesday night service. When our fraternity's time came, we held an all-night prayer vigil at the frat house. We asked God to speak in power and use one of our brothers, Charles Gray, to preach, in a special way. That night was one of the most spiritually moving services I have ever experienced. The Holy Spirit moved across students and congregation. People were saved and lives recommitted. My own life was deeply affected with a fresh sense of the presence and love of God.

The second event occurred in the same church. One evening, at the invitation time of the worship service, several went forward to make commitments to Christ and the church. Among them were two fellow students, Nigerians, whose big smiles and contagious hearts, blessed our campus. But, rather than being presented to the church, they remained seated. Some in the church apparently had voiced opposition to their membership because of their skin color. While most of us were away for summer vacation, the church made it more difficult for students to vote in church business matters. We turned out in a subsequent church session to vote them in as members.

This less-than-Christlike action jolted me. How could we send people and resources to Nigeria; lead them to the faith; have them come to our school; and, yet, be rejected and not offered the welcoming hand of fellowship? Being raised in the South, I knew something of prejudice. Some of my thinking was framed by the environment in which I lived, but this event was used by the Holy Spirit to erase much of my bias and widen my heart to see the world through the eyes of God.

The third life-shaping event happened at the beginning of my junior year. As upper classmen, we guys were always on the lookout for the new ladies on campus. One day I spotted a black-headed beauty being escorted by a member of a rival fraternity. Immediately, I discerned that I must rescue that lovely lady from the sinister grip of this menacing threat. I found out the future love of my life was from Cave City, Kentucky. The eldest of three children of a Kentucky farmer, Jeanette was named after a popular movie starlet of an earlier era. Her father had sent her to school with the instruction to find a rich son of a bluegrass farmer. This candidate for her hand should own a car so he would be able to ferry her back and forth between home and school. As it turned out, she fell for a Tennessee city dude who hitchhiked home and back, or who caught a ride with fellow students for nearly all four years of his college run.

Studies became more important as life became more serious. I worked hard to get on the dean's list—not the one for misbehavior, but for academic achievement. At the end of a semester, I was within one letter grade of making that elusive list. I had a required Bible class taught by a tough task-master, Dr. George Harrison. On a final test, I was within two points to have the higher grade that would have put me over the top and on that dean's list. I had a private meeting with my beloved professor to urge him to reevaluate my blue book exam paper and see if he could find two more points so that I could join that elite group. He promised to take a look at my exam. When I met him for follow-up, he said he could not find two more points. Despite my pleadings, he would not be moved. I walked away deeply disappointed. However, I worked harder and finally made that elusive list during the next semester.

Years later, I was preaching in chapel at my seminary alma mater, New Orleans Baptist Theological Seminary. Sitting in the chapel gathering was Dr. Harrison, now seminary professor in Hebrew and Old Testament at New Orleans. One of my points was on the difference between law and grace. There before me sat a real-life example of the point I was trying to make. On the spur of the moment, I decided to use my college experience with Dr. Harrison as a classic example of the difference: The law kept my grade as given; grace would have given me the two points. Some weeks later, I received a letter from my former teacher. He was most gracious in his opening remarks, and then shared the following information. He said something like, "Brother Henry, I listened with great interest to your message and your reference to your college days. You may not know it, but I retained all the grades of my students through the years. I went back to look at your grades in my class. After close review, the grade I gave you was grace!"

Georgetown was a wonderful experience. I love the school. It gave me a good education, interaction with excellent professors, great college experiences, eternal friends, a wife, and a deeper touch of God as my journey moved to its next turning point.

With All My Heart

To Those Who Carry the Henry-Sturgeon[24] DNA:

Jeanette's ancestry stems from English stock; mine is Germanic in origin. The name "Henry" is derived from two words that mean "home" and "power ruler." I think Jeanette must have some German blood in her as she is certainly a "home power ruler." We are all the better because she is!

---

[24] This is a note to our offspring. Sturgeon is Jeanette's family name.

CHAPTER SEVEN

SCHOOL BELLS, WEDDING BELLS, AND CHURCH BELLS

W**ITH DIPLOMA IN HAND**, it was time to fish or cut bait. Armed with my degree in history and certified in secondary education, I began fishing for a place to work. I was considering an opening in Ohio, when I made contact with Bill Ross, an elementary principal in Panama City, Florida. Two of his sons were my fraternity brothers, who became my connection points. I was offered an elementary position to teach the sixth grade with a promise of a position at the high school level the next year.

With anticipation and some trepidation, I headed south in my newly acquired Volkswagen Beetle. I rented a room in an old, two-story, Florida-style house which housed nine other single, male teachers and sat on a beautiful cove. It did not take me long to get settled and into my new life. I soon learned to eat raw oysters like a native Floridian.

Being fresh out of college, I quickly had to acquire the skills and patience to deal with thirty-two energetic sixth graders. My classroom was located on the second floor of Panama Grammar School. First Baptist Church of Panama City was down the street from the school and a short drive from home. It was Mr. Ross's home church. The church put me to work as a department director of upper school students.

At school, I was mentored by wise, mature teachers. I coached football and basketball with fellow teachers—one of whom was Chuck Seal. I had met Chuck and his new wife, Virginia, at Ridgecrest.[25] Many of the teachers and staff helped me learn the ropes. Needless to say, I formed many friendships I cherish to this day.

It was not just my colleagues who taught me about being an effective teacher. I was also educated by students with whom I worked at the school and at the church. "My kids" were wonderful individuals—and each one touched and shaped my life. I loved the classroom situation where I was privileged to get to know these great young people, and form relationships with them and their parents.

At Thanksgiving, I decided I wanted to give the children the opportunity to learn more about the joy of giving. In my class, there was a little girl who came from a family that was desperately poor. She often arrived at school in dresses that were patched or poorly fitted. I decided that our class would collect food and money to give it to her family. My plan was to do this without divulging the names of the recipient and family members so as to protect her/their dignity. The children responded enthusiastically. Soon the corner of the room was piled high with food.

[25] Once I got my teaching position, I could recommend the hiring of my friend Chuck Seal to school leaders. After he was hired, he and his wife, Virginia, moved to Panama City. They both became greatly loved members of the educational and church community.

On the final collection day, I headed for my classroom. In the mornings before school began, we teachers arrived first, and the students were not allowed inside until the bell rang. As I approached my class, I saw the child whose family we were going to bless inside the building. Taking the firm posture dictated by my teacher role, I said, "Ann, (not her real name), what are you doing in here before the bell rings?"

She had both hands behind her back, but swiftly brought them out. In her hands was a brown paper sack. Meekly she said, "Mr. Henry, I just wanted to help that poor family who doesn't have anything."

I opened the bag and looked at its contents. Inside was a lone can of beanie-weenies. My heart melted as I gazed at this sacrificial gift given by this precious youngster. From a small child I was the one who was taught a big lesson in generosity.

I learned many life lessons at my tenure in Panama City. One Sunday morning, I walked into the student department at church and found a large crowd assembled. To my dismay, I saw them huddled into small groups and many of the students were weeping. Stunned, I quickly asked what was happening. They told me that Dewey—an exceptional teenager who was active in our student ministry, president of the student government at Bay County High School, and beloved friend of many—along with two other student government leaders and their sponsor teacher had been killed in a terrible automobile accident near Panama City. The group had been returning home from a student government conference in Nashville, Tennessee. Wanting to be home for church and family, the group had driven into the early morning hours. Just outside Panama City, their car plowed into a steel bridge abutment. All were killed instantly. Apparently, they suddenly drove into a fog bank and had no time to react and avoid disaster. Our city was shaken and heartbroken.

Procuring someone to look after my class for a short time, I was able to attend Dewey's service at First Baptist. The church was so packed, I had to slip into the baptistry area to get a glimpse of this tremendously moving service. By the time the funeral procession had formed, by necessity I was back in the classroom.

The cortege proceeded down Harrison Avenue. My classroom's windows faced the street. Some students asked if they could stand at the window and watch. With a promise of their silence, I agreed. They stood still and watched reverently and quietly. One of my girls moved from the window and stood by my side with her arm around my waist. She said nothing for a few minutes. Then she said, "Mr. Henry, Dewey's in heaven, isn't he? He was a Christian. Wasn't he?"

"Why do you think so?" I asked.

"Because you could just tell by the way he lived," she responded matter-of-factly.

While I know good living saves no one, I also know God's children should be "good-living." When we get it right, those who walk behind us see our example, and a powerful influence is generated.

During this time in my life, I struggled with a call to ministry. I regularly pushed it down inside of me, and it kept bobbing up like a floating cork. Finally, I made an appointment to see my beloved pastor, Dr. Julius Avery. When we got together, I shared what was on my heart. He listened intently, and then this godly man offered words of wisdom that gripped me: "Jim, I cannot tell you what to do. However, you can be certain the devil never put it in a man's heart to preach about Jesus."

I prayed, read my Bible, and spent much time in thought. I examined my motives. I looked at my family history: no preachers since my early ancestors. And what about Jeanette? We had talked about the possibility of ministry. However, would she sign on to a lifetime of service that could be anywhere in the world?

A few weeks later, on a Saturday night, alone in my room, I committed my life to serve God in full-time ministry. I knelt down and told my Lord Jesus that the best I was able to discern His will and His voice, I was His man. I asked that I would not bring harm to His name, and I promised I to give Him my best. I determined that I would make it public the next morning at First Baptist, Panama City, and ask the church for their prayers and confirmation.

Sometime later, Mom told me that when she was pregnant with me, she attended a midweek Bible study at First Baptist Church in Nashville. It was a class taught for young women by Mrs. King, a godly and excellent teacher. While in prayer with the ladies, my mother told the Lord, "If You give me a boy, I will dedicate him back to You for You to use him as You please." Oh, the power of a mother's prayers! In my ministry over the years, as I have prayed for expectant mothers, I have made it a practice to pray that prayer for their babies. I believe the impact of the prayers of parents, grandparents, Christian friends, pastors, and teachers carries far greater influence than we can imagine

Dr. Avery and First Baptist licensed me to preach. Later Dr. Avery had me preaching in both morning worship services. I was nervous, to say the least. I totally changed my first service message before the second service began. I do not remember what I preached; however, I am pretty certain it wasn't the greatest.

While living in the big house with my teacher buddies, I had the opportunity to get to know a delightful lady who came to the house on Saturdays to fix us a country breakfast and then clean the house. Her husband was the pastor of a small church with a black congregation. When she heard of my going into the ministry, she asked if I would preach at their church. I gladly accepted, told my sixth-grade class, and prepared a message on John 3:16.[26]

It was a cold, February morning when I pulled up in my Volkswagen to the church. A pot-bellied stove on one side of the church served as the only heat source. Everyone had on overcoats and warm clothing. When we sang, you could see puffs of air turn to clouds. When I rose to preach, the pastor sat behind me. Doing as black preachers and congregations so beautifully do, he shouted, "Amen!" and "Yes!" throughout my sermon. Somewhere in the message I apparently got it going, as I heard him say: "You've got it! You're in it! Now, go on!"

Several of my sixth graders rode their bikes to the church, which delighted me. However, I soon found out that some of their parents were not happy. A visibly upset father of one of my precious students showed up at the door of my classroom later in the week. He demanded his daughter be moved out of my class because of my preaching in a "black church." He informed me that he was also going to appear before the local school board and ask the principal to have me fired. Thankfully, I was able to stay on as teacher. When the little girl was moved to another class at the request of her angry father, she came to my desk, began to cry, told me she loved me, and said that she did not want to leave. The raw edge of senseless prejudice had crossed my path, and would reappear again and again throughout my ministry. It was a learning experience that broke my heart and challenged my resolve to listen to God's voice over the too often negative, and even hateful, culturally and religiously biased rhetoric I was to hear.

---

[26] "For God so loved the world that He gave His one and only Son, that whoever believes in Him shall not perish but have eternal life" (John 3:16).

Back to happier memories. In the process of seeking God's will, I had not talked a great deal to my family or Jeanette about my surrendering my life to ministry, although all knew it was on my radar. After making my decision known that Sunday morning at First Baptist, I called Jeanette to tell her what was going on in my life. Before I could tell her about my decision, she told me she had something to tell me. "This morning at Georgetown Baptist Church I made a public commitment to follow Jesus wherever He wants me to go," she told me, " with or without Jim Henry."

We were in awe of God's direction in our lives. Hundreds of miles apart, He clearly spoke to both of us. That sealed the deal for me. I asked, "Will you marry me?" With a joyful "yes" whispering in our hearts, we moved toward becoming one in Christ.

Our wedding date and time—December 27, 1959, at 3:30 p.m.—were set. We were to be wed at Salem Baptist Church, Cave City, Kentucky. Christmas time is probably not the best time for a wedding; however, we were ready to move on. Everyone worked hard to make our day special. Jeanette and her mother, Bertha Mae, made her wedding dress, (which our daughter Betsy wore on her wedding day twenty-four years later). They also made all of the bridesmaids' dresses. The church was decorated with flowers and foliage from the countryside.

Our wedding day dawned bright and clear. I had breakfast with Mom and Dad. I distinctively remember the weird feeling I experienced as I realized this was my last time to have breakfast with my parents as a single man.

Our wedding party consisted of family members, as well as high school and college friends. Jeanette's brother, Larry, rang the church bell outside the church three times to signal the start of the wedding procession. The church was packed. I was slightly nervous, especially when, at the last moment, I noticed I had put on a white shirt with a slight trace of polka dots sprinkled

on it. (Thank goodness the spots were faint enough not to be seen by others).
Not exactly elegant formal wear!

Two songs were sung that still remain etched in my heart: "Savior, Like
a Shepherd Lead Us" and "The Song of Ruth" ("Whither thou goest, I will
go…"). Bolstered by my best man, Uncle Bascom Gunn Henry, I somehow
got through the vows. As husband and wife, we exited down the aisle of the
crowded church—the church where Jeanette had come to the faith, and
played piano for their worship services.

The reception was filled with countless hugs and best wishes. When the
festivities were over, we said our emotional good-byes to our parents. I went
over to thank PawPaw, Jeanette's dad. He did not have much to say, but I
noticed tears welling up in his eyes.

Amid a shower of rice and rain showers, we headed for our honeymoon at
a hotel in Park City, Kentucky. I think our room cost $10.00. As we shared
our first meal together, it was another stomach-churning moment as we realized we were married! I had a tossed salad and vegetable soup, which proved
prophetic as these have remained a staple in our day-to-day meal planning
through the years.

We honeymooned for two days at Cumberland State Park. Then, we had
to part. I headed back to Panama City to teach, and Jeanette returned to
Georgetown to finish her term. Talk about a tough good-bye! It was so hard
to leave my new bride.

Returning to Panama City, I found a small, two-bedroom house to rent.
As it was rather dull looking, I (without Jeanette's knowledge) made the decision to paint it yellow. Yes, I did! I thought it would tie in beautifully with
the yellow refrigerator in the house. After completing the task, I applauded
myself for my great decorating taste.

The time came for Jeanette to join me after her college graduation. With tremendous excitement, I headed to Kentucky to pick her up and drive her to our first house. She kept asking about it. I told her it was a surprise. When we rounded the corner and looked down the street, I asked her to guess which house was ours. She said, "All of them look all right, except for that yellow one. It's awful! Who in their right mind would do such a thing?"

Our first marriage crisis! I hung between anger and embarrassment. I nearly decided to drive by it, but I really had no other choice. When we stopped in front of the yellow house she thought I was kidding. When she found out this was no joke and the "awful" yellow house was our first home, it became apparent to my new bride she needed to do a major makeover on her tasteless husband.

You could guess that we did not stay long in those digs. As soon as we could, we rented an apartment near my school. The apartment was owned by a delightful widow, Mrs. Reddick, who mercifully let us move in without a down payment. Money was extremely tight during those early years. By the end of our first month of marriage, my spending exceeded our income. Too proud to ask our parents for help, I found a rural store whose owner gave me enough groceries to get us to our next paycheck.

It took us a while to learn how to manage our finances—and our impulses. Even though we were strapped for money, we foolishly bought a German shepherd, whom we named Rommel. Immediately, this quickly growing and easily bored pup devoured our shoes and chewed up our furniture. While we dearly loved him, we came to the sad realization that apartment living and financial limitations were not smart for us or the dog. We were relieved when we found a couple in the country who bought Rommel from us. The education of the Henrys in "Real Life 101" continued. We were learning the hard way.

Jeanette and I finished the school year. We said our emotional good-byes to children and colleagues we had come to love and cherish. We were headed for Ridgecrest Baptist Assembly in North Carolina, where we both worked for the Baptist Sunday School Board.[27] It was a great working environment that God used to mold our lives and shape our ministry as we were constantly being exposed to great preachers, missionaries, staff members, godly mentors and directors like Wayne Todd, Keith Mee, Adeline Dewitt, and Jackie Anderson. Our lives were also greatly enriched through meaningful relationships with a crew of high school and college students, who became lifetime friends, including a witty kid named Jan Williams, who later became dean of the Business School at the University of Tennessee.

While at Ridgecrest, God affirmed in our hearts that we were to look South and West for a new challenge in our lives at the end of our summer staff experience at Ridgecrest. He pointed us to Cajun country to the city of New "Awlins." With our wedding bells and school bells behind us; and with seminary and church bells before us; off we went as we sought to follow God's leading.

With All My Heart

To Anyone Going Through an Intense Period of Stress in Your Life:

Ringing bells are markers. This letter focuses on three of the biggest. Sometimes life seems to have long stretches where nothing seems to be happening, except the routine. But there are also periods when life happens fast and events telescope into a smaller framework of time.

---

[27] The BSSB is now LifeWay.

It is like boating on a tranquil river and suddenly finding yourself caught up in white-water rapids. While it can be wildly exhilarating and breath-taking, it can be dangerous, too. Keep your eyes and trust on the boat Captain. He will steer you through those seasons, as well as all of life. He has written a book called the Bible that directs you in both the rapids and the still waters.

CHAPTER EIGHT

I MOVE WE FIRE
THE PREACHER

ITH OUR VOLKSWAGEN BEETLE piled to the ceiling
and a little U-Haul van attached behind, Jeanette
and I headed for New Orleans and the Baptist seminary there. We chose New Orleans Baptist Seminary,
because it, like our second choice, Southwestern Baptist Seminary in Ft.
Worth, Texas, excelled in missions, evangelism, and preaching. We ended
up at New Orleans primarily because my former college president, H. Leo
Eddleman, a man I greatly respected, was now the president of New Orleans
Baptist Theological Seminary.

Because there was not enough housing on campus our first year at seminary, Jeanette and I lived off campus with a number of other students,
including Paul and Mary Kelley, whom I later had the joy of pastoring
at First Baptist Orlando. Once at seminary, I settled into a new world of
vigorous academics, and Jeanette became a substitute school teacher at the
elementary school level.

In her new work, Jeanette was introduced to a new kind of student, too. An insubordinate sixth grader told her one day, "I'll have my mom come down here and whip you!"

Jeanette responded by lifting him up by the collar, pinning him against the wall, and saying, "Bring her on!"

Today, she would be sued and hauled into court; however, that was the last trouble she had from that boy! She often said, "My main job is to keep the kids from crawling out the windows."[28]

Hungry to preach, my first opportunity came when Dr. Eddleman shouted at me one day from across the campus: "Do you want to preach this weekend?"

"Yes!" I shouted back.

"Come by my office for details," Dr. Eddleman replied to this excited seminarian.

Mt. Pisgah Baptist Church, (located between Quitman, Mississippi and Melvin, Alabama), needed a supply preacher. I threw a sermon together and drove the 210 miles to Mt. Pisgah on a Saturday afternoon. The church was having a fish fry when I pulled up in my car. People stared at me until one of the men, M.D. Lucas, approached me and asked if he could help. I told him I was their supply for the next day. He brightened up and took me around to meet the good people of Mt. Pisgah. He later told me that I looked so young they thought I was a stranger wandering the piney backwoods.

---

[28] After the birth of our first child, Kitty, Jeanette worked at Charity Hospital in downtown New Orleans, (which is now closed after major damage from hurricane Katrina). I worked part-time at J.C. Penney in household goods for $1.00 an hour. Because of our meager income, our young family ate lots of carbs in those days. We occasionally celebrated by splurging on shrimp, which periodically went on sale for three pounds for a dollar!

I was invited back for the next Sunday with the exhortation to be sure to bring my wife. Jeanette proved to be the selling point. They promptly asked if I would consider being their pastor. I was so excited, I am not sure I even prayed about it!

On a Sunday night, they sent us out of the front door of the small, white-framed building to discuss my calling as pastor. No pulpit committee, search team, or anything; just simple church. We were called in from the back, sat down at the front where the church patriarch—who had both hands on a cane that he moved back and forth like a pendulum on a grandfather clock—told us the terms of our call: "You will come up on the weekends. Visit on Saturdays. Preach on Sundays: morning and evening services. We will handle Wednesday nights. We will put you in someone's house every weekend. (There was no pastorium,[29] although later we built one.) You will be paid fifty dollars a week as long as the money holds out. If the money doesn't hold out, you'll have to go." These were the terms in which we began an eventful three years among a people we came to greatly love.

School put me under the scholarly yet warm teaching of men like Thomas Delaughter, Roy Beaman, Samuel Mikolaski, Claude Howe, James Taylor, Harold Souther, Helen Falls, Vernon Stanfield, and Malcolm Tolbert. Students were required to go beyond their classroom studies to preach or do ministry in New Orleans on a regular basis, and report on our work as a graduation requirement. As I went beyond the seminary campus to walk and work among some of the broken, hurting, and lost souls of a pagan culture, I had my eyes opened. Beyond getting to know individuals outside my Christian circles, I also made some tremendous, lifelong, ministry friends in Junior Hill, Don Bouldin, Jimmy Dusek, Mike Dawson, Jerry Vines, Larry

---

[29] A Baptist parsonage.

Black, and Jack May. In later years, Don came to be my associate at Two Rivers in Nashville, and Jimmy Dusek joined me as senior adult pastor at First Baptist, Orlando.

Church life was filled with dinner-on-the-grounds, especially on Memorial Day, when our members remembered deceased loved one with a memorial service—often held in a cemetery—followed by a covered dish dinner, complete with huge tables laden with lots of delicious Southern cooking. At one such occasion, a young man passed out while I was preaching. I thought we were going to have a death and burial on the spot!

During those years, I preached revivals, visited church members and others, and hauled kids to vacation Bible school. One day I crammed seventeen kids in my Volkswagen—maybe a feat worthy of the Guinness World Record! It was during those years I attended my first Southern Baptist Convention in St. Louis as a messenger. I had to sleep in my car on the way home, because I did not have enough money to pay for a motel room.

My first baptism experience was at Mt. Pisgah. I had the privilege of leading a young mother named Lucille to Christ. She, her husband, and her children lived a stone's throw from our church. As our church did not have a baptistry, I was informed that we baptized in the Buckatunna River when the weather warmed up. Having no experience or seminary instruction in baptizing, I went with my seminary friend Harry Couch to practice in Lake Pontchartrain. I am sure it was a strange sight for drivers passing by us to see one man with his arms raised to the sky, standing in the lake next to another guy with arms folded, waiting to be dunked!

Baptism day arrived. With nervous excitement, we headed for the river. Most of the congregation of fifty joined us. Of course, we sang "Shall We Gather at the River." I read Scripture on being baptized after one trusts Jesus and then waded into the cool waters of the slow-moving stream. The deacons assured me this was the perfect place—where the water was just the right height and baptisms always took place. But there was something we failed to consider. That spring a tremendous flood had occurred, altered the river bottom, and filled it with sand.

When practicing baptisms with my seminary friend, Harry, I had moved my right foot out to gain some leverage in handling the candidate. I desired baptism to be as dignified and beautiful as the symbol it represents. Having observed some pastors immerse candidates like they were trying to slam dunk á la Shaquille O'Neal, I had developed a strategy in which I instructed the candidate to fold their arms on their chest, imagine they were sitting down in a chair, relax, gently fall backwards as I supported them, and be assured that, just as they entered water, I would place my hand over their mouth and nose to protect from water inhalation.

On the day of the actual baptism everything worked masterfully, just as planned, until I started to move my foot to the right and realized the porous sand had sucked my anchor foot down into the muck. It was embedded as surely as if it was in concrete! Meanwhile, the baptism candidate, Lucille, had closed her eyes, relaxed, and peacefully fallen backwards, with my right arm gripping her neck. By the time her head reached water level, I was panicked. As Lucille fell back to water level, she was oblivious that she lay stretched out, as if she were a corpse bobbing on the water surface. Panicked, I threw up a silent prayer of desperation.

Remember the song, "You Took the Wrong Time to Leave Me, Lucille?" I felt that was about to become a reality! What if I could not get her under the water, lost my grip, and let her go floating downstream like a boat without an oarsman? Mercifully, the Lord gave me an adrenaline rush. I basically baptized her with one arm. I do not think I could do that again if my life depended on it. Later, some of my men told me they saw we were in trouble and were about to jump in for the rescue before my miraculous recovery. I assured them if I had lost Lucille, they would have had to find a new pastor!

Things were moving along well. Life was full of awe and wonder. On Halloween night, October 31, 1961, our Lord sent our firstborn, Jamae Kathryn—whom we call Kitty and who now sings under the handle of Kate Campbell—into our lives at the Baptist Hospital of New Orleans. In those days, fathers could not go into the delivery room. I waited in the waiting room and studied for a biblical language test that was coming up the next day. I will never forget when first saw her. Born healthy with no complications, our beautiful baby girl had a head full of dark hair and brown eyes like her mother. The awe of seeing a part of yourself reproduced with the lady you love is overwhelming. With much joy and excitement, we brought Kitty home to commence the new era in our lives: parenthood.

One Sunday night, we were wrapping up the monthly business meeting at which I, as pastor, served as moderator. At the time, Mississippi was caught up in a raging fire of racial tension as James Meredith became the first black student to enroll in Ole Miss. That tension spilled over and touched our little, country church. It was all routine until I asked for new business. One of our men—a man whom I loved, and who we had visited often in their home, and he in ours in New Orleans—rose to his feet and said, "I move we fire the preacher."

Our peaceful world quickly exploded. At first, I thought he was kidding, but I quickly realized he was serious. As moderator, I called for a second. (Have you ever called for a second to your potential demise?) There was a prolonged silence, followed by a muffled second. Tom proceeded to tell me why I needed to go. Basically, in his own words, "You are a n---- lover."

Then he went into a litany of things I said. Taking minute conversations and messages out of context, he proceeded to attempt to justify his recommendation.

No one else spoke. The people were in as much a shock as I. I asked them to table the motion, give me some time to gather my thoughts, and bring it up at a later date. I went into the nursery where Jeanette was rocking our Kitty, knelt by her chair, and blurted out what had happened. My lady has some Irish blood in her DNA. I think her first reaction was to just walk out the door, and let them have the church!

Instead of acting out of hurt and anger, Jeanette and I prayed about this disturbing state of affairs. I knew that racial bigotry was an affront to the love and grace of God for all people. In the truest sense, this was a mountain to die on. The Lord gave me a game plan. I asked the church not to vote as I knew the potential for division among longtime members and friends. I promised that the following Saturday I would visit every home. When I appeared at their home, they just had to say one word—either "Yes" or "No": *yes* if they felt I should continue or *no* if I needed to move on.

I told the congregation I would announce my survey results the following Sunday. I would continue serving as their pastor if they responded with *yes* or resign on the spot if the answer was *no*. We drove home with heavy hearts and our romanticized concept of ministry shattered. All kinds of thoughts raced through my head as I processed what had transpired. On a practical note, I thought about how I might note being fired on my résumé.

On Wednesday night, Paul Patrick, a deacon, called us in New Orleans. "Brother Jim, do not visit any homes. You are our pastor. Come by the station and I will give you the details." (He ran the local gas station in the small, logging village of Melvin.) Greatly relieved, I made that gas station my first stop on Saturday morning.

Mr. Tom apparently had decided to circumvent my request, made visits in homes, and encouraged people to show up on Wednesday night to handle some church business. Word reached two faithful deacons who made some calls, and urged the people to pray and not act in haste. They crafted a statement that another deacon, Bob Brewer, read at the outset of the Wednesday gathering of a much larger than usual crowd. I wish I had a copy of that statement. It went something like: "Our Baptist forefathers fought, bled, and died that the pulpit would be a place where the preacher could freely preach the Word of God as the Holy Spirit led him. That has been the history of our church. Therefore, we move that our church continue to be a free pulpit, where the pastor can preach in freedom the Word of God." The motion was made, seconded, and then passed by a strong majority of the church. It sustained my continuing ministry there for another year.

I have pondered these questions a thousand times: *What if they had voted to fire me? Would I still be in the ministry? What kind of attitude would I carry if I continued as a pastor? Could I ever trust people again?* One thing is for sure: The courageous action of those two deacons and the affirmation of a people living in the midst of racial conflict with enormous ramifications carved a monument of deepest gratitude in the heart of a young preacher.

One of the most memorable experiences of our lives occurred much later in our lives in 2008, when Mt. Pisgah Baptist Church invited me to come back and preach at their one-hundred-and-fiftieth anniversary celebration. I saw children whom I had pastored, who were now parents or even grandparents. I visited with some older members who were still alive and also walked in the cemetery where I saw the resting place of some of those beloved members of earlier days. The master of ceremonies that memorable Sunday was none other than Bob Brewer, who, along with Paul and others, had, in a very real sense, risked their lives for me.

One other thing comes to mind as I remember these outstanding deacons and members of this church. Some time ago, I made a series of videos to assist deacons and pastors in their common roles of leadership and ministry, which have been seen by thousands of pastors and deacons for nearly twenty years. If I were to have a dedicatory page to that video series, I would dedicate it to those men and that church, who sustained me in a critical time in our personal and national history.

As young marrieds at seminary, Jeanette and I learned something else about our Father and Savior that became a life lesson for us. One day, early in the week, I came in from class, and Jeanette, in tears, met me at the door. She had taken Kitty for a checkup when her doctor advised Jeanette that Kitty needed more Vitamin D. "What's the problem?" I asked.

"Jim, we don't have enough money, and we won't have any more until Sunday night."

I tried to comfort her and assure her God would take care of us. I went outside and flung up a desperate prayer. Asking the Lord who called us and sent us, I begged Him to provide for our baby.

The next day as I walked in from class, I was met with a huge smile. "Jim, look at this!" Jeanette exclaimed. She handed me a card from a Sunday school class at the Dalewood Baptist Church in Nashville, Tennessee, where I had been ordained in November of 1960. The class had written a nice note to assure us of their love and prayers, and signed their names. A "P.S." was added at the bottom of the note: "*Please forgive me for not getting this to you sooner. It has been in my pocketbook for some time. I had just overlooked and forgotten it. Hope you can use it now.*" Enclosed was fifteen dollars! Could we use it? We prayed a thanksgiving as we knew our faithful Lord had kept that money tucked away until we needed it and could learn a lesson of His providence.[30]

Graduation time was nearing. I was not certain about the direction my ministry should take after leaving New Orleans. At a chapel service about midway through my seminary years, I had yielded my life afresh to the Lord and His will. Some professors wanted me to pursue a doctorate. I had been interviewed for student pastor positions in larger churches. The campus pastor positions at Ole Miss and Vanderbilt were also available. Since I had four years of Army Reserves under my belt and I loved my country, I struggled with the possibility of becoming a military chaplain. The Vietnam War was just beginning to expand, and I saw the opportunity of ministry to young people deployed far from home and open to the gospel. I struggled with all these options; however, I felt confident God would direct my path.

Close to graduation, I went to see Dr. Eddleman and told him of my uncertainty, as well as my deepening interest in student ministry at the college level. He spoke a word that stuck in my mind and heart: "I cannot tell you what to do. However, if you will do the job in the local church as a pastor, you will probably touch more students, who sit under your ministry, than you will on a campus." That was a word that settled it for me.

Dr. Eddleman's counsel was right. Throughout the years of my pastoral ministry, the Lord has placed large numbers of students in our congregations.

---

[30] The word *providence* comes from two words that mean to "see beforehand." Sometime after God's provision of the money we desperately needed, I ran across the passage in Joshua 3 and 4: God had shut down the flood waters of the Jordan River when the priests put their feet in the water. He stopped those raging waters twelve miles upstream so that the children could cross the river on "dry ground," a phrase repeated four times in those chapters. I call that passage "The God Upstream." Our all-knowing, all-powerful God always goes ahead of us to lead us and provide for us as we walk the journey on dry ground or through flood-water experiences.

Many of them, in turn, have gone to a host of colleges and universities. Through these relationships and my exposure to many Christian leaders, I received numerous invitations to preach at college retreats, revivals, and conferences. In God's providence, He has allowed me to reach many more students through my ministry than I may have done had I not become a pastor in a local church.

What next? The wonderful people of Mt. Pisgah could not afford a full-time pastor, and I needed the financial means by which to provide for our growing family. By this time, our second beauty, Jane Elizabeth Henry, arrived in July of 1963. Betsy, as we call her, saw the light of day at Baptist Hospital in Memphis, Tennessee. We now had four mouths to feed, which meant we needed God to provide another church for me to pastor.

Jeanette never let me forget the circumstances around the birth of our precious second daughter. The hospital's policy on fathers not being allowed in the delivery room was still in force. Rather than staying in the waiting room while Betsy was slow in arriving and Jeanette was being induced, I decided to make some hospital calls on our people. I got back in time to see another black-haired, brown-eyed doll come into our lives; however, I am not sure Jeanette has yet forgiven me for my temporary lapse of judgment!

My old friend, Harry Couch, was pastoring in Sledge, Mississippi, in Delta country. A rural church nearby, which sat nestled in the middle of cotton fields, had a vacancy for its pastor. Harry recommended me. Excited about this potential opportunity, I preached a "trial sermon" at Sledge Baptist Church. They liked us enough to call us. We were off to Hollywood: Hollywood, Mississippi, that is!

With All My Heart

To Anyone Who Is Facing Job Security Issues:

You never know when that pink slip, letter, e-mail, or visit from the manager or boss can come out of nowhere. It can come as suddenly as a bolt of lightning on a seemingly calm summer afternoon. It can devastate your life in nearly every way: your identity, confidence, relationships, and ability to pay the bills. Add to that the highly stressful advent of an uncertain future. It is in these experiences you realize our Lord Jesus is all you need when He is all you have. These life-shattering times throw you back to your understanding of embracing a genuine, personal relationship with God. Do you truly understand He is absolutely sovereign and in control of all of life? Can you trust Him in all things— even in the most uncertain times of life? Yes. Absolutely, yes!

CHAPTER NINE

WE'RE GOING TO HOLLYWOOD

OUR MOVE TO NORTHERN Mississippi was not exactly glamorous. The day we moved from our apartment on the seminary campus—which, providentially, was named Florida—we were met by a deacon and his son from the new church. They were there to help us move our belongings in their truck, which was covered by a rustic beam adorned with a canvas canopy. They assured us the makeshift covering would protect our meager worldly possessions should we run into rain. Amazingly, the only item that sustained any moving damage was a minor crack in a small mirror.

Our "moving van" pulled up beside a modest, brick house—the church's parsonage which was located twenty yards away from the other church buildings, and right in the middle of acres of cotton fields: the "white gold" of Delta country. Our new home was adequate but challenging. Its water came from a well. To purge the iron out of the water, the pump required a filter that demanded regular changes. If not filtered, the iron turned everything orange. One day we missed the much-needed filter change. The result was a full load of my T-shirts and underwear in Tennessee orange right out of the washer!

There was no air conditioning in the parsonage. The hot Delta summer days took their toll on us. It was hard to sleep, get dressed, cook, do just about anything—especially entertain guests. On one such occasion, when it was hotter than blue blazes, Jeanette and I hosted a seminary friend Shelby Newman—an excellent preacher and immaculate dresser—who stayed with us while he preached for our church's revival services. Since there were no motels within an hour's drive, our home served the purpose. While we tried to be the perfect host couple, our home had some challenges we could not control.

On the first night of his stay, Shelby called for me from the guest bedroom. Perspiring profusely and lying on top of the sheets, Shelby said, "Jim, I'll make you a deal. Get an air conditioner, and you can have my honorarium to pay for it!"

Jeanette and I did not take our friend up on his generous offer; however, soon after, we purchased a window unit for the living room. Men from the church came to install it. When the window was opened to install the unit, mosquitoes swarmed in by the hundreds. They were so thick, they literally lined the walls like a black border. Jeanette, the pragmatic one, got the vacuum cleaner and proceeded to suck those bloodsuckers up. Finally, we were cool in the Delta!

Since our church was an island in the cotton fields, we soon experienced another episode in the discovery channel of our lives. Crop dusters came roaring down the rows of cotton, a few feet above the growing plants. It always seemed like they were going to hit the church or our house; however, at the last second, these skilled pilots would yank the stick, pull up, and avert disaster. They passed so closely over us, I could see their face and often, a wave and a smile. One of those pilots was Jim Gargus. His wife attended our church, as he, too, did on occasion. I shared the gospel with him, as did others, but Jim would not accept Jesus. One day I received word that his crop dusting plane had crashed, and he was in critical condition.

The church and neighbors rallied in support and prayer. The appeal came for blood donors as Jim had lost a considerable amount. I joined with others in giving the desperately needed blood. To the glory of God, Jim survived. Sometime later, he trusted Jesus as his Lord and Savior. One day in conversation, we were talking about recent events, expressing gratitude for his physical and spiritual life that emerged from the near tragedy. He told me, "You gave your blood, so I could receive the gift of Jesus' blood."

Life was soon immersed in revivals, home visits, and steady congregational growth. It was decided we needed an education building as we were out of space. Our babies and children were in the old church worship center, which was now dilapidated and not fit for man or beast. We set a financial commitment goal, had a Harvest Day when the people gave generously; and soon a fellowship hall and education space rose to accommodate our growing numbers.

The usual church operations challenges surfaced. One day the heater for the baptistry broke. No one tested the water to see if it was comfortable. To our dismay, it was ice cold. As a large number had prepared to be baptized, we made the decision to plunge ahead. None who were baptized will forget that momentous occasion. Teeth chattered and audible gasps rent the air as cold water hit warm bodies, and their breath was nearly taken away as they experienced total immersion in those chilly waters. There were some near shouts as these brave souls expressed their sheer relief in having survived the numbing experience. Another time the heater went the other way. The baptistry looked and felt like a sauna. We poured in some water to help lower the temperature, but those newly baptized members still looked like boiled lobsters!

Most of us have experiences for which we wish we could have a "do-over." I had one of those on a warm afternoon. Driving my car with open windows across a canal near the church, I crossed the bridge where I heard some whimpering and weak barking. Wondering what I was hearing, I stopped to investigate. Soon I spotted the source of the sound. At the water's edge was a gunny sack that was jumping like a Mexican bean bag. It was tied at the top. I realized that someone had thrown a litter of puppies into the canal, hoping to drown them, and drove off leaving the helpless pups to meet their fate. The sack missed the water, and the little ones were scrambling for life and air. I love animals, especially dogs, so my normal response would have been to rescue them. But I didn't. Instead, I drove off and left them there, and I have regretted ever since. The sights and sounds of that day still echo in my memory. I have asked the Lord to forgive me, and while I am certain He has, the memory of my poor decision-making still hurts. I am grateful that He is a Savior who did not leave me in my desperate state, but, in His great compassion, chose to rescue me.

During those years, Mississippi and the South were in the midst of racial tension. Marches, murders, cross burnings, and confrontations happened often. Word came that the "freedom riders" were coming to our area. Freedom riders were civil rights activists who rode interstate buses into the Deep South in the early 1960s to uphold the Supreme Court decision[31] that ruled segregated buses were unconstitutional, since there had been little enforcement of that ruling. One of the tactics of the freedom riders was to visit churches to test if they were accepted in houses of worship.

---

[31] Boynton v. Virginia, 1961.

I decided to be proactive and called a meeting of our deacons. We met at the church, where we discussed what we should do in the event that a contingency showed up at our place. There was a healthy discussion. The motion was made that anyone who came to worship our Lord Jesus with us was to be welcomed as a fellow worshipper. If anyone came to disturb the worship experience, they would be asked to leave. The deacons voted unanimously that this would be our attitude and response. I was so proud of these men for their maturity and for their Christlikeness in addressing this concern. When many churches were insisting, "You cannot come in," our members were saying, "Welcome in Jesus' name!"

Subsequently, there came a fuller joy and passion in my life for Him and all His people. A fresh anointing came on our ministry. I was at peace with myself and my Lord. The Lord surrounded me with godly men and their spouses. They modeled so much of Christ for me, Jeanette, and our little girls. I will be forever grateful for the Bud O'Neals, the Darnell Jenkins, the Zack Jenkins, the Travis Allreds, the Junior Aldisons, the Gary Mayos, the Buddy Fausts, the Stan O'Neals, and so many others who deeply loved and cared for us.

Doors began to open for me after my tryst with the Lord.[32] Preaching, association meetings, and pulpit committees became a part of our life. Invitations came for me to pastor at other churches that were more attractive in location, opportunity, and salary, and I met many more godly people on search teams. By this time, our salary was up to seventy-five dollars a week, in addition to the pastorium and our utilities. Additionally, fresh vegetables, fruit, and meat often appeared on our front doorstep. We were totally satisfied. Jeanette and I would pray, listen, and wait on each invitation to move, but no green light came. So, we dug in.

---

[32] Refers to the deep soul-searching experiences I described near the end of Chapter 3 in this book.

One Sunday morning, a well-dressed group of about five people showed up in our morning service. To say they were obvious is to say, "There's an elephant in the room. Can you see it?" They left in their rental car without saying a word. I noticed our usually friendly folk were not going out of the way to welcome them. That night in the evening service, I castigated them for the seemingly cold shoulder they had given our guests. There was an awkward silence, then one of our precious saints, who was sitting near the front responded. She held up her hand, I recognized her, and she stated, "Well, I'll tell you why we did not seem glad to have them. We thought they were a dad-blamed, pulpit committee!" The church broke into yowls of laughter. I couldn't help but join them in this honest retort to my inquiry.

As it turned out, the group was a search team from Two Rivers Baptist Church in Nashville, Tennessee. It was a fledgling church, formed in the basement of the home of Harold Bennett, former president of the Executive Committee of the Southern Baptist Convention. Their first pastor, Fred Jolly, had stayed only a brief time before returning to seminary for additional study.

A dialogue with the church commenced. Initially, I was hesitant in pursuing this ministry opportunity. My current congregation was twice as large—which should not be a factor, but I thought about it! Plus, Two Rivers was located in my hometown. [Didn't the Bible say something about "*a prophet being without honor in his hometown*" (Luke 4:24)?] Our family visited Nashville, met with the search team, and still I struggled. *Could I minister in my home town where I would probably be remembered as "Little Jimmy"? What if I failed on my home turf?* I realize these were carnal thoughts, but I had to get beyond them to discern God's will. The question could not revolve around what I wanted, or whether I would fail or succeed. I truly had to seek to ask and know: "Father, is this Your will?" Jeanette and I talked and prayed. However, we had no clear word from God.

My usual habit was to study and have my time with the Lord in the mornings in my study. On one unforgettable morning, I went into the church and checked the mail. There was a letter from Keith Mee, chairman of the Two Rivers search team. It simply said, "We are praying for you," to which he had attached the Bible verse Acts 16:9. I went to the study for my quiet time. That year I was reading through the Bible, and unbelievably my reading for that day was Acts 16. Recalling the note from Nashville, I bypassed the first verses and searched out verse nine, which read: "*During the night Paul had a vision of a man of Macedonia standing and begging him, 'Come over to Macedonia and help us.'*" For me, I translated the verse to read, "Come over to Nashville and help us." I got on my knees, thanked the Lord for His leadership and revelation, and headed for the house. Once there I called out to Jeanette: "Start packing! We're moving to Nashville!"

With All My Heart

To Anyone Who Thinks You Are Not Where You Ought to Be:

One of the propensities of life is to think more highly of ourselves than we should. Self-confidence is a good thing; however, it should always be in the yoke of humility. One of my seminary professors made a statement I have never forgotten. (In fact, it is the main thing I remember from the class.) He said, "God knows where you are, and He will move you when He's ready." When I thought I was ready for prime time, I was not ready to come off the bench. I needed to be in Hollywood, Mississippi. I learned a great deal from that pastorate and that time in our lives.

CHAPTER TEN

MUSIC CITY, HERE WE COME

W E WERE CRYING WHEN we left the good people of Hollywood. Though our tenure was short, the bonds we forged were deep, and we gained meaningful relationships that continue to this day. They and their current pastor, Roy Hartzell, have been kind enough to invite me back several times through the years.

Our new church, Two Rivers Baptist Church, was located on a road that ended at the Cumberland River, where an eight-car ferry (piloted by Two Rivers member, Hugh Dixon) transported passengers back and forth; and tied the Inglewood and Donelson communities together.

Two Rivers was a young church, primarily made up of young adults with young children. Many in the church were college-educated, mid- to upper-class, and upwardly mobile. Much like the good folks of Mt. Pisgah and Hollywood, the members of Two Rivers had a heart for God, and were willing to take a chance on a twenty-seven-year-old, Nashville-native preacher. The church was blessed with a strong core of spiritual leaders. Many were professional people, and several were employed at the Baptist Sunday School Board. With a heart to grow, Two Rivers' leaders and members were visionary, hard-working, and patient with their young pastor.

One of the first breakthroughs in reaching our young community was when we joined with a couple of other churches in presenting a student musical entitled *Good News*. It was a fast-paced, upbeat, vibrant presentation of the gospel. This musical was accompanied with guitars and drums, which I (and most of our people) had never previously heard played in a worship setting. The packed audience was surprised when the kids who had been sitting among them in the congregation, sprang from their seats, and rushed to the platform, singing joyfully while the drums and guitars ravaged and banged. The people were startled! So was I!

Soon, a few, who had looked unhappy, got up and left. Some of these gathered for prayer outside the sanctuary. I immediately saw the abrupt end of my brief ministry there. However, the Holy Spirit did a marvelous thing. Those there experienced and saw God at work through this modern musical presentation. At invitation time, several teenagers accepted Jesus as their personal Savior. They subsequently brought their families and friends to our church, where they found a people who accepted them as they were.

Those who had been concerned that we were going the way of the world adapted to this contemporary musical expression as a way to reach these young people and their families. Because of this willingness to change, Two Rivers was soon welcoming a steady stream of youth, with several coming out of the drug culture.

In an effort to reach young people outside the walls of our church, I began hanging out at the football practices at Two Rivers High School. Coach Hewitt allowed me on the sidelines and in the locker room. We had the joy of seeing several players come to faith in Christ. Youth retreats and aftergame "fifth quarters" added to the atmosphere of excitement and buzz about the church. I am still in touch with some of those now mature adults, who continue to faithfully follow Jesus.

One experience remains forever branded in my memory. Our baptistry, which was located behind the platform and choir loft, had an unusual design. A stained glass window behind the baptistry allowed light to come through at certain times of the year, which caused a strong glare. As it made it difficult to see the platform without hurting people's eyes, we had something similar to vertical blinds—which extended from the ceiling to the front edge of the baptistry—built to deal with the issue. The blinds could be closed when the sun's rays made it difficult to see. The bottom portion of the blinds could be opened by sliding them horizontally to reveal the baptistry, and then closed again to maintain the beauty and symmetry of design. As I was preaching one Sunday, I saw one of our members, Ernest Mosely,[33] suddenly jump up and run out the door. Even though he was seated near the back, his quick departure from our small sanctuary was noted.

After the service, Ernest said, "Pastor, I guess you noticed my exit. We nearly had a disaster!"

Bewildered, I asked, "What do you mean?"

"As you were preaching, I saw the sun's reflection on the wall, coming off the baptismal, and then the waters began to move. It occurred to me that our children and little ones were in the basement below us. I was concerned one had wandered out of the room and fallen into the baptistry. I dashed up the steps, looked into the baptistry, and was amazed to see a teenage girl swimming "buck naked"' (in Tennessee language) right there in the baptistry!"

---

[33] Ernest Mosley, who was a vice-president of the Executive Committee of the Southern Baptist Convention, added immensely to our church, my family, and all the Southern Baptists through his life, ministry, and wonderful family.

Ernest went on to explain, "Quickly running downstairs, I got a couple of our ladies and some covering. With their help, we managed to get her out. Miracle of all miracles, no one saw anything except us. (God must have blinded everyone's eyes!) I found out she had come to Bible study with some friends, had a drug flashback, saw the water, and thought, *There's nothing that hinders me from a swim.*"

Ernest, whose dry sense of humor was famous, said, "Pastor, I was thinking, '*What if she had stood up in the baptistry, opened that part of the blinds we open for baptisms, and said, "Welcome to Two Rivers!"?*' We would have to have three services for the crowd next week!"

On the somber side of those exhilarating days, was the fact that my first seven funerals were teenagers, who either by accident, illness, or suicide went into eternity. One of the most gut-wrenching experiences came early in my Two Rivers years. John and Betty Fuqua with their two little boys began attending our church. They told me of another son—an outstanding athlete and school leader, who was a Green Beret fighting in the steamy Vietnam jungles. They were so proud of him, and kept me posted on his well-being. Then, the sad call came. John had been killed in action. The grieving parents asked me to go with them when his body arrived at the Nashville airport. I stood by their side as we looked through a chain-link fence that separated us from the tarmac and the plane that bore the body of their eldest son. After all the passengers had disembarked, the military moved to the plane and gently lowered the gray casket from the underbelly of the plane. Never shall I forget the sobs of the broken-hearted mother. Nor can I erase the memory of Mr. Fuqua, leaning hard against the fence, tears streaming down his face, and repeating, "My son, my son, I wish I could have died in your place." (The deep sorrow of this father has caused me to pause many times to wonder what our heavenly Father must have thought when His only Son died on that cruel, Roman cross: "My Son! My Son! You alone must die in their place for their salvation.")[34]

Years later, a beautiful bridge was built across the Cumberland near our church, linking the north side and the east side of Nashville,[35] as well as the interstate systems. When the span was opened, I was asked to attend and offer a dedicatory prayer. Politicians and other dignitaries showed up for this ceremony to mark important progress for the Nashville community. The bridge was named "The Duke-Fuqua Bridge," as a memorial to Kenneth Duke and John Fuqua, Jr.

Kenneth Duke was an All-State, All-Southern, football star, who graduated from my high school alma mater, Isaac Litton. Ken was killed in action in Korea. Though I did not know him personally, I knew much about him as he was and remains a legend in our school, as well as in local high school football lore. The impact of his life was strongly experienced by me and others. The news of his death came when our school was playing Oak Ridge High, a perennial Tennessee powerhouse. Undefeated and unscored on, they were number one in the state. Our team dedicated that game to Ken Duke's memory. When the final whistle blew, Litton had prevailed 55-19. Two wars. Two heroes. United in the struggle for freedom, and then in death. I never drive over that bridge and see those names that I am not solemnly reminded of the terrible price of freedom.

Happier memories for me revolve around the Lord's favoring our family for a third time with the birth of another child: a baby boy. James Bascom

---

[34] "*While we were yet powerless, Christ died for the ungodly*" (Romans 5:6).

[35] The need for the eight-car ferry ended with the building of this bridge. On the ferry's last trip, I took our son, Jimmy, to ride in the ferry's pilot house with Mr. Hugh, before he and the ferry were retired.

Henry II, entered the world on June 7, 1966, at the Baptist Hospital in Nashville. When Jeanette's labor pains began, we rushed across town to the hospital in our Volkswagen. Jeanette was timing the contractions as I was putting the pedal to the metal. Forty-five minutes after we arrived, our son arrived. I was in the waiting room alone. There were no family members, friends, or other expectant fathers around when our doctor walked in, congratulated me, and said, "Pastor, you've got a baby son. However, he is having a little problem. We are working on it. I think he will be fine, but hang around."

My elation turned to fear. I decided to go downstairs to the little chapel on the first floor to pray. The pastor now needed a pastor, a word of assurance regarding the uncertainties that lay before us. As I approached the chapel, my eyes were fixed on the words written on an announcement board placed just outside its entrance: *"My God shall supply all your needs"* (Philippians 4:19). Instantly, a peace came over me. It seemed as if my Father had spoken those eternal words directly to me in my time of need. This passage of Scripture has been a favorite since that day. Many times I have preached messages based on that verse.

We will be forever grateful to God that Jimmy's problem was handled. He is living a full and vibrant life as the director of the exhibition and convention space of the Gaylord Opryland Hotel (now Marriott), just across the street from the Two Rivers Church. Decades ago, I had the privilege of praying at the groundbreaking of that magnificent, three-thousand room facility, and recommending my younger brother, Joe, to Jack Vaughan, who was the president of the hotel.

Joe was then working for Sheraton Hotel in Lexington, Kentucky. Jack picked him as an associate. Joe with wife, Romelle, and sons, Michael and David, became a part of the Nashville scene. Shortly after their arrival, I was called to Orlando and missed the privilege of being pastor to my brother and his family. Someone quipped, "You had to go to Orlando as you Henry boys were working both sides of the street." I am proud of my brother. When he retired, he was senior vice-president and general manager of the hotel, and greatly loved by all who worked for and with him.

As the turbulent sixties faded into the rearview mirror, the tidewaters of national and international events were shaping a different world. The seventies proved to be chaotic and exciting nationally, and an eventful decade for the Henrys too. The times, they were a-changin'[36] indeed.

With All My Heart

To Anyone Contemplating Going Home Again:

Thomas Wolfe wrote the best-seller novel, "You Can't Go Home Again."[37] For years, I heard many people—even the some of the godliest folks I knew—say, "You can't go home again." After having that notion reinforced in my thinking, I came to believe it was true. However, our experience back on familiar turf changed my thinking. Returning to my hometown of Nashville turned out to be one of the most rewarding segments of our life. You can go home again if God wants you to do so. When you leave home, try to leave well. It smooths the road home if you travel that way again.

---

[36] Reference to the popular song from the sixties: "The Times They Are a-Changin'" by Bob Dylan (1964).

[37] Thomas Wolfe, *You Can't Go Home Again, 1940.*

CHAPTER ELEVEN

BUCKLE YOUR SEAT BELT

URING THE YEARS WE were at Two Rivers, God's hand was on our church. Rapid growth brought the need for additional staff, as well as buildings and land. We prayed, fasted, and sacrificed. Through only what can be described as miraculous circumstances, land became available. We went from five acres to over forty acres located on one of the most visible and desirable locations for a church in the area.[38]

By God's providence, we were able to secure airtime on two nationally affiliated, local television stations: NBC and CBS. We prayed for those doors

---

[38] Sadly, through a series of circumstances that occurred years after we moved to Orlando, the church became fragmented. I never thought that would have happened to one of the great churches of our country—a leader in evangelism and missions for many years after I left. Driving by it today, it is hard to look at what has happened to that awesome group of people, who were so strategically used by the Lord. The redemptive thing about what occurred is that some of the most godly, mature, and faithful disciples have joined a host of other local churches, and bless those congregations with their hearts, spiritual gifts and pocketbooks. That beautiful property is now in ownership of the Nashville Catholic Diocese.

to open. One of those opportunities to reach a broader number of people came through a connection with Tommy Erwin, the program director of the local CBS affiliate. His wife, Pat, and her family were my high school friends. I had an appointment with Tommy during which he promised to think about it. Shortly thereafter, he gave us an hour of prime time on Sunday morning to televise our worship, tape delayed.

The other entrée came when Mr. Irvin Waugh, President of WSM, Inc., came by our church as construction began on the Opryland complex. I asked Mr. Waugh if I could do something like a morning devotional—a "Coffee with the Parson" type of program—for two to three minutes, Monday through Friday, before the popular and widely viewed "Ralph Emery Show" aired. He thought for a moment and said, "Lad, I owe something to you Baptists. When I was a teenager, I went to a church of another denomination; however, my eye fell on a lovely Baptist girl. I went to the Baptist church, not for spiritual reasons, but for her. Her pastor was good to me. I liked him, and he did not try to run me off. I enjoyed my time there, although I did not get the girl. I will let you try it for two or three weeks, and we will see how it goes."

Two or three weeks stretched into several years on the air. Taking several changes of clothes, I went to their studios every couple of weeks to record three- to five-minute segments. With a Bible and a cup of coffee in front of me, I taped informal spiritual (and spirited) talks. That program reached thousands of teachers, construction workers, business leaders, homemakers, and others, who tuned in every morning for *The Ralph Emery Show* and the weather. I continued taping that daily talk until I left for Florida in 1977. To this day, I still meet or hear from people who tell me they watched that morning segment.

I was also often privileged be the pastor guest of Teddy Bart on *The Noon Show*. Teddy was a popular, local TV favorite. Each week he hosted a local pastor for a five- to seven-minute dialogue. For some reason, I found favor with him. Though he was Jewish by birth, he was most inquisitive and knowledgeable about the Christian faith. I tried to share the gospel message every chance I could. I am not sure if Teddy came to saving faith, but I always hoped that the good news gripped his heart, and he came to Jesus.

Several other events—some of historical proportions—took place during my twelve-and-a-half years at Two Rivers. One such event was the Jesus Movement. It was a great move of God that swept our country beginning in the late 1960s through the late 1970s. In a very real sense, this awakening of people's hearts to Jesus was very similar to the historical First and Second Great Awakenings that tilted our nation toward God hundreds of years before. It began in the Haight-Ashbury district of San Francisco, where drug addicts and free-love advocates were dramatically saved. They dropped their former lifestyles, and became bold witnesses for Christ and His transforming love. One of the hallmarks of this movement was the development of contemporary Christian music as well as several new denominations.

Kent Philpot was one of those whose life was dramatically changed. He and several of his friends began to fan out across America. They came to Nashville, and somehow got in touch with me. I worked with them and accompanied them when possible with my schedule. One day they decided to witness on the Vanderbilt University campus. I was amazed as I saw them walk into classrooms and boldly state the claims of Christ before professors and students. I was afraid we might be reprimanded or arrested; however, no one interfered.

This move of God spilled into local high schools. Students stood up in class and bore witness to Jesus. Classes were dismissed or ran overtime as the

Word was spread. I was invited to some campuses as an advisor or counselor. Some might think it was simply an emotional time that had no roots. But the evidence is in the fruit, and thousands around the country and in Nashville were eternally changed. I pray that God would visit us like that again. Our culture desperately needs a heavenly fix to stop its current death spiral.

During that time I was strongly moved by the Holy Spirit to make an appointment to see John Jay Hooker—a young, prominent, promising attorney, who aspired to attain political office (later making several runs for governor.) He was gracious enough to see me, a young preacher, whom he did not know. In our brief meeting, I told him I believed God would use him in a special way if he was committed to Jesus Christ. In our subsequent dialogue, I shared Jesus with him and asked him to receive Christ. He did not make a commitment that day, though I recall he told me he attended church. I pray that he made his peace with God. I have followed his career with interest, although he has not yet attained his political ambitions.

During those Two Rivers days, I witnessed some other cultural phenomena. A fad began when college students would run naked across their campuses. They were called "streakers." Some thought they were idiotic or nuts, while others thought the streakers were simply expressing their inner feelings. Most university and college presidents ignored them. Not so for Dr. Herbert Gabhart of Belmont University. I was a trustee there when streaking was rampant. We were wondering what would happen if some clueless pinhead decided to do the same at Belmont. We did not have to wait long to find out. At a trustee meeting, Dr. Gabhardt addressed the situation: "If a Belmont student streaks across our campus, he can streak by his room, get his belongings, and keep on streaking somewhere else, because he will no longer be a student here."

As far as I know, no one ever streaked at Belmont. Current university presidents would do well to have some of that good man's backbone. It often looks like the animals are running the zoo at many of our institutions, instead of mature adults who should be modeling and teaching civility rather than coddling pampered students.

During those years, not all was well on the local/community front. We received word that a casino-type gambling boat was to be launched on the Cumberland River, not far from our church and the homes of many of our members. This venture was to take advantage of the growing number of tourists who would gravitate toward the Opryland complex. At a public hearing, I appeared before the city council, and spoke strongly against gambling and its accompanying corruption invading the tranquility of our neighborhood. Not long after, I received a special delivery letter from a local law firm. In the letter, the firm, advocates for the riverboat casino, were charging me with slander and threatening a lawsuit. In retrospect, it was an intimidation tactic to shut us up, something we see a lot of today. But it scared me as I thought: *What would they do to our church? What would they do to our family?* Shaken and seeking some guidance and peace from my Lord, I hit my knees in prayer.

As this was transpiring in my study, my secretary, Dot White—a great godly lady—knocked on the door to inform me there was someone to see me. I composed myself to greet the visitor. In walked a faithful, vibrant member of our church. His name was Jim. He said, "Pastor, I hate to interrupt you. Won't take but a few moments of your time. I was driving by the church on Briley Parkway, and the Holy Spirit told me to come in and pray with you and for you. Do you mind?"

Did I mind? This messenger from God knelt down with me and put his hand on my right shoulder. I do not remember all of his prayer; however, I do recall the Scripture he quoted: *"Though a thousand shall fall at your side and ten thousand at your right hand, but it will not come near you"* (Psalm 91:7).

He left, and the peace and presence of my Lord settled on me. I am awed at the goodness of God: that from His omniscience and compassion, saw a frightened, young preacher, touched a sensitive layman to pray with me, and brought tremendous comfort immediately. As far as I know, only the lawyer from the threatening law firm and the Holy Spirit knew about my crisis.

I contacted Frank Ingraham—a well-respected, competent, godly, Christian lawyer—to assist me with the issue. Frank took it on at no charge, assured me things would be okay, and went to work on the situation. I do not know what he did; however, the threatened lawsuit was dropped. I am eternally grateful to both of those men, Jim and Frank. God used them in my life to calm my soul and increase my faith in the One who called me to faithfully serve Him. What an awesome God we have! We are not alone in life's battles.

I experienced another life-changing event that affected my family. I was having the time of my life. God's blessings were showered on us. There was love and unity in the church. Our family was a joy to me. All was well on the home front, so I thought, until one day, my secretary, Dot, told me my wife, Jeanette, was here to see me for her "appointment." I thought: *Appointment? My wife?* I played along with what I thought was a practical joke. I met her at my study door, greeted her, and said, "Mrs. Henry, have a seat. What can I do for you?"

I sat down behind my desk and waited for Jeanette to break into a smile as we began our pleasant visit. No smile. Only a glare. Her laser, brown eyes zeroed in on a target right between my eyes as she stated, "You've got time for everybody else. Now, how about taking time for us?"

She was right. I had not given my family their proper place. The church, in a sense, had become my mistress. I apologized to my precious wife and to the Lord. We began to live differently, intentionally filling our calendar with family outings, recitals, ball games, and family nights, giving them their proper priority. One time I was in a group where nationally known speaker and pastor Peter Lord encouraged us: "Either the Holy Spirit and you will plan your calendar, or everybody else will." Jeanette and I began to do just that.

Dr. Edgar Arendall, longtime pastor of Dawson Memorial Baptist Church in Birmingham, added another truth to my growing family vocabulary. I was visiting in his study and gleaning all I could from his experience to assist me in leading our growing church. As I was leaving he said, "I know you are not making a lot of money. What are you doing with your family? Let me encourage you to save what you can, and spend your money with your family on events and experiences. They will forget nearly everything you buy them; however, they will never forget a shared experience."

Whoa! What great wisdom. We put it to work with our children, and then with our five grandsons. It works! I have passed that on in sermons, at seminaries, and in pastors' conferences. Many have told me they started practicing that maxim and received the same happy results.

One such event I experienced with our daughter. A local church had an invited guest, the governor of our neighboring state of Georgia. I heard he was a "born-again" believer and unashamed of his commitment to Christ. With young Kitty in tow, we headed for the church. She wondered why we were going. As a lover of history, I flippantly replied, "He may be president someday."

After the service, we stayed to meet him. Kitty had Jimmy Carter, the future president of the United States, autograph her Bible. Years later she was singing at 16th Avenue Baptist Church in Birmingham, Alabama, when President Carter was present and spoke during the service. Afterwards, she met him, recalled her youthful encounter, and got him to autograph that same Bible a second time. He first signed it as the governor of Georgia and then as the president of the United States of America. My guess is that not many people possess that kind of historic memorabilia.

The Lord opened many doors for me to preach in a variety of places and events, including Ridgecrest Conference Center in North Carolina, where I have preached or taught every decade since the 1960s. Those mountain-top experiences are forever "gentle on my mind." Often I meet people who tell me they were there at a certain week and that they, or others in their group, were touched by the hand of God.

From time to time, I had the opportunity to preach at churches I respected for their influence and history. One of those was Bellevue in Memphis. Dr. R. G. Lee, one of my heroes in the faith, led the church to be one of the most influential in the area. His power in preaching and painting pictures with words was legendary.

My opportunity to get to know Dr. Lee better came when he spoke on two different occasions at Two Rivers after he retired. The first time I had Kitty with me when we met him at the airport. He returned a couple of years later. The instant he saw her, he said, "Hello, Kitty!" By then he was in his late eighties. He preached his famous "Payday Someday" sermon to a packed Sunday night crowd.

One morning when we pulled up to the church, he said, "Preacher, what do you want me to preach today?"

Dr. Lee was asking me! I was flabbergasted, and blurted out, "What do you have in mind?

"I have got two in mind. With one sermon I just go from A to Z and talk about a variety of things. It is like bologna, which I can cut it off anywhere. It's good. The other possible sermon in one that is really focused on Jesus alone," he explained.

"Let's do the Jesus one," I suggested.

Dr. Lee quickly agreed and enthusiastically responded, "You can't beat Jesus, can you?"

When Dr. Ramsey Pollard—the senior pastor who succeeded Dr. Lee—retired, a series of pastors, including me, were invited to preach. All of us jumped at the chance. I am sure that many of us were wondering the same thing I thought of: would the church choose me to succeed Dr. Lee? Looking back, I realize it was most unlikely, but it was something that flitted through my mind.

Jeanette and I drove to Memphis on Saturday. I worked feverishly on a message. I could not push back the thoughts: *What should I preach? What could I say as I stood in the shadow of such great preachers and pastors?*

There was no need for me to be anxious. Late Saturday, the chairman of the pulpit committee called our room. In somewhat of an apology, he said, "Brother Jim, I hate to do this. Our search team has found who we believe is to be our next pastor. He is here, and will be preaching tomorrow in view of a call. We need to ask you to step aside, so we can make this happen. However, you can preach tomorrow night?" Disappointed, we certainly understood.

The next morning, we were a part of the congregation, eager to hear a dynamic young pastor from First Baptist Church of Merritt Island, Florida. What a preacher! With a powerful voice, keen grasp of Scripture, unction from the Holy Spirit, a graceful and fluid delivery, he preached. Bellevue unanimously called him as pastor.

Jeanette and I joined Adrian and Joyce Rogers, along with the selection committee, for a celebration luncheon. Adrian was a man for the times. Greatly used of God, deeply loved and respected, he became the voice of pastors and people in the drive to keep our Southern Baptists true to the Word of God. I am convinced he was one of the key individuals God used to keep our denomination from being thrown into the wasteland of apostasy in to which so many denominations have drifted. In retrospect, being "bumped" by Adrian Rogers was not such a bad thing!

Things could not have been better for us in Nashville. The children were happy in their schools. We lived near the grandparents. The church was booming. Pulpit committees occasionally called or visited. We usually prayed about each approach, not wanting to turn a deaf ear to God if he had work for us in other places. Some we turned down. Some turned us down.

We visited one church in a nearby state, and had a good meeting with the pulpit team at an evening meal. The next morning the senior member of the committee took us to breakfast. We were praying for the Holy Spirit to give us some hint about further pursuit of this invitation. During breakfast the older gentleman said, "We have visited your services and really enjoyed them. However, I noticed you go past twelve o'clock. We expect to be walking out the door in our church at twelve o'clock."

With that statement, Jeanette kicked my leg under the table rather sharply and rolled her eyes. I can assure you that was not the only time the Lord used a nudge from my bride, my best teammate in life and ministry, to help make His intentions known. We both had great peace on closing the door on that situation.

Another invitation really pulled at us. We had said no to another church that came after us strongly. I think we may have entertained it further, except for a couple of ladies on the team that were adamant in their opposition to us.

When First Baptist Church of New Orleans contacted me in the latter part of 1976, I wrestled deeply over that decision. Other churches had come knocking; however, New Orleans really got our attention. The chairman of the search team was Dr. Marvin Thames. The committee was made up of gracious, godly people. However, in January of 1977, I told them I could not get the green light from the Lord. They were persistent and asked me to pray some more. We did. A couple of weeks later I wrote Dr. Thames to tell them I could not come. Jeanette was disappointed for she loved the city, the seminary, and the church. Dr. J. D. Grey, long time pastor of the church, was the charismatic spiritual voice of New Orleans. As seminarians, we loved to hear him preach in chapel and in his pulpit. On his 25th anniversary as pastor of First Baptist, they had a huge celebration in his honor, and even made coins with his image on one side.

One of the events was a men's dinner at which they brought in one of his contemporaries, Dr. W. A. Criswell of First Baptist Dallas. One of my friends Billy Murphy, who was on the staff there, wrangled a ticket for me for the evening. Dr. Criswell brought his usual eloquent and powerful message. Afterwards, they asked Dr. Grey to say a few words. He began to reminisce. Looking across the packed room, he asked, "How many of you were here when you voted to call me as pastor?"

Several hands went up. Then he called the name of a man, whose name I do not recall. [For the sake of the story, I will call him Bob.] "Bob, weren't you here when I was called as pastor?"

From the back of the room, Bob shouted, "Yes, but I didn't vote for you."

It broke up the room and was one of the few times the articulate Dr. Grey was at a loss for words!

Those memories and that strategic church on St. Charles Avenue pulled at me; however, I could not get the green light from the Holy Spirit to accept their gracious invitation. On the same day I wrote the letter turning down the church in New Orleans, I received a letter from one of our members who was a winter visitor to the Central Florida area. They had visited First Baptist Orlando, reported pastor Dr. Henry Parker was retiring after a good, twenty-year tenure, and included a newspaper clipping of his decision. In my journal, I wrote these words: "I felt impressed some months ago that I may go there as pastor. Sensed it again today. Why? I do not know."

We jumped back into the joyous daily grind at Two Rivers. One Wednesday night the phone rang and the voice on the other end said, "This is Mac McCully. I am on the pulpit committee of First Baptist Church, Orlando. We would like to talk to you."

I laughed, thinking it was one of my preacher brothers pulling my leg. (Pretending we were on the committee of some prestigious church, we did that to each other from time to time.)

Mac said, "No joke. I am from the First Baptist Church of Orlando. We will be visiting your church. When our team comes, we hope we can meet discreetly and talk with you."

Thus began our journey to First Baptist Orlando.

I found out later that they had run through several others on their potential pastor list and on which my name was not listed! Humbling. However, that June I had been the morning platform preacher at Fellowship of Christian Athletes (FCA) summer camp at Blue Ridge. I had bypassed my usual attendance at the annual Southern Baptist Convention to preach to this assembly of a thousand coaches and athletes. Some of the students, coaches and the FCA director of the Orlando area, Doug Scott, were members of First Baptist, and were at the assembly. They brought my name to the attention of the search team, which brought them to Two Rivers to check me out.

For weeks, Jeanette and I prayed and discussed: *Why leave family, a dynamic church, and an extensive television ministry to go to a downtown church that is smaller than ours?* As we talked to the committee the decision seemed to have more of a downside than an upside: Earlier in the summer in revival with Richard Jackson, we had sixty-eight additions at Two Rivers. From the human standpoint, it made no sense. Yet, we could not shake this incessant feeling in our spirit. We struggled deeply. We fasted and prayed as we begged God for some evidence, some sign, as to whether we should stay or go. Heaven was silent.

I called Ray Dorman, the chairman of the nine-member team, and told him we could not get a release to come. Ray was most gracious, and said he would inform the Wednesday night attendees that we were not coming. The church had been asked to pray. They had not publicly released my name; however, the word was out that someone had been asked.

After the call, I headed for our Wednesday night service, which was usually full and packed with excitement. I totally expected to find the same sense of relief that I had experienced in turning down other invitations. When I came to the platform and looked out over the sea of faces I dearly loved, something strange happened. It was as if I was no longer there—like I was having some strange out-of-body experience. My Lord had changed my heart!

I went to the house and gathered our family. Kitty was a rising junior, Betsy was a rising freshmen, and Jimmy was headed for the sixth grade. I told them that God was calling us to leave everything and everyone they had known and loved. Kitty was quiet. Betsy started crying. Jimmy had visions of Disney World. We prayed together. I told the Lord we believed He was leading us to Orlando. There was no doubt in our minds; however, we asked

God, "If You do not mind, would You please have someone from Orlando call and just say, 'We're sorry you're not coming' or something like that?"

Since they were on eastern standard time and we were on central standard time, the church had already heard we were not coming. As I was saying, "Amen," the first of three calls came within a few minutes of each other. They were not from anyone on the pulpit team. God had graciously confirmed our decision.

Finally, I called Ray to tell him we were coming. I asked him not to share my decision until I had the opportunity to tell our people of our call and the details on the following Sunday.

My devotional reading that day was from Joshua 14, which includes one of my favorite texts: "*Lord, give me this mountain*" (verse 14). One of the search team members had read this scriptural passage when we met with the deacons in our recent visit. In my journal I penned these words on August 14, 1977: "Bless, O Lord, the work of Thy hands. Give us, O Lord, this new mountain!"[39]

Somehow the news of our decision leaked out. The front page of the *Nashville Tennessean* told of our upcoming move. Telling those wonderful people of our exodus was one of the most difficult things I have ever done. They wept, and so did we.

Commending us to the work in Orlando, the members of Two Rivers were gracious to us in every way. To this day, we continue to cherish the deep friendships we developed with those great people. Two Rivers was a kind of spiritual Camelot to us, and, I think, to our people. I pray that every pastor

---

[39] Later, when we encountered some difficult days on that mountain hike, I could relate to Elvis Presley, singing, "But this time, Lord, you gave me a mountain!" (*You Gave Me a Mountain* was written by Marty Robbins during the 1960s and recorded by Elvis Presley in the 1970s.)

has a Two Rivers-type of church experience. My sense is that it was church as it was meant to be. Not a perfect pastor or perfect people, but a people united in a common bond of love for our Master and His mission.

I often wept, even after we moved to Orlando, as I thought of the people there. Sometimes I wondered if they might call, and say, "Brother Jim, did you make a mistake? Will you consider coming back?" (Several years later, they did just that.) In my heart of hearts, I knew if they did, I would have to say no. God had clearly sent us on a new mission—a venture so unique that if I had been given a preview, I would not have believed it.

Packed with all we owned, our family said our tearful good-byes to our family, our church, and a city we loved. Off we headed for Mickey MouseWorld!

With All My Heart

To All Who Are Experiencing Life Coming at You Too Fast:

In retrospect, all of life seems to move at warp speed, except when you are in school or waiting for Christmas, especially before you get to middle school. Now, as I am approaching the eighth decade of my life, I look back at how chock-full each decade was. My thirties were a whirlwind! I wonder how I survived those years and emerged in one piece with my mind intact. Only by the grace of God! If life is coming at you at breakneck speed, take time to slow down, smell the roses, drink a cup of coffee, and enjoy the timeless One who set eternity in our hearts.

CHAPTER TWELVE

WE'RE GOING TO DISNEY

W E HIT THE GROUND running upon arriving in Orlando. First Baptist Church had a solid reputation. With their long-tenured pastorates of a combined sixty-plus years, Dr. J. Dean Adcock, Dr. J. Powell Tucker, and Dr. Henry Allen Parker had given the church stability. The charismatic movement had made an impact on the church. Some people came to our church for Bible study and then went to Calvary Assembly of God for its music. First Baptist had two morning worship services. The early service was youth-oriented with more upbeat music and the second was more traditional. I decided to combine the two into one service for a better sense of unity.

The Lord blessed us. Our attendance swelled. Soon we needed to go back to two services to accommodate the growing numbers. The same was true of Bible study classes. In time, we had to go to three morning worship services, three Sunday School class hours, and two evening worship services.

We began to run into a few snags as we moved along. The church had operated for some time under a committee structure, headed by the operations committee. The committee—a group composed of leaders in the various organizations of the church—met monthly for giving reports and granting approvals of programs, resources, and ideas. Some good people comprised that committee. However, that system of operating the church fostered a situation where we were spending a lot of time doing church work, instead of doing the work of the church. I think this is a common trap in which many churches get caught.

Too often, we had to jump through several hoops to get mundane tasks accomplished. We would come up with a fresh idea or direction, only to find it stonewalled or difficult to move forward. An example of this was the possibility of doing a "Singing Christmas Tree," an idea that our Minister of Music, Ragan Vandergriff, had proposed. We shared this idea with the operations committee. A vote was taken as to whether we might get the go-ahead for this new venture. It ended as a tie vote; however, one member of the committee—Karick Price, a citrus grower—had to leave early. He said, "If you vote, count me for it."

So, by that one vote reported after the tie vote of those present was added, the "Singing Christmas Tree" came into the fabric of First Baptist.[40] It has continued for over thirty years and been instrumental in bringing thousands to faith in our Lord Jesus. Through this outstanding music ministry, people of faith have been greatly blessed as its message of hope is presented with excellence by committed and talented members.

---

[40] Voting to go ahead with the Singing Christmas Tree meant that we had to amend the 1980 church budget by $50,000, which meant we had to go to the deacons to authorize this increase. Stan Hand, Sr., made the motion to amend the budget. The motion passed. Visionary leaders, like Stan; far-sighted and faithful laity; and gifted pastors and associates who possess God-sized faith make it a joy to pastor.

Our church had an antiquated constitution and by-laws that not only hamstrung us often, but became a weapon by some to make it difficult to navigate efficiently and effectively. I have noticed that constitutions and by-laws tend to serve as obstacles rather than instruments to preserve the mission of the church. Some church members know their church constitution better than the Bible! I decided to have a committee to see how we could adjust our constitution in ways to preserve order, yet allow it to be a channel through which we could work well (rather than one that would work against us). I designated associate pastor Bill Curl—a college fraternity brother and long-time friend—to represent us. Things were still not operating smoothly. Our staff and I would send changes to the current documents that we thought would be helpful, only to have Bill report to us that they did not like, or refused to do anything about, our suggestions.

Finally, in desperation, I decided to take it to our deacons. I could not see spending the rest of my life climbing a fence that was leaning toward me. I dedicated two deacon meetings to sharing a vision of what First Baptist could be. I used the Bible, charts, the church fathers' vision for the church, and history as tools to explain the biblical pattern of church function. At the conclusion, I asked the men to affirm a more biblical pattern. A rousing discussion followed. I could not tell how it would end.

Prior to the meetings, I had not asked one deacon to vote for what I was teaching. I did not want to politicize the matter. It had to be of the Holy Spirit, the Word, and the heart. Ernest Hungerford—a Georgia Tech grad and a Campus Crusade volunteer, who, along with wife Helen and children, had brought maturity and passionate evangelistic hearts to our church— rose to speak. Holding the Bible in his hand, he asked, "How many of you believe this is the Word of God?" As far as I could tell, the hand of every one of the approximately eighty to ninety deacons in the room went up.

Ernest went on to read the following passage from the Bible: *"Obey your leaders and submit to their authority. They keep watch over you as men who must give an account. Obey them so that their work will be a joy and not a burden, for that would be of no advantage to you"* (Hebrews 13:17). Ernest pointed at me and said, "You see that man? He is the leader the Bible is talking about."

With that he moved that the deacons affirm the biblical pattern of leadership. Most of the deacons voted in strong affirmation for his motion; however, some still were not convinced this was the best way to govern our church. It was to the dissenters Ernest spoke next: "Let me add one more thing. You who oppose this, this is your right. But if you are going to remain unhappy, kindly go to another church and take any ill will with you."

I was stunned by the turn of events. That was a tipping point in our church. We sensed a freedom—not the license—to lead our church. With the exercise of this freedom came innovation, excitement, and, most importantly, tremendous blessings from God.

We were privileged to host a number of great Christians who taught and encouraged us: David Wilkerson, Arthur Blessitt, Andraé Crouch, Mrs. B.B. McKinney (whose late husband had penned many of the great hymns of the church), Jack Taylor, Peter Lord, Sam Cathey, Richard Jackson, Perry Sanders, Bailey Smith, Bill Bennett, and so many others.

The Billy Graham team accepted the invitation of pastors and lay leaders to come to Orlando for a Central Florida crusade at the Citrus Bowl. It was my honor, along with Dr. Howard Edington—the courageous pastor of First Presbyterian of Orlando—to be co-chair of that powerful spiritual event. On the Sunday of the crusade's beginning, Cliff Barrows and George Beverly Shea led our praise service. Our church and our community were blessed beyond words by the ministry of this exceptional team.

During those downtown campus days, I had the opportunity to go to South Korea to preach in crusades in Taegu and Pusan. We were a part of a joint venture with the Florida Baptist Convention to partner with the booming evangelistic movement in that country. Fellow staffers Bill and Lucy Pat Curl, both excellent musicians, also joined me. While in Pusan, I walked through the American cemetery there and was overwhelmed by the gripping sight of the graves of our brave soldiers.

We initially stayed in a hotel in downtown Seoul. A riot occurred while I was there. It was disconcerting to see soldiers in gas masks, and with fixed bayonets and shields confronting the demonstrators, in addition to having tear gas waft into my room. Because of the unrest, the authorities decided there would be no public gatherings, which meant the canceling of our crusades. The host pastors were in great anguish. I heard them, with tears and loud voices, appeal to God to change the minds of the military. God did! Permission was granted. To guarantee our safety and prevent disruption in our crusade meeting, the government posted soldiers to guard the perimeter of the stadium.

Billy Kim—the former president of the Baptist World Alliance (2000-2005)—was my host for a part of the tour. Even then, during the 1980s, Billy had great influence as a pastor and spokesman for the faith. Because of the respect and reputation he had attained, Billy had arranged for us to have tea with the commanding general at an Army base. It was an incredible opportunity, where we both witnessed to the general and prayed for him.

In the crusade services, Billy was as animated and intense—as strong and forceful as I, probably more so. Because of Billy's having to translate for me as I spoke to those in attendance, I felt some uncertainty about my effectiveness in getting across my message. At the end of the service I said, "Billy, I hope you and everyone listening understood what I was trying to say."

"Oh, yes, Brother Jim," Billy assured me. "They got yours, plus some of mine. I made yours even better!" We have maintained friendship to this day. He is truly a remarkable Christian leader.

Growth at First Baptist was a blessing and a challenge. We maxed out our space and meeting times. Desiring to stay in our historic, downtown location, we tried to buy up everything in proximity to our facilities. There was one property, which was owned by an elderly couple and located in the middle of the block near the church. We needed that piece of property in order to build a larger worship facility, as well as much needed parking. We fasted. We prayed. Deacons visited this couple in their home and offered them far beyond their property's value. The older couple could not be budged. Purchasing that property was not an option.

With very little parking, we often saw people drive up, try to find parking places unsuccessfully, and drive away. This compelled us to consider future options. We desperately needed a solution for this dilemma.

To help us move forward, I appointed a "dream team," a visionary group of individuals to whom was given the charge of considering not only our present situation, but the possibilities for the next fifty to hundred years. For months, they prayed, talked to church growth experts, considered the demographics of our community's growing population, and studied the projected areas for future growth in the Orlando area. In due time, they reported and recommended we purchase at least one-hundred acres to give room for plenty of parking, a Christian school, recreational fields, and senior adult retirement housing. The church almost unanimously adopted this ambitious, future-oriented plan.

Next, I appointed a property search team to find some property and report back to the church. The team found twenty-five acres north of the city at a key intersection on busy I-4. We had a business meeting to look at their recommendation. With a large crowd assembled, I was in for a shock when substantial opposition showed up. Some even petitioned the community into which we were considering moving and asked them to take a stand against our relocating there. Other substantial voices, including several of long standing local and family roots and another local denomination, also spoke against this plan. The discussion pro and con went back and forth until late in the evening. The best I can recall, we finally took a vote around 11:00 p.m. The vote to purchase carried, but only narrowly.

Not comfortable with the results and with a heavy heart, I drove home with a strong sense that we should not move forward. After praying further about the decision, I knew in my heart we would not move forward with this plan, which I announced on the following Sunday. I sent the committee back to work. Somehow, I sensed God had a better plan. I just did not have the foggiest idea what it was!

With All My Heart

To Those Who Faithfully Serve and Follow God's Call:

When things are going well and life, for the most part, seems to be comfortable, God can pull the plug and send you on another mission. You can feel your life and service are being disrupted. While questions may fly, you sense something else is going on. When God led our family to Orlando, I only thought of Disney World as a magical destination for vacationers. As one who moved into this new kingdom, I can tell you that it was an adventure of a lifetime. With God as our Guide, following His lead to this new home was anything but boring!

CHAPTER THIRTEEN

THE BETTER PLAN

THE LORD CONTINUED TO rest His favor on the church. The recently elected mayor of Orlando, Bill Frederick, and his wife, Joanne, joined our church from another denomination, and asked for baptism by immersion. In my opinion, Mayor Frederick, a man of great integrity and wisdom, was one of Orlando's finest leaders in the last fifty years. A forward-thinker, he helped changed our city's law enforcement procedures to become a model for many cities across our nation. Mayor Frederick's legacy includes securing the Orlando International Airport and bringing the Orlando Magic basketball franchise to our city.

God also blessed our church by bringing other great community leaders to become members of our congregation. Randall James, staff aide to three Orlando mayors, joined with his wife, Irma. (Years later, I invited Randall to become a member of our staff, which he did—a tremendous blessing for everyone.) Athletes, professional golfers, business leaders, educators, ordinary folks, students, as well as an increasing number of people with diverse national and racial heritages became a part of the loving and welcoming heart of the First Baptist family.

The ongoing search for property was difficult. Orlando was booming. Available property of any size was expensive. Because of our charter, to be First Baptist Orlando, we had to be in the city limits. A new member, who knew of our search, came across a 156-acre property in southwest Orlando on the interstate I-4. The land was somewhat swampy, not in a high-rent district, and a dumping ground for everything from old stoves to scrap metal—you name it.

The possibility of our attaining this property came before the deacons for discussion and their recommendation. When it came to a vote, the deacons passed it; however, the vote was not overwhelmingly in favor. This greatly disturbed me. When we took a break in our meeting, I asked Don Easter, our deacon chairman, to ask the deacons to go to prayer and reconsider their vote. I felt I could not go to the church without stronger deacon support. Don did. We prayed. Then we revoted. This time the vote was much stronger to affirm the recommendation.

Decades later, I saw Don at this grandson's wedding and thanked him again for taking a second vote. I told Don that if he had not, history would have been changed dramatically. Tears welled up in his eyes and he said, "I am glad I did. Under the same circumstances, I would do it again. It was the right thing to do."

Thank God for godly leaders like Don Easter. These courageous people are the kind of people that make eternal differences—most of whom quietly do their work, desiring no personal glory, only seeking the Kingdom of God.

When we brought the acquisition of this property to our church for a vote, we decided to have three possible vote options: yes, no, or "whatever the majority decides." Believing we needed a significant majority of our members in favor of this faith venture to make the move successful, I prayed for at least a sixty-six-percent vote. When the vote was tabulated, it came in at a fraction over sixty-six percent.

We set our hearts and hands toward raising capital for the purchase. Our leadership joined with me in deciding we would raise the owner's asking price of 2.6 million dollars without borrowing. With a short-fuse time we prayed, fasted, and asked God for a miracle. We called commitment day "Miracle Day," and asked our Lord to do a mighty thing for the glory of His Name, for His Church, and as a larger witness to bless the Body of Christ everywhere.

On the Sunday before Miracle Day, I preached a message from Matthew 26:9-13 in which I challenged our people to give their sacrificial "alabaster box," as the woman did for Jesus. At the invitation time, a young couple in tears came forward. In her hand was her wedding ring. She said, "We do not have much to give. Could you sell my ring and put it in the offering?"

I was stunned. I had never seen this kind of sacrifice. I asked her husband if he agreed. He nodded yes. I knew this was special. They were of limited means.[41] When they returned to their seats, I held up her ring and challenged the people: "What will you do next Sunday?"

Miracle Day was unbelievable. Our people brought money, stock, property, automobiles, motorcycles, and antiques. One man came forward with papers in hand and said, "There are the papers on my prize bull. I cannot bring him forward; however, I want you to sell him and put it in the offering."

When the smoke cleared, our people had given over a million dollars in cash and gifts of kind. It was so significant it was reported on the front

---

[41] His work as a painter was sporadic. We had assisted this couple from our ministry from time to time.

page of the *Orlando Sentinel* with a picture of one of our pastors, Bob New, surveying the array of gifts and money the people brought.

Newspapers all over the country reported the story from Detroit to Ft. Worth, from coast to coast. The Armed Forces paper, *Stars and Stripes*, even wrote it up. As I was driving into the office, I heard Paul Harvey say, "Did you hear about that offering at First Baptist Church in Orlando, Florida?" He told the story two other times on his national broadcast that day.

Churches wrote and called us to say that what God did for us had encouraged them. They were going to try to raise money, rather than borrow it. Our prayers were answered beyond our imagination. Oh, yes, the ring! Seven people offered to buy the ring, return it to the giver, and put the money in the offering!

We closed on the property before the first of the year. A building team was organized. We traveled across the nation—in fact, all the way to San Francisco—to glean ideas from other churches. Several were incorporated initially; others later.

Construction began with our people going to the property, reading Scripture, and praying over the property and the workers. Grateful to God for His protection, we had no one who was critically injured in the massive construction project.

Another miracle along the way was our experience with the Ford Foundation. They owned ten acres in the vicinity of our present worship center. We could build around it; however, we thought it would be wiser to acquire the property so it would not be a problem in the future. We got no response from them, even when our senator and congressman appealed on our behalf. As only God could orchestrate it, Bob Robinson moved to Orlando and joined our church. Bob had connections with the chancellor at Vanderbilt University, who had served as president of the Ford Foundation board. Bob had built a house for him in Nashville. He got in touch with the chancellor. Soon the Ford Foundation was in touch with us. A reasonable asking price for the property was presented to us. We gobbled it up! We built a beautiful and functional worship center that graces that part of our property. The rest is history—another chapter in the providence of God.

On February 10, 1985, we gathered for the ribbon-cutting and our first worship service. Nearly seven thousand people packed the worship center. When we ran out of parking space, we parked cars on what is now the John Young Parkway (which opened shortly after we did).

We dedicated our new place with guests Pat Boone, Sandi Patty, Larnelle Harris, and comedian Jerry Clower—whose first words were, "Praise the Lord! All of this with no federal aid!"

Our original plan in relocation was to continue a strong presence downtown. For several reasons, a number of our people wanted to stay in the downtown location. We determined to have a church in two locations—a fairly new concept then, but more familiar now. I would preach and Ragan Vandegriff, our Minister of Music, would lead the choral music and congregational singing at the downtown service. Then the downtown campus would have Bible study classes, while Ragan[42] and I jumped into his red Land Cruiser—fully equipped with lights, siren, and official Fire Department Chaplain markings—and raced to our new location to lead the services there.

Both campuses did well; however, some in the downtown church wanted to be an autonomous congregation. We formed a committee to facilitate that desire, which resulted in our parting ways. This was difficult for me. I wanted

---

[42] In addition to his pastoral duties at First Orlando, Ragan has faithfully served thirty-eight years as the chaplain for the fire departments of Orlando, Orange County, Reedy Creek (Disney area), and Orlando International Airport.

to continue being the undershepherd to all, but it was not to be. To make it financially viable for the downtown church to become an autonomous congregation, we sold off a portion of the downtown property. The group that soon formed Downtown Baptist Church purchased two of the buildings. (In one of those ironic twists in the current of God's river, I was invited to return as their "preaching pastor" in 2014 to prepare Downtown Baptist for their next pastor. In the sovereignty of God, both church locations will be lighthouses for Christ in the growing Orlando metropolitan area.)

Adjustments were many and fast in our new facility. Almost immediately, we were out of room. Classes met in the worship center. Portables were brought in. We added more facilities. The Lord kept sending people as we kept going after them. Under the dedicated leadership of Gerry Leonard—a convert under the ministry of D. James Kennedy, who authored *Evangelism Explosion*, a powerful, evangelistic training curriculum—our people learned how to share their faith, which they effectively did all over central Florida. The Lord not only added to the church daily, He multiplied the church!

We had to make changes on the fly. Things were fast, furious, and fun. I made a lot of mistakes; however, God in His grace and the people with their patience stood with our leaders and me. Together, we steered the ship of faith without wrecking it!

There were so many magnificent events and transforming personal moments for the people, my family, and me. It would take another book to tell the story; however, two events and decisions proved to be monumental in their present- and long-term effects. One Sunday I preached a pro-life message. Later in the week, Rick Fletcher, a lawyer and fairly new convert to Christ, asked me to lunch. Over lunch he told me he agreed with what I had to say. He then posed the question, "What are we going to do about it? It is one thing to talk; another to act. Here is my proposal. I will financially underwrite whatever it costs to launch a ministry to save babies. I will pay all the expenses the first year, if the church will assume it thereafter. I will continue to support it; but it needs to be a church ministry."

We prayed. The church agreed, and our Center for Pregnancy was launched. In the years since its inception, we know that at least 2,397 babies have been saved rather than aborted; over three thousand individuals have come to saving faith; and our center has been used to facilitate the launching of other similar ministries around the country. Our first director, Lynn Kennedy, is now a lifetime missionary in Burkina Faso. This important ministry is staffed by a large number of compassionate volunteers.

The second decision was the launching of a Christian school. Shortly after coming to Orlando, Tom Gurney, a locally and nationally renowned and respected attorney, was a faithful member of First Baptist. Over lunch one day, he said, "If our church ever decides to have a Christian school, I have set aside some seed money to help." I assured him we would keep it in mind.

As I was a public school graduate and advocate, I saw no pressing need to start a private Christian school. It was not on my front burner. However, parents began asking me if we were going to start a school since we had listed it as a possibility in our future vision. They showed me examples of things their children were dealing with and the deterioration of some of the public schools in our area. After study and prayer, we launched The First Academy (TFA). In 1987 we launched grades K-5 with Fred Chase as our first headmaster, followed by Ed Gamble and Steve Whitaker—all of whom have provided superb leadership. Blue and gold, which symbolized the royalty of Jesus Christ, were chosen to be the school's colors. The lion—as Jesus is the Lion of Judah—was chosedn as its mascot.

After growing to grades K-8, parents wanted to know if we were going to add an Upper School. I knew this would require more buildings and more money, already in tight demand. A meeting was held to listen to parents, church members, the school board, and leaders. I struggled with what to do. I was determined to be a listener, and asked for God's wisdom as we decided. At the end of a healthy discussion, they turned and said, "Brother Jim, what do you think?"

At that moment, I sensed the Holy Spirit saying, "Yes." And that's what I said.

The Upper School was launched in 1987. We added a grade a year, and had our first graduating class in 1994. In the years following, we graduated 1,257 students; won state championships in nearly every sport against public and private schools; awarded scholarships totaling an estimated 85 million in the last eleven years for academic excellence; seen our athletes compete at the university and professional levels; rejoiced over hundreds coming to faith in Christ; reached countless family members; had graduates return to teach and coach at TFA; had the privilege of encouraging other churches to launch their programs in Christian education; and, as an added blessing, experienced the joy of having three of our grandsons graduate from The First Academy.

The church continued to grow. When we added another worship service and had three Bible study periods sandwiched around and during those services, Carl George—a church growth consultant, who had wisely counseled us since we had begun relocation possibilities years ago—asked me, "Do you have the same pattern of worship services in both services?"

Replying to the affirmative, he said, "Pastor, you need to add a different type service. If you always do what you've always done, you will always get what you've already got."

Not knowing what kind of a response we would have if we added what most call a contemporary service, I prayed and contemplated if we should give it a go. Finally, after numerous prospective members inquired if we had a contemporary service, I decided we should try it. I preached a series of messages on worship, styles, history, and biblical types of worship. At the conclusion of the series, I announced that we would have a contemporary service to model what we could expect in the future. Then, they could choose their preferred style of music. I would preach the same message. We would keep one service in the same style we had used for years.

Truett Cathy, the godly founder of Chic-fil-A, told me one day as we were driving, "I made a big mistake in my business. I had added something to our menu that was basically a giveaway. Looking at the bottom line, I realized it was costing us a lot on our bottom line, so I stopped it. The reaction was swift and horrible. We got hate mail. People stopped coming to our stores, and so forth. I learned a lesson: don't give them something and then take it away."

We did not. Instead, we added, and God blessed. As far as I know, we lost no one over the change and addition, though I did hear some complaints about the "loud music." Our people were gracious, mature, and cooperative. The result was we reached more people and survived what could have been a potential division.

Our people at First Baptist stood with us on every issue we dealt with in the swirling, cultural waters around us. Our deacons always had our back, and were not timid about putting their names and their voices on record.

One such occasion was when we received reports from some Stetson University students about some of the teaching and textbooks they were using in class. They were not what Baptist theologians had written and did not adhere to historic Christian theology. I invited the president and the dean of Stetson to come to our deacon meeting to address our concerns. We had given "over and beyond" financial gifts to the school, in addition to the monies they were receiving from our Southern Baptist Cooperative Program. I respect the fact that they came and talked with us; however, I was saddened to hear that they spoke from a different perspective than what we had believed they were supposedly teaching.

Stetson later removed itself from desiring support of the Southern Baptist Convention. It has gone the way of so many other universities that were founded on propagating Christian education on the precepts once delivered to the saints. Still a respected school, Stetson is removed in many ways from its bedrock. And it has been my studied observation that when a Christian school deviates from its historic roots, it nearly always drifts left. Mr. Gurney's wise observation to me years ago still holds true today: "When an institution removes itself from the umbrella of the church, it will always move away from its biblical moorings." Sadly true.

At our new campus we continued the annual tradition of presenting the Singing Christmas Trees that began at our downtown church. Although one of the most demanding, yet most rewarding, undertakings of our church, this magnificent Christmas under the direction of Ragan Vandegriff grew from one Christmas tree structure at our downtown church to two fifty-foot-high tree structures—each of which holds two-hundred-and-five singers—in our new worship center.

"The Light: The Story of Christ" was the next huge musical-drama production our church presented for many years. The script was written and produced in 1987 by Wayne Johnson, our talented drama and media pastor, who codirected these presentations with Ragan Vandegriff. Utilizing the abilities and service of hundreds of our people as actors, singers, and support teams, "The Light" told the story of the life of Christ in a highly impactful way. Presented during the Easter season, large crowds attended, and our church parking lot filled with buses of church groups and tourists.

It became a fixture in many Christian's celebration of the death and resurrection of our Savior. As with the Trees, thousands can point to that production as being an eternally transforming event in their lives.

Later, we took "The Light"—first, in concert format with preaching—to Liverpool, England and then to Coventry, England, and Cardiff, Wales. I shall never forget the first night in the magnificent cathedral at Liverpool. At the conclusion of the music, I gave a brief gospel message and invited the hearers to respond publicly since we did not have a response card. Knowing the reserved nature of our English friends, I did not know what to expect.

At first, there was no response; and then a man came down the center aisle, then another, and another. We were privileged to see an awesome response to Jesus. The by-products of those efforts were not only people coming to saving faith, but lasting friendships being established, churches being encouraged, lay people and pastors being emboldened.

Another fruit of these presentations was that children, students, and adults were able to use their spiritual gifts and talents. Many of the younger ones who performed nightly before thousands, went on to successful careers in theater, music, and arts in the church and secular worlds. It was a divine derivative that allowed us to penetrate the world as salt and light.

With All My Heart

To Those Whose Best Laid Plans Do Not Seem to Be Working Out:

There are times when you think you've got it all figured out. You pray, plan, and prepare. You feel like you had heard from God as to the best course to follow. While that may be the case, God intervenes and seems to be upgrading your vision. A professor in a theological insti-tution said he could tell rather quickly when he heard his students preach if they were "big Godders" or "little godders." If God is in your plans, He may upsize His orders for you. Be prepared to give Him the glory and live out the song "Our God Is an Awesome God." [43]

---

[43] "Our God Is an Awesome God" was written by Rich Mullins (1988) and recorded by Michael W. Smith and others.

CHAPTER FOURTEEN

NO ONE ELSE BELIEVES IT EITHER

DURING THOSE WILD AND wonderful days, we were blessed with our first grandchild, Caleb—son of our daughter, Betsy, and her husband, Danny—who was later joined by siblings, Seth and Asa. We had the joy of holding them in our arms, praying over them, and whispering the name of Jesus in their ears. They and now their spouses—Cali, Catherine, and Kinsey—have brought beauty, talent, and joy to our family.

Our son, Jimmy, found a Tennessee lady, Tammy, whom he met while working at the Opryland Hotel. I had the privilege of officiating at their union, as well as all of the others, except Caleb's. Jimmy and Tammy produced two sons: Trey, who was named after me and his dad; and Will, who was named after his great-grandfather and great-great-grandfather.

Jeanette and I celebrated our twenty-fifth year of marriage as I took my first sabbatical, which the church graciously allowed for personal renewal. We went to Liverpool, England with our choir and drama folks. After that amazing experience with our church group, Jeanette and I took a car tour of France, Italy, Austria, and Switzerland with Bob and Miriam Vickery. Following our European experience, Jeanette and I headed to the mountains of western North Carolina to stay in the Boone area mountain home of Gene and Lois Wenger—godly, dedicated, and generous members of First Baptist Orlando.

While there, I wrote my second book, *The Pastor's Wedding Manual*, a practical tool to help my fellow pastors in directing, preparing, and officiating Christ-centered weddings. I wrote it because there was very little on the bookshelves to help pastors with this most important ministry. The Lord blessed it. Thirty years since it hit the Lifeway bookstores, the book is still widely used.

I know that is not exactly a romantic way to celebrate one's silver anniversary. I did promise Jeanette I would not work on it full-time. Plus, I spiced up the deal by loosening the purse strings so my bride could do some extra shopping!

Meanwhile, in the wider Southern Baptist world, I found myself and others engaged in a denominational crisis. It was a war of historic proportions, often referred to as the "Battle of the Bible" for our denomination—the largest Protestant denomination—and Christendom. The Lord gave me an inside seat on the struggle that was gripping our institutions. The controversy centered on the claims that some of our seminaries no longer considered the Bible to be inerrant. Reports from students and others contended that what was being taught in seminary classrooms was opposed to the theological teaching that most had heard from the pulpits and classrooms of their local churches. Sermons, public utterances, and published material gave added credence to these concerns.

With the election of Adrian Rogers in 1979 as president of the Southern Baptist Convention, a strategy of returning schools and institutions to their foundations began. Attendance at our denominational annual conventions increased. I remember having my son-in-law, Danny, going early to reserve seats for us, so we could participate in the discussions and voting. Tensions were high. Charges raged back and forth. Others have written in more detail about this period.[44]

In the midst of the turmoil, the Southern Baptist Peace Committee was formed to ferret out the truth and report its findings to the convention. The committee was nominated by Bill Hickem of Florida. It was composed of twenty-two members with Charles Fuller as its chairman, and sought as much balance as possible. Over twenty-five thousand messengers approved and appointed the committee.

I was appointed as a member of this group. Our first meeting was in Nashville in October, 1985. Dr. Herschel H. Hobbs, who had drafted much of *The Baptist Faith and Message* (1963), shared how it came to be and its intent. Cecil Sherman felt it would draw us into blind attachment to a particular creed. Article I of our tenets defined our belief about the Bible as being "without any mixture of error." Adrian Rogers and Charles Stanley said that if a professor signed it and did not intend to teach as Article I and the other articles outlined—as commonly believed by most Baptists—they were dishonest. These professors should quit or be removed. We broke into three subgroups to discuss our 350-word paper on "Theological Concerns." Later, we broke into small prayer groups, where I had the privilege to pray with Rogers and Stanley.

I noted that this group was more conservative than I first imagined. Among the most verbal were Ed Young, Adrian Rogers, Charles Stanley, Dan Vestal

---

[44] The work of James Hefley is some of the most accurate and helpful concerning this period in the life of our denomination.

and Cecil Sherman. Dr. Hobbs was adamant that we take a strong stand for total inspiration of the Bible, underscoring "all," as he did on exegesis on 2 Timothy 3:16, "*All Scripture is God breathed....*" We concluded that *The Baptist Faith and Message* document was to be used to guide our work. I journaled: "In time, we will have to deal with some seminaries and professors. I don't see how we can avoid it, nor should we."

Our peace committee was divided into subgroups to visit all of the seminaries and agencies supported by Cooperative Program money. I was appointed as the chair of a group that included Jerry Vines, copastor of First Baptist, Jacksonville; Bob Cuttino, a pastor from South Carolina; and Bill Poe, a lawyer and member of First Baptist, Charlotte, North Carolina.

Our first visit was to Southwestern Theological Seminary in Ft. Worth, Texas—at that time, the largest of all our seminaries and probably the largest in the world. We started at 7:30 a.m. on a cool morning on January 29, 1986, and went until 4:00 p.m. Dr. Russell H. Dilday, the president; Dr. John Newport, academic dean; and Jerry Gunnels, pastor of the Spring Hall Baptist Church in Mobile, Alabama, represented the school. Cuttino, Vines, and I represented the Peace Committee. The meeting was cordial with very little tension, except when Dr. Dilday and Dr. Vines got into an exchange when Dr. Dilday insisted there was a "hidden agenda" to take over the seminaries by Paige Patterson and Judge Paul Pressler. Dr. Vines avowed he did not know of such "a plan." Other items were discussed. We ended our meeting with prayer. Our group's consensus was that Southwestern was basically conservative and very stable.

That was not the scenario at Southeastern Baptist Theological Seminary, which occupied the former Wake Forest University campus. Arriving on February 4, we were hosted by Dr. and Mrs. W. Randall Lolley at the president's home for a delicious meal. Dr. Morris Ashcraft, the dean of the school;

his wife; and Dr. Charles Horton, the chair of the board of the trustees, also were on hand. All of our team—Poe, Cuttino, Vines, and I—were present. Later in the evening, our team met with about fifteen students from a group who called themselves the Concerned Evangelical Fellowship (CEF). They had contacted me previously and requested to meet with us. (A part of our instruction as Peace Committee members was to listen to any and all parties if they requested it.) They were kind-spirited, not angry, but concerned. We met for three hours. They gave to us a long list of grievances, which we promised to pass on to the entire Peace Committee.

We met on the seminary campus the next day, February 5, from 8:00 a.m. until 6:00 p.m. The same group that had met for dinner was gathered over some of the things that had surfaced when we met. Dr. Ashcraft was guarded and defensive. They were evidently upset that we had met with the students the night before. I sought to allay their fears and remind them of our mandate to hear from all parties. Their stance reflected the opinion that the CEF were renegades and not representative of conservatives on campus. I think the thing that really grabbed our attention and, perhaps, highlighted the concerns that had pushed our convention into divisiveness, was when I asked about a comment one of the students made to us. He said that one of his Old Testament professors did not accept the first eleven chapters of Genesis as being authentic and taught that Adam and Eve were not human beings but allegorical figures. I asked Dr. Lolley if this was true. He turned to Dr. Ashcraft for a response. The dean said something like, "Not only him, but no one else in that field does either." That lit the fuse. Dr. Vines was aghast, as was I. A rather pointed discussion followed. We were told that no one on the Old Testament faculty believed in the inerrancy of Scripture.

I reported in detail to our full committee meeting in Atlanta on February 24. The committee affirmed us in our approach and our attempt to be fair with our inquiries and report. In March, we received a report that the CEF group had been put on probation for a year. I later heard that was true. If so, it is a sad thing when honest concerns cannot be voiced without fear of reprimand.

In July, 1986, the subcommittee came up with a statement that well reflected our several concerns about Southeastern Baptist Theological Seminary, which included: a sense that we received evasive responses about some professors teaching outside *The Baptist Faith and Message* parameters; the need to include more conservative speakers and lecturers; and more conservative books and parallel reading in classroom work. Our subcommittee unanimously adopted it. Subsequently, at the full Peace Committee meeting with the six seminary presidents at Glorieta, New Mexico, in October, it was adopted.

There were several more substantive meetings as we worked hard to maintain our historic position on Scripture and reach out to those who had different persuasions.

The Peace Committee brought our final report and recommendations to the Southern Baptist Convention meeting in St. Louis in 1987. When our report time came, the convention center was packed. After much discussion, the vote was taken to affirm the report. From our vantage point on the platform, as well as by the estimate of others, the vote was ninety-percent to approve. Our work was completed. It had been a tough and demanding two years for all of us; however, in the long run, I believe it succeeded in preventing a major split in our denomination.

Perhaps my greatest satisfaction from the experience was that we had dealt substantively with the reality that our Southern Baptist Convention had been slipping away from its roots that had made us the most evangelistic, mission-focused, largest Protestant denomination in the country; and we were turning it around. That was a first. Once most denominations start down the road to liberalism and undercut the authority of Scripture, they never get out of that downward spiral.

As I write this thirty years later, the dinosaurs of once great denominations lay scattered on the ash heap of irrelevance and compromise—paper tigers, toothless, and inconsequential in the face of secularism: a tragic picture of apostasy. As Southern Baptists, we continue to be strong in articulating God's truth, and in offering hope to the moral and spiritual dissolution so rampant around us. We have done something else. By God's grace we have remained firmly anchored in the absolute, infallible truth of God's Word.

Around this time, I found myself on a plane seated next to a businessman who identified himself as a "disillusioned Episcopalian." He asked me about my faith; I told him I was Southern Baptist. His face lit up, he turned in his seat, and said, "Thank you. You have stood up for the things our church preached and believed early on. We began to drift away. I began to look around. When you took a stand on the authenticity of Scripture, I felt hope again. We found a conservative Episcopal church that stands where you do and has the heart to stand on the truth. You have helped a lot of us—though not Baptists—to take heart and stand up. We are not alone. Thank you."

It was worth it.

Conservatives continued to be elected as president of the Southern Baptist Convention, who, in turn, appointed committees that nominated trustees to our institutional boards who have been true to our historic roots. The trend toward regaining control of our schools and entities continued unabated.

By the early 1990s it seemed that the resurgence was successful, but some uncertainties continued. When Morris Chapman became the nominee for conservatives, I hosted a meeting for interested pastors in our area to come to our church to meet Morris, ask questions, and pray.

During this period, several of my contemporaries—who had not been as vocal or as deeply involved in the struggle as others—came out in strong support of Chapman's candidacy and the positive trajectory of our convention. These included Joel Gregory of First Baptist Dallas; John Bisagno of First Baptist Houston; Ken Hemphill of First Baptist Norfolk; Charles Fuller of First Baptist Roanoke; and others. My support was not only vocal, I wrote about it in an article in our church's periodical, *The First Baptist Church Orlando Beacon*, on March 8, 1990:

A Time to Be Silent and a Time to Speak

For eleven years, our Southern Baptist fellowship has been engaged in a struggle. I understand that struggle to be around the nature of the Holy Scripture. I must confess that in the early years of this conflict I felt it would quickly abate. As far as I could tell, all the Southern Baptists I knew believed the Bible was infallible, inerrant, and authoritative—the historic Baptist position. I had run into a few who taught and believed otherwise, but I considered that position an aberration.

Therefore, I kept quiet, voted my convictions, and tried to keep focused on the challenge of our church to evangelize and edify. I removed myself from active participation in the political life of our denomination, except for intercessory prayer. Five years ago, the Lord gave me the opportunity to serve on the Peace Committee. We went to work to find the root causes of our problems. When all of the smoke blew away, there was unanimous consent that, indeed, in certain institutions supported by the tithes and offerings of our people, there were those in the place of instruction and leadership who had drifted far from the heart of our spiritual roots. In our 1987 Southern Baptist Convention in St. Louis, the messengers voted by a ninety-plus-percent majority that we expected those in our institutions to clearly reflect the heartbeat of our heritage: that (among other things) God's Word was to be elucidated as free from all false-hood, fraud or deceit; and that its truth was not limited to spiritual themes but to all fields, including science and history.

There are those who say that, in spite of basic differences on the nature of Scripture, we can unite under the auspices of missions and evangelism. But can that be? There is a strong link between right doctrine and life. *Right doctrine is right thinking.* Once the doctrine is diluted, the life-style soon follows. A house of missions and evangelism will soon fall in on itself if its foundations are not deep and sure. Evangelical Christian theologian and pastor Francis Schaeffer said, "As I see it, the Christian life must comprise three concentric circles, each of which must be kept in its proper place. In the outer circle must be the correct theological position, true biblical orthodoxy and the purity of the visible church."[45]

Right doctrine does not necessarily mean that one agrees on the millennial question, etc. There are Scriptures that we interpret differently. But the mindset, the heart attitude, must be: this is God's Word. I approach it in reverence and faith, and trust the Holy Spirit to lead me in understanding its rich treasures.

To most Southern Baptists, the authority of Scripture is non-negotiable. It is or it isn't. I was raised in Southern Baptist churches, taught in Southern Baptist schools, and have pastored Southern Baptist churches for nearly thirty years. I am loyal to our way of doing God's business grounded on our spiritual moorings: a basic fundamental trust in an infallible Scripture on which to anchor every other aspect of our life and fellowship.

As we headed toward our Southern Baptist Convention assembly in New Orleans in June with the election of a new president, the questions with which I dealt were: *Who best reflects that historic tradition? Who can lead us to continue in the pathway of correcting some of*

---

[45] Schaeffer, Francis A. *No Little People: Sixteen Sermons for the Twentieth Century.* Wheaton, IL: Crossway, 2003. Chapter 4: "The Lord's Work in the Lord's Way."

the Trojan horses that had slipped into our ranks until recently exposed? Who is most strongly committed to the faith of our spiritual forefathers and will not compromise it?

A couple of years ago, I stood with a fellow pastor in the tower of the great naval carrier, the USS Kennedy. He told me of going out to sea on her one day. He said that at one point the commander told him there could not be any conversation while they traversed a certain span of the sea. When finished, the commander explained that he had to give his total attention to the direction of the great ship: for if he was off by just the tiniest bit in his calculations, a few miles away, they could find themselves aground, putting the ship, its men, and its mission at jeopardy. That lesson at sea carries a powerful parallel in our doctrine and destiny.

Eleven years ago we caught the ship of faith in time to correct her course and lead us confidently into the twenty-first century! For these years that the correction has been going on, things have been said and done from all points of reference that have caused pain and embarrassment, but we have made decisive and constructive progress. I believe we must continue on that path. For years I have prayed for and desired a widespread participation of like-minded brothers and sisters in that process that was begun years ago. I see that consolidation beginning to happen at a quickened pace as we unite around principles larger than any political aspirations.

Two godly men seem to be the major nominees for the strategic position of presidential leadership in the Southern Baptist Convention. I know and love them both, but I can only vote for one. In deciding for the first time in my ministry to speak out on a presidential election, I am doing so not on the basis of personalities, but of a far greater concern—a principle: the integrity and nature of Scripture. Our leader must be one who will affirm the course that will keep us off the reefs of denominational destruction the "spiritual oil spill" that has polluted and practically destroyed every mainline denomination, the environmental hazard that has wasted too many lives and evangelical pursuits, the toxic waste of biblical compromise. John Wesley put it succinctly: "If there be one error in Scripture, there might as well be a thousand. It would not be the truth of God." The Jesus whom I know and serve believed the Bible was true and was the very Word of God. As one scholar said "He commanded His disciples to believe it and obey it. He rebuked those who disregarded it or sought to interpret away its obvious instructions. And He held its teachings to be binding for Himself."

I am confident both Dan Vestal and Morris Chapman believe this. But, I feel only one appears willing, according to my information, to appoint capable men and women who will adhere to the spirit and intent of the Peace Committee Report as adopted by the messengers to the 1987 Southern Baptist Convention held in St. Louis, Missouri.

The writer of Ecclesiastes said, "*There is a time to be silent and a time to speak*" (Ecclesiastes 3:7). In my time to speak, I speak for Morris Chapman as president of the Southern Baptist Convention when we gather in New Orleans. I encourage others to do so also, in this crucible year in our denomination. I encourage you to now join with me and thousands of our beloved Baptist fellowship elsewhere in praying God's will to prevail and a growing consensus in the course plotted for us by His Word and our Baptist heritage.

In Him Who Is the Word,
Brother Jim

At the pastor's conference prior to the convention, John Bisagno preached what I consider one of the most powerful and persuasive sermons I have ever heard about what was at stake. The meeting place was packed. For those who may have been on the fence about their voting choice, that message, I believe, was decisive; and the direction was settled.

Some whiplash remained and I saw it firsthand. I was invited to be the chapel preacher at Southern Theological Seminary in 1994. Dr. Roy L.

Honeycutt, Jr., was leaving his position as its president. The young and brilliant Dr. R. Albert (Al) Mohler, Jr. was his successor. Not all at Southern were happy about the forthcoming transition. Apparently, a memo went out to those who were not enchanted with his choice to make it known in the chapel service the following day. I met for prayer prior to the service with Dr. Honeycutt, who was most gracious to me.

What took place in the chapel service still astounds me. As the service began, some students stood with their back to the pulpit area. As we continued, some walked out. When I stood to preach, some stood with their back toward us while I preached. I did not consider it so much an affront to me as a rebellious action against God. A worship service is not the place to air disagreements.

When I finished preaching, a number of students gathered around me. In the group was a seminary professor whom I did not know. He got in my face and took umbrage with my message. In the course of my sermon, I had used some parodies of today's moral ills such as "a culture that is more concerned about protecting turtle eggs than unborn babies." I do not know what set him off, but he was visibly angry, got red in the face, and raised his voice several octaves. I wondered if he was going to hit me.

Afterward, Dr. Mohler said, "Jim, when I become president, this kind of stuff will not happen. We will have you back in a different setting." Twenty years later, he kept his word. I preached in chapel and heard great music. I observed a faculty and student body in love with Jesus. And the only faculty in my face were those who offered encouragement and thanks. What a difference elections and direction make!

During the same period of time, something else took place on the national scene that imbedded itself in my heart and mind. I received an appointment from President Ronald Reagan's office to serve on a commission to bring a report to Surgeon General C. Everett Koop about the impact of abortion on the nation. We were asked to come to Washington, D.C., on November 16, 1987, for a meeting convened by Dr. Koop. I admired Dr. Koop. He was a strong evangelical Christian. I looked forward to, perhaps, assisting him and the president with any strategy to curb this terrible blight of abortion.

Our group of eight had lunch at the famous Hawk 'n' Dove restaurant on Pennsylvania Avenue, and later convened in Dr. Koop's office. He was genial and laid back. Over seventy years in age, he conveyed vigor and youthfulness. He propped his feet on the table, put his hands behind his head, and started talking with us. He expressed his gratitude for Southern Baptists. He thought we were the most homogenous group. He felt our response could help them in drafting a paper for President Reagan.

When it came time for us to leave, I suggested we pray for him, which we did. Dr. Koop said, "That was better than the Planned Parenthood prayer!" He autographed his book *Sometimes Mountains Move*, which recounts the tragic, accidental death of his son. Later, his son's fiancée met and married a young man. The Koops financed a medical trip for them to Swaziland, where the young man became a Christian. Tears welled up in his eyes as he recounted the story.

While our meeting with Dr. Koop was fruitful and meaningful, the ultimate outcome did not move the mountains for which I had hoped and prayed. Prior to flying to Washington, D.C., I told our people from the pulpit on a Sunday morning about that upcoming meeting. I informed the church that our committee members were asked to bring any pertinent material about the issue to the meeting. I asked the women in our church that if any had had an abortion, would they please write a letter conveying its effects on them: emotionally, spiritually, and physically. They could conclude their letters by signing their names or remaining anonymous.

The response was overwhelming! In a few days, I had fifty to sixty letters. During my flight to Washington, D.C. for that meeting, I began to read them. The transparency, the honesty, the pain, and the brokenness of those who had aborted their babies overwhelmed me. I wept nearly all the way to Washington. I am saddened to say, like many other things that fall through the cracks in the government bureaucracy, the report we sent to the president did not seem to make much impact. However, it did serve to intensify my commitment to speak up, vote, and support every effort to protect the unborn. Since God is a life-giver, why should anyone who believes in God support a philosophy or ideology that is life-taking?

With All My Heart

To All Who Take Seriously Their Faith:

Martin Luther called Lucifer "Our ancient foe," who "doth seek to work us woe."[46] Lucifer's insidious strategy is to get Christians to ask, "Did God really mean what He said?" The attack on truth is relentless. It is always an attempt to dilute, dismiss, or destroy the Word of God. The foe is tricky.

A pastor friend had an idiom that fits much of what goes on today in seminaries and churches: "They use the same words but different dictionaries." I implore you to hold fast to the Word of God. Defend it. Delight in it.

When I first began to follow Jesus, my pastor gave me a Bible he had autographed. He had noted the Scripture 2 Timothy 2:15: "Do

---

[46] Reference to the Martin Luther hymn entitled "A Mighty Fortress Is Our God" *(1527-1529).*

your best to present yourself to God as one approved, a workman who does not need to be ashamed and who correctly hands the word of truth." He told me to memorize it, which I did. At age 8, I had no idea that when I was nearly 80 that verse would anchor me through personal, church, denominational, and cultural struggles. I urge you to the same, so that God's Word will be a lamp to guide your feet and a light for your path.[47]

---

[47] Psalm 119:105.

Mom and Dad photographed shortly after their marriage in 1936.

Mom and Dad on their 50th wedding anniversary in 1986.

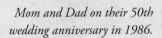

Elementary school days. I still part my hair—that is, what's left of it—on the right side.

The first 11-year-old registered as a Boy Scout in Tennessee, I received my Tenderfoot badge from my mom (1948).

1

Proudly displaying my athletic prowess for this 1951 cover of Home Life Magazine.

Chosen as the main character in the Broadman film Lift Up Your Eyes *(1951).*

Basketball "powerhouse" at Bailey Junior High School (1952).

Posing in 1955 for my favorite high school sport: track.

Thumbing a ride to Georgetown College (1957).

Pictured with C.L. Miffin (left) and three-term Governor Frank Clement (center) after he spoke in chapel at Georgetown College and flew me home to Nashville on his Tennessee National Guard plane.

Jeanette and I were married on December 27, 1959.

Our first home: the canary yellow house I painted for Jeanette (1960), which flabbergasted her.

The Henry clan in 1969.

Jeanette and I with our family at my 20th anniversary celebration at FBCO. Front row (left to right); Seth de Armas, Asa de Armas, Trey Henry, Caleb de Armas. Second row (left to right): Betsy & Danny de Armas; Stan & Kitty Campbell. Third row (left to right): Joe & Kim Henry; mother Kathryn Henry; Jeanette & I; Jimmy & Tammy with grandson Will.

Jeanette and I with son, Jimmy, and daughters, Kitty and Betsy (2014).

Jeanette and me celebrated our fiftieth wedding anniversary in 2009. Front row (left to right): mother, Kathryn Henry; me; and Jeanette. Back row (left to right): Kim and (brother) Joe Henry; daughter Kitty holding a photo of her husband, Stan (on military duty as an Air Force chaplain); grandson Asa de Armas; daughter-in-law Cali de Armas holding a photo of her husband, grandson Caleb (on military duty in Iraq in U.S. Army); Danny de Armas and daughter Betsy; grandson Seth de Armas; grandson Trey de Arman; grandson Will de Armas; son Jim Henry II and Tammy.

So proud of my brother, Joe.

Jeanette: the love of my life!

Fifty-six years of marriage to my remarkable journey partner have flown by too quickly.

Jeanette & I aboard the Queen Elizabeth 2 (1988), a gift cruise from some members of FBCO.

Jeanette on the night we attended one of the inaugural balls for George H.W. Bush (January, 1989).

Jeanette and I with Vice-President Dan Quayle when he visited Orlando (1989).

Jeanette and I with President and Mrs. Ronald Reagan when he was presented a special award by the House of Hope in Orlando shortly after leaving office (1990).

Press conference following my election at the President of the Southern Baptist Convention in Orlando (June, 1994).

Tennessee Congressman Bob Clement (left) and Florida Congressman Bill McCollum (right) hosted a reception for me in Washington, D.C. after my election as the President of the Southern Baptist Convention in 1994.

I took this picture of President Clinton signing the Israel-Jordan Peace Accord (1994). He is seated on the left next to Prime Minister Yitzhak Rabin, who was assassinated a year later. Just behind Clinton is Secretary of State Warren Christopher. Seated on the far right is King Hussein of Jordan.

To Dr. James Bascom Kerry Best Wishes, Bill Clinton

Pictured with President Bill Clinton at Andrews Air Force Base prior to our leaving for the signing of the Israel-Jordan Peace Accord (1994).

With Hillary Clinton at a reception in Jerusalem following the Israel-Jordan Peace Accord signing (1994).

*Praying with one of my spiritual heroes
Billy Graham before I introduced him at
the Southern Baptist Convention in Atlanta
in 1995. It was his last time to address his
fellow Baptists at our annual gatherings.*

*Jeanette; my mom, Kathryn; and
I thoroughly enjoyed our time
with Billy Graham prior to the
SBC gathering (1995).*

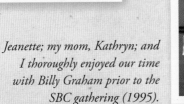

*As the current President of the Southern Baptist Convention, I had the privilege of
joining former presidents of the convention for their annual dinner prior to convening
the 1995 gathering in Atlanta. Seated (left to right): Adrian Rogers (deceased), Wayne
Dehoney (deceased), Ed Young (Senior Pastor of Second Baptist Houston), and Franklin
Paschall (deceased). Standing (left to right): Jimmy Draper (retired President of Lifeway),
Jerry Vines (retired Senior Pastor of First Baptist Jacksonville), Morris Chapman
(retired President of SBC Executive Committee), Bailey Smith (evangelist), and me.*

Posing in front of Air Force Two before take-off from Jerusalem back to the U.S. following Rabin's funeral service (1995).

Pictured with President George H. W. Bush '41 when he; his wife, Barbara; and son Jeb, then Governor of Florida, visited FBCO for an evening worship service and Fall Festival in November, 2000.

At the invitation of my long-time friend Florida Senator Bill Nelson, it was my privilege to be the U.S. Senate Chaplain of the day on two occasions. All prayers have to be written out, submitted, and vetted before being prayed before this august gathering.

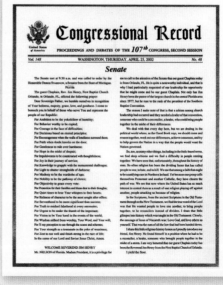

MT. PISGAH BAPTIST CHURCH
1858 – 2008

My first pastorate (1960-1963): Mt. Pisgah Baptist Church located between Quitman, Mississippi and Melvin, Alabama.

My second pastorate (1963-1965): Hollywood Baptist Church, Sledge, Mississippi.

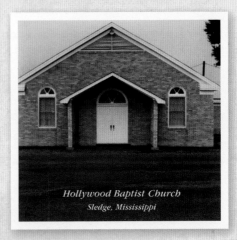

Hollywood Baptist Church
Sledge, Mississippi

My third pastorate (1965-1977): Two Rivers Baptist Church, Nashville, Tennessee.

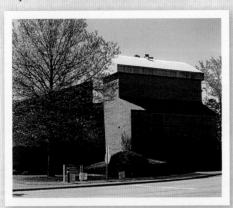

My fourth pastorate (1977-2006): First Baptist Church, Orlando, Florida. This original location is now called Downtown Baptist Church.

My fourth pastorate (1977-2006): First Baptist Church, Orlando, Florida. This is the current 130-acre campus of FBCO.

The interior of the 5,500-seat worship center of FBCO completed February, 1985.

The choir and orchestra leading Sunday worship at FBCO.

The twin Singing Christmas Trees under the direction of Ragan Vandegriff at FBCO.

My presiding at the Singing Christmas Trees, where I gave the welcome and shared the Gospel for more than 200 presentations (1979-2005).

Pictured standing next to me (from left to right): Orlando Mayor Buddy Dyer, astronaut John Young, Congressman John Mica, and pastor Randall James at the groundbreaking for I-4 exit overpass for which FBCO donated part of our land to make it possible.

Every decade since 1979 I have had the joy to lead tours to the Holy Land. Pictured is my teaching at the site of the future battle of Armageddon: Megiddo, located in northern Israel.

Jeanette and grandson Caleb leaving the Garden Tomb, always a place of inspiration.

My successor as senior pastor at FBCO, David Uth, has done a remarkable job, as well has been more than gracious to Jeanette and me.

Pictured with my scrambled golf team at Arnold Palmer's Latrobe Country Club, Latrobe, Pennsylvania, where Mr. Palmer presented us with our third-place award. I had one of my best rounds of golf ever. (Must have been helped by a visiting angel!) Photos with Christian leaders/"celebrities":

Pictured with André Crouch at downtown FBCO (1979).

Pictured at a Bible Conference at which I was privileged to speak at Southern Theological Seminary with (left to right) Dr. Lewis Drummond, President of Southeastern Baptist Theological Seminary; T.W. Wilson, Billy Graham's staff aide and dear friend; and John Stott, eminent theologian, author, and pastor.

Pictured with Zig Ziglar, one of Jesus' greatest salesmen!

Picture with Christian singer, comedian, and song-writer Mark Lowry at FBCO.

Pictured with Dr. Robert Schuller of the Crystal Cathedral when we were a part of the team accompanying President Clinton for Rabin's state funeral.

Pictured with dear friends (left to right): Junior Hill (evangelist), Jerry Clower (country comedian), and Bill Cox (music pastor) at my 20th anniversary celebration at FBCO.

Pictured with Rick Warren (Senior Pastor at Saddleback Church and author) at a conference.

Pictured with good friend Josh McDowell (evangelist and author).

CHAPTER FIFTEEN

WHITE HOUSE CALLING

L IFE WAS NEVER BORING around our home with a growing number of grandsons. Likewise, life around the church was fulfilling beyond measure with a growing church and all its building programs and expanding ministries; taking sabbaticals in Israel and Scotland; serving our denomination; preaching; working with a gifted and dedicated staff; and serving as chaplain for the Orlando Renegades.

Coached by Lee Corso and owned by Don Dizney, the Orlando Renegades were a professional football team that played in the United States Football League in the mid-1980s. Not a Christian at the time, Don gave me the opportunity to be the team chaplain and around football, a sport I greatly enjoy.

Years later, it was my joy to greet Don, who had married Irene—a lovely, gracious member of our First Baptist family—when he came forward during the invitation time at a worship service to profess his faith in Christ. Don has maintained his commitment to Christ. He and Irene have had a significant influence in the business, academic, and athletic community.

Coach Corso was a delight to be around. Even during a tough football season, he was constantly upbeat. I often ate with the team prior to games, and then gave the locker room devotional. Coach Corso always came. The team was in a losing streak when I gave the message "When Your Back Is to the Wall." In it, I gave the application that in tough times we look to God and He always shows up. The Renegades won that night. Before the next game, Coach asked me to repeat the same message as it seemed to bring celestial support!

The Florida State Seminoles came to the Citrus Bowl one New Year's bowl season. I was asked to give the chapel address. Coach Bobby Bowden showed up with all his team. I brought two of my grandsons with me. Just little tykes, they took it all in and absorbed the buzz of a locker room, a big game, and a great coach. Coach Bowden graciously autographed an item or two for them. A Gator fan, I observed that years later they had become big Seminole fans instead of Gator fans. When I asked why, they said, "It's your fault! You took us to the locker room chapel with the Seminoles and Coach Bowden. We were hooked!"[48]

For several years, some of my pastor brothers had encouraged me to consider being nominated for the presidency of the Southern Baptist Convention. I had not seriously entertained the notion as my cup was so full. Plus, we had a number of men more qualified than I for such an undertaking. When the annual Southern Baptist Convention meeting was to be

---

[48] A few years ago, I had the privilege of taking Coach Bowden, his wife (Ann), his son (Tommy), and daughter-in-law (Linda) to Israel and Jordan. He was a real pilgrim, who soaked in every bit of Bible, history, and archeology that was communicated. I soon discovered his fame was not limited to football fans in the U.S. While at the traditional site of the Upper Room in Jerusalem, a Jewish man stopped as he walked past our group, pointed to Coach Bowden, and announced with a loud voice to all in hearing distance: "Coach Bowden! Coach Bowden!" It's a small world, indeed.

held in Orlando in June, 1994, and Ed Young's second term was winding down, the calls and letters urging me to let my name be put in nomination began to increase. By this time, my good friend, Fred Wolfe—the dynamic pastor of Cottage Hill Baptist in Mobile, Alabama—had announced his intention to be nominated. He was supported by a number of my fellow pastors, including Adrian Rogers and Charles Stanley. As I prayed and pondered, my deepest concern (beyond my being in God's will) was the fear that some would perceive my nomination as a sign that there was a split in the conservative camp. That could open a door for a third candidate, who might not support the resurgence. I prayed over this a lot, and finally decided to allow my name to be presented.

Not one to often ask for signs, I did on this occasion. I asked the Lord to have someone whom I held in high esteem get in touch with me and encourage me to be nominated. Within hours, I received a phone call from Dr. H. Franklin Paschall, the pastor of First Baptist, Nashville and a former Southern Baptist Convention president. Then I opened a letter from Dr. James Sullivan, president of the Baptist Sunday School Board (now called LifeWay) and another former Southern Baptist Convention president. I feel God gave me these signs as I had prayed. The die was cast. I decided I would not ask anyone for their vote or support, not call or write anyone to help me. If the Lord wanted me there, He could make the arrangements.

Subsequent days were filled with interviews, phone calls, and inquiries about my position on everything from theology to politics. Our church staff and family were totally supportive. Some weeks later, I saw Adrian Rogers, who said, "Jim, you know I have already given my support to Fred. However, if you are chosen, you will be my president, and I will have your back." That's Adrian. I appreciated his candor and integrity.

The nominating speech can be a strong determiner in our election circles, especially for those who are what we call "under voters." After praying about whom to choose, I asked Jack Graham, pastor of Prestonwood Baptist in Dallas, to nominate me. Jack prayed and told me he would.

Election night was electric, to say the least. The Orlando Convention Center was filled with our conventioneers. Dr. Stanley nominated Fred. Dr. Graham spoke for me. Dr. Graham did such an excellent job that I was not sure he was even talking about me! He used one phrase—"he is one of us"—that probably carried the day. (Some had felt I was not conservative enough, outspoken enough, or had enough "blood" on my hands.)

Jeanette and I waited for the results in our room at the Peabody Hotel near the convention site with our family, friends, and church members. Suddenly, the door burst open and our son-in-law, Danny de Armas, rushed into the room, shouting, "We're going to Disney World!" I was overwhelmed and somewhat surprised. After the hugs and well wishes were completed, we got on our knees and thanked God for His grace. We asked for God's wisdom and strength for the days ahead.

The day following our election, we had the usual press meeting with religious and secular news reporters, who were present to ask their questions. One that came up was the matter of President Bill Clinton's home church, Immanuel Baptist in Little Rock, Arkansas. Prior to the convention, an effort had been made to remove him from the church membership due to his position on some moral issues—particularly his stance on abortion. Pastor Rex Horne had handled it wisely by reminding all that Baptist polity directed that local congregations determined who was or was not a member. The matter had created quite a brouhaha, and I was pressed for a response. I underscored what Dr. Horne had stated and added that, although I disagreed with President Clinton on several issues, we, as Christians, were under a biblical mandate to pray for those in authority: *"I urge, then, first of all, that requests, prayers, intersessions, and thanksgiving be made for everyone for kings and those in authority..."* (1 Timothy 2:1-2). I added that our church and I practiced that biblical directive, and would continue to do so.

In the late afternoon of June 23, 1994, I was "minding my own business"—as one of our favorite, former members, evangelist David Ring often says—while still trying to get acclimated to my new role as president. Requests for interviews, invitations speaking engagements, appointment requests, meeting schedules, letters, and advice were pouring in from all directions. I noted in my journal, "I need the wisdom of God more than ever in my life." The regular demands of pastoring were always present: funerals, weddings, and "Sunday's coming" preaching preparation were constant banners flying at the forefront of my mind. My routine was abruptly interrupted when my executive assistant, Sandi Mathis, rushed into my office and said, "It's the White House! The president is on the line. I'm not kidding!"

Picking up my phone I was greeted by the White House operator, who clarified my name and church. Then President Clinton came on the line and said, "Congratulations on your election."

Addressing him as Mr. President, I thanked him. The next seventeen minutes were fascinating. He told me he talked to his pastor—Rex Horne of the Immanuel Baptist Church in Little Rock, Arkansas—every Saturday. He also shared that Rex had been supporting me to be Southern Baptist Convention president. Then he added, "Vice-President Gore and I were talking about you yesterday."

The whole conversation seemed surreal, yet amazingly comfortable. As our conversation seemed to be coming to a close, I asked President Clinton how I could pray for and with him. He replied, "North Korea—a little country; however, if we cannot negotiate in the next three months, they may make ten to twelve atomic bombs, and sell them to terrorists or small nations. I fear for our children."

During that conversation (as well as in subsequent meetings with him), I found the president to be very conversant about our denomination, its history, and contemporary issues. He mentioned that he sensed "the battle for inerrancy had become a political battle." He then shared a couple of personal items: "We're all frail and make mistakes." He spoke of personal attacks against him and named a well-known televangelist. "I regret that we cannot debate things, because of the political climate. There used to be a day when people with honest political convictions used to debate."

As we closed our conversation, he asked, "Would you come to the White House if I invited you?" I said "yes," and stated that I believed in submission to those in governmental authority (unless it contradicts the Word of God). I told him I would pray for him every Wednesday and at other times. I told him while I did not vote for him and had differences with him on several issues, I cared for him as a person and would be available to talk at any time. He said, "I'll invite you." (That he did. More about that later.)

In reflection, I found him to be very personable and down-to-earth. It is easy to see why he became president. He is the consummate politician, who makes you feel as if you are the most important person in the world. My major regret of that initial contact with the president was that I did not pray with him on the phone. I kept thinking, *He's got a world to deal with, and I must not corner his time.* If life gave me mulligans, I would take that one as a "do-over." I prayed that day I would have the opportunity to pray with the president which I later did.

During this same period of time, I received another unforgettable call. I had been preaching at The Cove, a beautiful mountain retreat near Asheville, North Carolina—the vision of Billy and Ruth Graham. Jeanette and I were at the airport when I was paged. Dr. Graham had tried to reach me earlier; however, we were unable to connect. An airport page always gets your attention: emergency, death in the family, or something. I picked up the phone to hear the voice on the other end say, "Jim, this is Billy Graham. I heard of your election as our Southern Baptist Convention president. I wanted to call to congratulate you and assure you of my prayers."

As we talked, I told Dr. Graham how much he meant to so many, to Southern Baptists, and to me. While I had Dr. Graham's attention, I decided to ask if he would address our annual meeting. I knew he had done so in the past; however, he had not recently done so. He said, "I want to preach at least one more time to a Southern Baptist Convention before I leave." He then instructed me to send the request to his planning team.

I asked Dr. Graham if there was anything about which I could pray with him. He said, "My health. I have the problems of an old man—arthritis, prostate, and Parkinson's—but it hasn't affected my preaching yet."

As Dr. Graham and I wrapped up our phone conversation, he asked to speak to Jeanette. By this time she had realized to whom I had been talking. I turned to her and said. "Jeanette, it's Billy Graham."

Her eyes grew big, she shook her head *no*, and gave me a *no go* hand signal. I pointed at the phone and mouthed, "*It's Billy Graham. He wants to say hello.*"

Adamantly, she continued to indicate *no way*. Finally, with gritted teeth, (and I'm sure exasperation showing all over me), I whispered, "You will talk to him!"

Rolling her eyes, she took the phone, with her voice under control and her lovely Kentucky drawl, she said, "Hello, Dr. Graham."

Instantly, he insisted, "Jeanette, please don't call me Dr. Graham, just call me Billy." His genuine humility, so typical of him, melted her heart and she relaxed. They spent several delightful minutes in conversation. Though she had met him years earlier at the Central Florida crusade, and respected him greatly, those words and that attitude put him on an even higher pedestal for her.

Of course, I did take the opportunity to officially invite him to address our annual convention meeting in Atlanta—the celebration of our 175th anniversary as the Southern Baptist Convention. The Georgia Dome was filled with our "messengers"—the delegates from the local churches across our convention—for his closing address. I do not think anyone left early, even though Dr. Graham was a little late in arriving. The toll of his busy years had brought health issues and left him physically weak. (T.W. Wilson, his close friend and aide, told me that whenever Dr. Graham got up to speak, he assisted him to the pulpit and stood right behind him in case he faltered.) As the moments passed for his arrival, I asked our praise leader to sing some extra songs to fill in the gap until Dr. Graham made it to the stage.

As Dr. Graham arrived in the golf cart that was used to transport him and was assisted on the platform, the people quit singing and burst into a prolonged ovation. The atmosphere was electric. After I introduced him, another sustained ovation occurred as he came to preach. Dr. Graham gripped both sides of the pulpit. Then, as T.W. had told me would happen, Billy Graham seemed to go into another zone. Weakness seemed to disappear as his characteristically strong, familiar voice—the distinctive one that had touched millions of individuals around the world, including me in my teen years—powerfully resounded throughout the huge arena. I believe it was the last time he spoke to any of our annual Southern Baptist Convention gatherings. I will forever cherish those moments.

During these momentous times in my life and ministry, I was blessed by having our church be totally supportive of my two year term as president of the SBC. The deacons gathered around us at morning worship and prayed for us. I never received one complaint about my time away or about not doing some of the pastoral things I normally did. I placed a table in our welcome center on which I displayed where I was going, what I was doing, and any memorabilia from events. That kept our people involved and informed. I sought to be there on Sundays, except for my usual vacation times.

I was off and running literally: to institutional trustee meetings, seminary chapels, answering phone calls, letter writing, fielding media requests, and planning toward the next year. My co-officers elected at the convention were Gary Frost, an African-American pastor from Ohio, and Simon Tsoi, a Chinese pastor from California—both wonderful men. From the South, the Heartland, and the West Coast, our team was a picture of the widening diversity of our denomination and a harbinger of good things to come.

With All My Heart

To Any Who Thinks Your Life May Not Matter:

There are no little things with God. He shapes our lives in many ways of which we are not cognizant. As I write this, I am thinking of the teachers, professors, church librarians, and family who gave me a love and an appreciation for history. It never occurred to me that in the middle and later stages of my life, God would arrange for me to be an eyewitness and participant in some historical occasions with leaders who made and continue to make history. I would encourage you to not treat the mundane lightly. I am forever grateful for the people who were not necessarily in the spotlight, yet they illumined my path by pouring their lives into mine.

CHAPTER SIXTEEN

STANDING, SITTING, PRAYING...IN HISTORY

R EX HORNE, THE PRESIDENT'S pastor from Immanuel Baptist in Little Rock; Henry Blackaby, the head of spiritual renewal and prayer at the Home Mission Board, as well as author of *Experiencing God* and other books; and I were among sixty religious leaders invited to the White House for breakfast with President Clinton on Thursday, September 8, 1994.[49] Our invitation did not arrive until that Tuesday. We spent the next couple of days ascertaining if the president would also privately meet with Henry, Rex, and me. On Wednesday that affirmation came.

Early Thursday morning, we went to the White House, where we went through identity checks. Our group gathered in the Red Room. We were surrounded by portraits: a brooding, meditating President Kennedy, a smiling Harry Truman, and a pensive Dwight Eisenhower.

---

[49] This chapter is based on "White House Notes," the notes I wrote about the events of September 8, 1994, in my personal journal.

Then we were escorted into the State Room that functions as the site for many state and important dinners. I was told we had open seating. However, as we took our seats about halfway back, someone came and told me that I was to sit at a table at the front. When I approached the table, I noticed that there were place cards at that table. Around the table to my right was Dr. Bob Dugan, Jr., Director of the National Association of Evangelicals of Former Congressmen. Beside him was Betty McNamara, who is head of the Women's Ministers and Catholic Diocese of Washington, D.C. Beside her was Arthur Caliandro, pastor of Marble Collegiate Church in New York and successor to Norman Vincent Peale. To his side was a rabbi from New York. To his right was Margaret Steinfels, who is the editor of *Commonweal*, a Catholic publication. The president sat in the middle. To my left was Sam Wise, a black pastor who had served at the Assembly of God Church in Washington, D.C., for twenty-five years. This seating arrangement placed me one person away from the president.

It was a diverse group. Several Jewish rabbis, Catholics, a wide range of Protestants and Evangelicals, including several conservatives, were there. Vice-President Al Gore, who had just returned from the Cairo Conference, came in on crutches. In a few moments, the president entered the room, and we all stood up. He was smiling broadly as he approached our table and shook hands with one or two people. I extended my hand to say hello to him and introduce myself. Before I could say anything, he said "Good morning, Jim. I'm so glad you came." Then we were all seated for our meal. Prior to eating, Arthur Caliandro led in a prayer of thanksgiving.

The President's face was red. I did not know if that was from his playing golf at Martha's Vineyard, where he had just been vacationing or from his jogging that morning. He looked to be a little more slender than I had seen him in pictures. He was a very animated conversationalist. He was asked about the baseball strike. He said the man representing the owners was a close personal friend and had been one of his early supporters. However, he did not think it was the government's place to intervene at this point.

President Clinton also gave an animated discussion about Martha's Vineyard. He said it had been built as a summer retreat for Bible study, and the houses had been built three-fourths-size to impress a sense of humility to those on retreat as they came before the Lord in the study of His Word. He also shared about his visit to Bath, Maine, the day before, in which he had encouraged workers who were seeking to turn a former shipyard into another kind of industry. He said they were very enthusiastic, and he was hoping it would be successful.

When I had the opportunity to chat with him, I asked him about jogging. He said he had been running every day, and trying to run three miles in twenty-six minutes or less; however, he was getting ready to change the routine and go to only four days a week and run longer distances. We talked about Governor Frank Clement and how he had been a hero to me when I was younger. President Clinton told me that on his family's first television set he had watched Frank Clement in 1956 deliver his famous "How Long, How Long" address at the Democratic National Convention. An animated President Clinton waved his arms as he gave his imitation of that address. He said that Congressman Bob Clement had brought him a tape of that speech. The conversation around the table covered a number of issues, but I did not get to engage in great length with him.

When it was time for the president to address the group, he was introduced by Al Gore, who told two or three funny stories. I saw some humor in the vice-president, which differed from the wooden-like expression that I was used to seeing on television.

The president got up, gave opening remarks, and said he had a prepared text from his aides, but he had decided to throw that away and speak from his heart. He said that we were a nation out of rhythm. He said he had read that worship, work, and play all need to be in proper balance. Should they be out of balance in an individual's life, the person gets out of rhythm. He said he thought that was true of our country. That we were out of rhythm, out of sync. Three major events had occurred in this century: World War I which isolated us; World War II which engaged us properly in the world; and the Cold War in which we had a stated enemy that had been defeated. These left us as a people without a mission or a purpose. We were going through great change and not dealing well with it. The president said you can be going through change and good things are happening, but people do not realize it. He sensed that we are becoming more divided along ethnic, racial, and religious lines, which was making it more difficult to govern.

President Clinton recited a litany of things that he felt were successful in his administration, but, also, expressed his chagrin in not being able to bring the people together. He said that he encouraged people who disagreed with him to become involved in politics. However, he expressed that we had to find a way to be in the political process without screaming at each other. He pointed out how we are guilty of labeling each other and end up fighting with each other, instead of entering into civil discourse. He encouraged us not to demonize our adversaries, and gave the illustrations of Martin Luther King, Jr., William Wilberforce of England, and Nelson Mandela of South Africa—who, after being in prison for twenty-seven years, invited two of his jailers to his inauguration. He said that kind of spirit—the ability to disagree and talk through the issues must carry the day. He said we must talk to each other more about what makes us work and what we share. As Americans, we basically share a piece of land, and we have got to learn to get along together on that land. We must find specific and concrete things on which we can agree, and then act on these things toward common goals.

President Clinton talked about strong families several times. He said that our government cannot do everything. We must have help from the religious sector. He said that there were too many abortions; that people who could have children and have stable homes were not having any, or very few, children; and the people who could least afford to have children and were not married, were having more children. He ended by saying "Pray for me, because I need it. Sometimes, when I do the best I can, it is not enough."

He then opened the floor up for any questions or discussion and stood there for thirty minutes while the group asked questions and dialogued with him. He seemed to enjoy it very much, and was quick on his feet. He often began his response by saying, "Well, there are two things I would recommend..." or "I feel there are three things that could be done." The sense of the group could have been summed up as: *We all realize that we have some major problems—moral, spiritual, and ethical—in our country, as well as economic ones. What can we, as the Church, do to help you as a president?* Very little was said about what government could do for us; however, in reaching and helping across denominational lines, there were some things—such as a commitment to pray continually and give honest counsel when asked—on which we agreed we could do to help the president.

When time was called, Clinton moved out among the group and began to shake hands. Knowing that I would be with him later, I moved to his side. As I walked by, he caught my eye, turned and said, "Jim, I look forward to talking to you after a while."

I stood at the door with Linda Lesourd Lader, who was the volunteer coordinator for the president and the religious community advisor. She said, "He needed this. This is the kind of thing he really thrives on."

Henry Blackaby, Rex Horne, and I met at the hotel where we had a period of prayer before we went back to the White House. When we returned to the White House, we went back through checkpoints and were escorted into the West Wing and the outer offices of the Oval Office. As we stood there, we were told, "I hope you do not mind waiting for a few minutes as the vice-president has expressed his desire to meet with the group, too."

At approximately 12:00 p.m. we were escorted into the Oval Office. The president met us at the door. Just prior to our going inside the office, Al Gore came up to me on his crutches and talked to me about Tennessee. We talked about Carthage, Tennessee; Vanderbilt; his work at the *Tennessean*; and my ties at Two Rivers Baptist Church; as well as my brother Joe's being at the Opryland Hotel. Gore was not very animated, did not smile much, and seemed troubled. Actually, he did more responding than speaking.

When we went into the Oval Office, I was a little surprised: it was not as big as I had thought. It was very bright and had a warm feeling. I felt very comfortable in there. As I walked into the office, the presidential desk, which was in front of a huge glass window, was to my left. In front of the desk were two couches and a couple of chairs. At the far end of the couches, in front of the fireplace, were two chairs, which I had often seen in pictures. The president sat in one of those chairs. I sat on the couch closest to him with Vice-President Gore seated next to me. Alexis, who was in charge of the president's appointments, sat next to Vice-President Gore. To the president's right was Henry Blackaby, then Rex Horne, and Linda. While we were shaking hands and greeting each other, the photographer came in and took pictures.

Rex began the proceedings by saying that we had come to talk to him and encourage him. Rex introduced us: who we were, our positions, and some background information. The president smiled and said, "Well, Al, would you like to open up?"

Planned or not, Vice-President Gore, became the bad guy and voiced his concerns regarding the Christian Right. He expressed how it was hard for him to understand how people could claim to be Christians, and yet respond so bitterly when there were differences of opinion. That kind of got the ball rolling. We steered away from that the best we could. Henry Blackaby responded by explaining the reason we had come was not to get into those kinds of issues so much. Rather, we were there to affirm the president and tell him that we were there because we cared. We also wanted to assure him of the prayers and concern of the people we represented.

I do not remember the chronological order of the next few minutes, but we discussed several things. When I began my remarks, I told the president that I, too, loved Dr. W.O. Vaught, who had been his pastor as a teenager at Immanuel and had had such influence him. I told him he also had a great deal of influence on me. (Dr. Vaught had been a speaker at my graduation, and I had seen his wife the last spring.) As I talked about Dr. Vaught, a smile came on the president's face and tears welled up in his eyes. I also told the president that we did have some concerns about homosexuality and abortion. I explained that our people's perception was that he seemed to favor those positions. When I brought those two things up, Vice-President Gore got up and left. He did not say good-bye. He just left. I do not know if he had another appointment or he did not want to be involved in that discussion. Perhaps he had primed the pump to give it to the president. I do not know.

When the president said, "Well, let's just take one of those issues: homosexuality. As the president, by law, there are certain things that I must allow people to have: equal right to employment, protection under the law, etc."

I told him we certainly agreed with all of that. That was not the problem. However, the perception was that he seemed to favor homosexuals. He then mentioned the secretary of education, a known lesbian. He said that he had recommended her because when he asked for recommendations for that position, everyone seemed to like her and considered her to be the most qualified to serve in that arena. He also said that he had come under greater attack because of his recommendation that the ban that prevented homosexual individuals from serving in the military be lifted. He said, in actuality, what he had wanted done was much stronger than what had been accomplished. He said he wanted a law that actually aligned with the military code of conduct, which previously had stated no homosexuality, as well as no adultery—was allowed. He said the new law, which he supported, said you could do it, but should not talk about it.

Instituted by the Clinton administration, "Don't Ask, Don't Tell" (DADT) became the official United States policy on service by gays, bisexuals, and lesbians in the military.[50] The president said the outcome was what he had desired and much stronger than previous law.

I told him that often we, who are considered the Religious Right, were lumped into the category of conservative Christians who agreed on everything that Pat Robertson and Jerry Falwell—both men whom I respect and admire—said. In their pronouncements, Falwell and Robertson had hit on two issues—abortion and homosexuality—about which most mainstream Southern Baptists agreed, although we did not always concur with the attitudes and tactics of some on the far right. I encouraged him not to use the tactic of lumping all conservatives in the same camp in the future. He kind

---

[50] DADT took effect on December 21, 1993, and lasted until September 20, 2011.

of bowed his head and said, "I know I was wrong to do that. I am not going to do that anymore. I was definitely out of order in that."

He seemed to take my admonition, which I had given in a spirit of love and concern in the proper way. I also told him that we had tremendous compassion for homosexuals, and were not "gay bashers." I shared that our church had a ministry to homosexuals, and that there were homosexuals in our church. He said, "Let me ask you a question. If you were me, what would you do in dealing with homosexuals?"

I described our ministry to homosexuals, how we loved them, and how we prayed with them, but how we did not elevate them to places of leadership, stature, or visibility in the church. When I went on to say there was the perception he was doing that, the president responded, "Well, as a pastor, I could certainly understand why you would not do that. However, as the president, I have a different responsibility and I have legal ramifications that I must consider."

Assuring him I certainly understood and knew he had to do that, I went on to explain that there seemed to be the perception was there was undue favoritism being extended to homosexuals—a position that many people resented. He seemed to hear what I was saying.

Henry Blackaby picked up the conversation at this point to share that we realize the rhetoric has often been wrong and some of our people had not reflected the Spirit of Christ. Henry sad he had been calling people to repentance about this, and talked to our missionaries about it. He had addressed their feelings about the president and some's refusal to even pray for the president. Henry told our missionaries that Scripture told us we must pray for those in authority. When he had spoken to a group of missionaries in Kenya and told them they must repent of these things, Henry said they wept in brokenness about their less-than-Christlike attitude. These missionaries asked if it was all right to write the president and ask his forgiveness. Having encouraged them to do so, Blackaby told the president he would probably receive some letters from those missionaries in Kenya.

Henry Blackaby went on to explain that we were trying to help Christians and others realize the truth of an important teaching of Christ: that we will be judged by God with the same kind of judgment by which we judge others. Those who are harsh in their judgment will be held accountable for their actions and responses; and that same kind of judgment will come back on them in the future. We needed to understand God would not be mocked. The president listened very intently to Henry's words.

As we got ready to wrap up our conversation, Henry went on to encourage Clinton to do two critical, life- and leadership-defining things: The first was to always seek the mind of God, decide a course of action, and stay on that course of action, no matter what his critics on either side might say. He must persevere, not waiver, move ahead, take a stand, and not be seen as vacillating. The second was to seek to rise above the fray and be a statesman. God would vindicate him and handle his enemies or those who would seek to discredit him.

As Henry talked about handling difficult times and referred to a passage in the Psalms, the president immediately said, "Yes! I just finished reading through the Psalms recently. I found much with which I can identify in the Psalms. They have been very helpful."

Henry encouraged him to continue to read the Word of God, and especially the book of Psalms. While Henry spoke these final words, the president leaned forward and intently received what he had to say. Henry told him to ask for wisdom from God, to believe God would give him that wisdom, know that God would honor him for seeking His guidance in all things, and be confidant God would use him in a very special way in the life of our nation and the world.

Rex asked me if I had anything to say to the president in closing. I told him I wanted to assure him that Southern Baptists were praying for him, and I would continue to encourage more of our people to pray for him. Also, I would do what I could to try to ease the rhetoric against him. I told him I thought it was important to surround himself with wise counsel, as I felt like President Carter had had a difficult time because the people around him did not give him wise counsel. Since there is a difference between knowledge and wisdom, he should seek to have people around him who not only had great ability, but who also had God's understanding of things. I thought that having such wise counsel would provide a great source of strength to him. I also told him that early on I hadn't liked him; however, in prior months the Holy Spirit dealt with me about my attitude; gave me compassion and love for him; and that now I genuinely loved him. He listened very carefully, and again, tears seemed to come to his eyes.

At the conclusion of our time together, the president thanked us for coming to Washington and visiting with him. By this time we had spent a little bit over an hour in the Oval Office. We had been promised thirty minutes and we stayed over an hour. I knew there were critical international issues and other weighty matters hanging over his head. So, in my spirit, I felt that we were saying some things and relating to him in such a way that he did not sense it was a waste of time.

We stood to pray, and I asked if we could join hands, which we did. The president was on my right and Alexis was on my left. Rex led in a prayer, said "amen," and we began to disband.

Immediately, I asked, "Could I have a word of prayer? Earlier this morning I asked the Lord if I had an opportunity to pray with you, I would." Without hesitation, our group all rejoined hands, and I prayed. My prayer came from God's Word: James 1:5 (that he would ask God for wisdom and ask in faith) and Colossians 1:10 (that he would walk worthy of the Lord, fully pleasing Him, being fruitful in every good work, and increase in the knowledge of God). At the close of this, the president shook our hands again and thanked us several times.

As we walked by the president's desk, Henry Blackaby asked him, "I have my invitation to the White House. Would you, please, autograph it for me?" And then Henry added, "I would also like to have one for my children."

President Clinton sat down at his desk and genially asked, "How many children do you have?"

To which Henry replied, "Five." President Clinton graciously autographed five, little White House Oval Office Presidential seal cards.

While this was transpiring, I quietly mentioned to someone, "I wish I had brought mine. I have three kids who would love to have one."

The president overheard the conversation and queried, "Three? Who's got three?"

Seizing the opportunity, I spoke up and said, "I do!"

Necessarily aware of the president's schedule, Linda jumped in the conversation and suggested, "Mr. President, we can get those from you later. You have some other people who are waiting to see you."

Choosing to follow his own priorities in scheduling his day, the Commander-in-Chief politely insisted, "No, let's do it right now." At which point he reached into the right side of his desk, picked up three more cards, and proceeded to autograph his name on each, emphatically stating, "I want my name on these. I don't want it stamped. I want to sign these personally for you." He proceeded to put his *Bill Clinton* on three cards, which I put in my pocket, and which we will give to our children at a later time.

Henry also presented him with the book, *Experiencing God*, which had just come out the previous week, as well as a painting by Dick Button, a pastor in Texas, who is well known for his paintings. "You probably get hundreds of these," Henry commented.

Surprisingly, the president replied, "No, I don't get that many. When I get these, I usually put them somewhere in the White House." The way he responded gave me the feeling that this painting may have shown up somewhere upstairs in the White House.

When we walked out into the hallway, Alexis, who had been with the president for several years, turned to us and said, "Gentlemen, I want you to know this was a historic occasion."

"In what way?"

"You just don't realize the things you said, how important they are to the president, and the significance of this. Most people who come in there do not talk to him like that, are not open like that, and have other agendas. He rarely hears what you said today. These were things he needed to hear. I tell you, it was historic and very significant. I have been with him a long time, and I can assure you this was a very historic moment," she explained.

We were somewhat taken aback by what Alexis said; however, during our time with the president, we all had felt a strong sense of God's Holy Spirit within us. We knew many people were praying. We had asked God to speak to the president's heart and mind in such a significant way that what transpired would stay with him and bring glory to God. We, indeed, walked away feeling that it had been an important occasion. The fruit it bore will be known only to God.

Linda and Alexis assured us that if we needed to get a word to the president or needed any help in any way, we only needed to call or write them, and they would see to it that it was done. I will always remember their extending our time together in excited conversation as they profusely expressed their gratitude for what we had shared with the president.

In retrospect, I do remember meeting Thomas F. "Mack" McLarty III—a prominent Arkansas business and political leader who served as White House Chief of Staff—as he walked passed us. Rex commented, "This man is a real close friend of President Clinton's and has been with him for many years. He has a lot of responsibility."

In the course of our conversation, I commented, "He is small and thin, isn't he?"

Nodding in agreement, Rex said, "Yes, he has lost thirty pounds since the president was elected. He's on the go night and day."

We walked away from our visit with a sense of touching history, which we prayed was in a positive, eternal way. I remain eternally grateful that the Holy Spirit entrusted us with that moment. We left not knowing if God would give us a similar opportunity in the future. However, we did feel that a bridgehead of trust had been established. The president saw we were not pounding him or berating him, but trying to do what he said to do: to agree where we could and discuss our differences with respect for each other.

President Clinton also shared with us that he had done a lot of reading and studying about abortion. He told us he had probably done as much reading and thinking on abortion than any other important issue before him. This process was an agonizing thing for him, and he was continuing (and this was particularly interesting to me) to read and struggle with the issue. Clinton said, "I can see both sides of it: pro-life and pro-choice. Sometimes the pro-choice people seem to be as wrong as the pro-life people in their bitterness and anger. They will not listen or talk about anything else."

In retrospect, I felt the president did see the other side of the abortion issue, which I found encouraging. I did not believe he had closed the door. I felt that we, in the loving spirit of Christ and through persistent prayer, might see Clinton make some changes in his stance on the sanctity of life somewhere along the line. In my personal journal, I made note of Clinton's repeated focus on the family and family values as being our basic and only hope.

The next day, on Friday, the president spoke at the National Baptist Convention in New Orleans. While I was not present for that meeting, those who heard him said he did an excellent job. His tone was different, and he came down hard against people choosing abortions. They ought to make the life of the unborn child a higher priority. Young women should be encouraged to make better choices. We needed to reestablish the importance of family. With those remarks coming on the heels of the meetings the day before, it seemed he was working through the sanctity of life and the family's being the basic fabric of society.

My overall impression was that the president was very intelligent with an impressive grasp of a wide range of subjects. He entered into sweeping discussions of places he had visited in context of their historical ramifications. While Clinton was very gregarious and outgoing in many ways, I saw a kind of bashfulness and shyness in others. He was very knowledgeable of our Southern Baptist Convention. He quoted verbatim our *1971 Resolution on Abortion,* and told me that much of his position on abortion had been tailored after that 1971 Southern Baptist Convention resolution, but his own position about the sanctity of life was stronger than our resolution in 1971!

The president also quoted nearly verbatim that which I had said at the press conference after my election. I had said that the door was open to the president to be on our program in the future, and that my door would always be open for him to talk with me. Clinton said how much he appreciated my statement. Gore, who was sitting beside me at that time, said, "Yes, I read that. I agree with the president. It was well said, and we appreciate it."

Apparently someone had given my statement to them. They had read it and were responding. It may have been for politically motivated, but they were keeping up with Southern Baptist Convention positions.

One other little tidbit of trivia. At the breakfast table, I noticed that when we were eating, the president took his toast and leaned it beside his breakfast plate on the table, instead of placing it on the bread and butter plate—something Jeanette would have been horrified if I had done. It was a small habit that put a country boy like me at ease.

Later in the day, I noticed something else about the president that made him seem even more like someone to whom I could more easily relate. He had on the same kind of shoes that I wear: black, kiltie tassel loafers, which I have been reminded countless times by Jeanette should not be worn with a suit. Since my meeting with Clinton, I like to teasingly respond to Jeanette by saying, "Well, if the president can wear those kinds of shoes with a suit, I can!"

My time at the White House with the president was an unforgettable experience—one I pray God will use for His glory. I returned to Orlando with memories that remain with me to this day.

With All My Heart

To Those Who Speak Up When They Must:

It is easy to be intimidated by people, places, pressures, and procedures. Trying to keep steady when everything within you is churning is a formidable challenge. You run through various scenarios in your mind and practice what you might say if given the opportunity. You wonder about protocol or if you will be perceived as too preachy or too soft. When you have the chance to speak what you believe is the truth and a wise course of action, you can be filled with feelings of self-doubt instead of self-assurance. As you walk away from taking a stand, self-examination begins: "Why did I say that? Did I leave everything on the table that the Holy Spirit can use for His Kingdom purposes?" Only history and eternity will reveal those things. Jesus told a story about scattering seed and some "fell on good soil and produced a crop—a hundred, sixty or thirty times what was sown" (Matthew 13:8). This I believe. You must not fear scattering the seed when prompted by God's Holy Spirit.

CHAPTER SEVENTEEN

AIR FORCE TWO

J EANETTE AND I HAD just returned from a restful time at a beautiful resort called Chetola in the mountains of North Carolina. Phil Templeton, brother of our cherished friend Maurice, owned the place and gifted us with several days as his guest. While there I read a book on the second coming of Christ and decided when I returned I would preach a series based on that subject, entitled "Bible Sense, Common Sense, and Nonsense." I would have never guessed that in a few hours after returning to Orlando from our vacation, I would be working on that sermon series in the Holy Land in the midst of a long-sought peace accord for that troubled region of the world.

Upon returning to Orlando, Ragan Vandegriff, our minister of music, contacted me to inform me that the White House was trying to reach me. The administration wanted me to be a part of the U.S.A. delegation at the signing of the Israel-Jordan Peace Agreement, which was scheduled for the following Wednesday. Linda Lader, who made the call from the White House, had met with President Clinton to compile the list of invitees. She told me that he had struck off some names on the list, and said, "Put Jim Henry on this list."

After learning of this invitation, I got in touch with some of our deacon officers and Jimmy Knott, senior associate pastor,[51] for counsel and prayer. My struggle was realizing that if I went I could be criticized as being used by the president because the November elections were just around the corner. To resolve this in my mind, I called Linda Lader and asked her about the president's motive. She said, "Rarely does anyone have pure motives. However, he will not ask you to change your convictions or support him. He really wants you to go and be personal support."

Most people encouraged me to go. Sunday afternoon Linda called again to encourage me to go. Later on that same day Linda called me yet again to see if I had made a decision. She said, "I don't want to talk you into this, but I think it's important that you go."

After seeking prayer and counsel, I had no further check in my spirit. I informed her I had decided to be a part of the delegation. In retrospect, I am glad I went and I am grateful for Linda Lader's encouragement. She is a godly sister in Christ with a trusted position with the Clintons and I deeply respect her.

Arriving in Washington, I took a taxi to Andrews Air Force Base, procured my identification tags, and met several of my fellow delegates. We were surprised when the president came in from Ohio and addressed our group. While he was speaking, his assistant, Alexis, came to me and whispered, "The

---

[51] Jimmy Knott and his wife, Linda, had attended Two Rivers. Jimmy was an engineer at DuPont. Linda was a pharmacist. Jimmy came to faith and was called to the ministry while at Two Rivers. He went to New Orleans Baptist Theological Seminary, came back to serve on my staff at Two Rivers, and later joined us at First Baptist Orlando. I could always count on Jimmy to be analytical in his response and tell the truth. His counsel, as well as that of godly deacons, helped me make a wise decision in this situation and countless other times.

President wants to see you." She pulled me to the front row and instructed me to remain there.

After the president finished speaking to the group, she tapped him on the shoulder, he turned and told me he had talked earlier in the day to Billy Graham. President Clinton then shared that he had been to Israel years before with his pastor, Dr. W. O. Vaught, in 1982. He said, "I loved it. While we are there on this trip, I will have one-and-a-half hours in Jerusalem during which time I want to see more of the holy sites. Will you go with me?"

Of course, I said, "Yes!" (And if he were to ask me again today, I would gladly do so again.) Israel has a deep affection in my heart. I have probably been there thirty times through the years. Each time I am inspired and informed. Visiting Israel should be on every Christian's bucket list.

The president spoke to me three times that night. In one of our brief conversation, he commented, "Washington is so abnormal—not the people, but the atmosphere."

Our conversations were brief and casual because of the tremendous surge of people who were pulling on the president from every side. He was like a magnet. Everyone wanted to shake his hand and pose with him for a picture. As I did not know most of the people in the room, I spent my time observing, trying to identify people, and sizing up the significance of this moment in history, and in my life.

When it was time for us to depart, our group was carried out to Air Force Two, which formerly had been Air Force One. This iconic airplane was a thing of beauty. It was an awesome sight to see the beautiful flag of the United States of America painted on its tail and side. While on the plane, I met others in the delegation, checked out the plane, and enjoyed the delicious food prepared for us. Our delegation was in the front of the plane. The press, media, Secret Service, and White House personnel were in the back.

I saw the communications area, which was an awesome array of the latest in technology. We flew all night. I tried to sleep, but the excitement and anticipation inside me had me so wired that even two doses of Ambien could not have put me to sleep!

Upon arrival in Jerusalem our delegation was transported to the historic King David Hotel. After a brief time to refresh, we were escorted to the signing at the Arabah (in the Rift Valley). I was seated on the fourth row from the desk behind which President Clinton, King Hussein of Jordan, and Prime Minister Rabin of Israel were seated. Among those in attendance, there was a tremendous sense of excitement, and well there should have been. After centuries of conflict and bloodshed, hope for peace was on the horizon. Perhaps, the weapons of warfare could be retired. Quite understandably, in spite of the focus on peace, there was a huge display of security.

Twice President Clinton caught my eye, smiled, and waved. After the historic signing, amid much applause and celebration, we visited the fortress that Lawrence of Arabia had conquered in World War I, after the Ottoman Empire had dominated it for centuries. We were placed in a motorcade that whisked us past streets lined with curious onlookers. Then the president addressed the Jordanian Parliament. There I had a front row seat, fifteen feet from the First Lady and Queen Noor of Jordan. A great communicator, President Clinton did an excellent job in his speech, and was often interrupted by applause.

It was midnight before I got to bed. We departed early the next morning for a brief flight to Tel Aviv. From my window seat on the plane, I watched the pomp, as well as the heightened security. During the flight, Mrs. Clinton came by, introduced herself, and called me "Jim."

Once we disembarked and were en route to Jerusalem, I once again noted the tight security. Every intersection was barricaded and secured by soldiers with automatic weapons. I found it reminiscent of the scene I saw in Nashville, Tennessee, after the assassination of Martin Luther King, Jr., decades earlier. In Nashville most public transportation and automotive traffic was prohibited near major thoroughfares. At that time, because I was a pastor, I was granted permission to visit our people in the hospitals. En route to the hospitals, I traveled Broad Street, where there were armored vehicles and military with weapons at the ready. A few years later, while on a mission trip in South Korea, I saw it again. There were riots in protest against the government. From my hotel room in Seoul, I saw the same scenario with the addition of tear gas. None of these *deja vu* scenes were comfortable, to say the least, for this Tennessee country boy.

While in Tel Aviv, our delegation attended a luncheon for Jewish dignitaries that was held in the First Lady's honor. I had the privilege of being seated next to two Southern Baptist missionaries, John and Connie Anthony, who were serving in Israel. (John was an elementary school classmate of the president's.) To my right was Prime Minister Rabin's campaign director in his election bids in 1984 and 1988.

At the reception afterward, pictures were taken of our delegation, with each of us being photographed individually with the First Lady. With both hands to my side, I took my place by Mrs. Clinton's side. However, when she threw her arm around my waist, I did the same! She told me she had also come to Israel in 1982 with Dr. Vaught and how much it meant to her: "…especially Jerusalem and the Sea of Galilee. The experience stuck in my mind and heart."

I had the privilege of personally meeting Prime Minister Rabin, President Perez, and Yehuda and Esther Waxman, whose son, Nachshon, an Israeli soldier, was killed by Hamas. Later, the president came by, shook hands with all of us, thanked me again for coming, and said, "I had two tremendous nights."

We left Tel Aviv that night. Aboard Air Force Two, Mrs. Clinton served all of us chocolates and once again thanked us. During the night, her assistant, Melanie, asked me to "read an article in *Newsweek* about Mrs. Clinton's religious views on different issues and give your opinion. She values it. She was scared to do the interview." I did, pointed out a few areas of concern by making notes on the paper, and returned it. I never heard her response to my critique.

We arrived in Washington at daybreak. Again, the First Lady, who was wearing no makeup with her hair pulled back, came by and thanked us yet again. It was a fast and hectic four days that I will never forget.

I had one other interesting event involving Mrs. Clinton. In August, 2006, I received a call from a longtime friend and confidante of the former First Lady, inviting me to be one of six pastors to have dinner with her. Considering a run for the presidency, Mrs. Clinton wanted our input. She told me she liked and respected me because "I spoke truth into her ears."

In September, 2006, I flew to Washington, where I was housed in the infamous Watergate Hotel. Among the pastors invited were a Hispanic pastor, the president of the American Bible Society, and John, a delightful African-American pastor. Two taxis dropped us off at the Clinton's Georgetown home. The house was decorated in a "Hillary yellow" and lots of glass. Enabling them to host larger groups, their home had an extension they had added that looked out into gardens. I spotted an autographed picture of King Hussein and his wife on a motorcycle with words of appreciation and mention of the Peace Accord with Israel.

Hillary was late because of a meeting with an Iraqi minister. She told us over dinner she had urged him to put their oil in a kind of trust where everyone could benefit: stabilizing the country and vanquishing terrorists. I sat directly across from her at dinner. My friend, Don, said she wanted me to give the blessing because "she trusts you." Around the table we discussed health care, gay marriage, and abortion. One of the men said that evangelicals were together on those issues, and centrist on matters like global warming and the environment. She told us she was committed to traditional marriage—would be okay with civil unions, but not gay marriage. On abortion, she said we needed more education so people would not make "terrible choices."

I asked her about Iraq, told her our grandson Caleb was about to be deployed there, and shared that our church had buried one of our fine young men, Antoine Smith, a Marine killed in Fallujah. I added that Caleb felt freedom was at stake. He and others did not want to serve in vain. Mrs. Clinton agreed. She said our people should have the best equipment and support. She went on to explain the civil war there was on a "slow burn," and we had maybe a six month window to turn the tide.

Our conversation as a group also touched on immigration. Jessie, a fellow pastor, said that immigrants were "our brightest hope" and there needed to be a bipartisan move in Washington on the matter. Hillary spoke of how Republicans had manipulated the religious community. She did not understand why Southern Baptists, for example, would "lobby for tax cuts for the rich that reached beyond the church's primary mission." She brought up "Islamic terrorists" and her deep concern about them "because they, like Jews, had a commitment to a standard, traditions, and religious patterns that we as Christians did not seem to have." One particular example she gave was that we did not do more to celebrate Easter and Christmas. She thought we should participate in more rituals and our families should remember what it is truly about like the Jews do at Passover. I responded that the reason we did not have those kind of convictions and core values was because the Bible was not preached and taught in many pulpits.

As we closed I asked her how we could pray for her. She asked for "wisdom, discernment, courage, and strength," and mentioned some trying times in the past where their lives had been threatened. I gave her a CD of our daughter Kitty's most recent release and thanked her for serving us refreshments on Air Force Two after the memorial for Prime Minister Rabin. Our group prayed.

Afterwards, we went back to our hotel and did a reprise of the evening. I told the brothers that she probably could be elected if she became pro-life and supported traditional marriage.

My black pastor brother made an interesting comment. He felt that Jesse Jackson and Al Sharpton did not represent the majority of black people. He went on to explain how they were "out of touch" with blacks, who were socially conservative but politically aligned with the Democratic Party because of economics. In closing, he said, "…but that is changing."

Reflecting on the evening, I recalled that Hillary was wearing a cross— one that was not large or showy—around her neck. I sensed that she was trying to identify with our group by finding common ground in seeking our input and counsel. Whatever her motivation, I valued the opportunity to spend time with her. I know that there are conservative evangelicals who have sought to give biblical counsel to Hillary. My sense is that she does not listen to those sources as political expediency seems to have the loudest voice in her determined ambition. My observation is that as time moved on, Hilary appeared to feel that she could not or would not move toward the center on social issues. She cast her lot with those who opposed the pro-life stance of evangelicals. She, perhaps, deemed this a more expedient way to win the White House. Despite our differing views, I still pray for her and Bill on a regular basis.

But that happy historic moment was too soon shattered, and a dark cloud descended on the Holy Land. And then came another call from Washington.

With All My Heart

To All Who Struggle with Who and What to Believe on the Political Scene:

I struggle with political people. Sometimes I sense that they will say or do something for your vote, money, or influence. The positive side of me says, "I believe they mean what they say." The skeptical side says, "They did not mean a word they said. You're being used." The current political scene and probability for our future might best be summed up: "We are mad as all get out and not going to take it anymore." We'll see. My ultimate trust and hope are in placed in the King of Kings, who has always said what He means and meant what He has said. I place my hope in Him and confidently cast my vote for Him.

CHAPTER EIGHTEEN

WHEN ALL OF ISRAEL WAS SILENT

P ASTORS DREAD THE PHONE calls that come late in the night. When my phone jingled about 12:30 a.m. on Sunday, November 5, 1995, I wondered what bad news I was about to receive. It was bad. White House staff member, Flo McGehee, called with the sad news that Prime Minister Yitzhak Rabin had been assassinated by a Jewish zealot. The President wanted me to go with his delegation for the funeral on Monday.

Off I went to Andrews Air Force Base where I reunited with some friends I had met on our previous trip for the signing of the Peace Award. Dr. Joan Campbell of the National Council of Churches and Father Leo J. O'Donovan, president of Georgetown University, were among the group. Robert Schuller, pastor of the Crystal Cathedral, was my seat partner. We talked for hours. Two planes had been prepared: one for us and one for a congressional delegation. I was seated in the lounge area of Air Force Two. In our group were two rabbis, a lawyer, the president of the Jewish American League, and Henry Lyons—the former president of the National Baptist

Convention, USA, who, shortly after our journey, was charged with fraud, conspiracy, tax evasion, and other criminal acts, and sentenced to several years in prison. I liked Pastor Lyons; however, he seemed distant. Also aboard were several Secret Service agents, several Cabinet members, and Mickey Kantor, a Nashville native who was serving as the United States trade representative and was later appointed secretary of commerce.

We arrived in Jerusalem and were again housed in the historic King David Hotel. My suit bag and travel kit had been misplaced, so I borrowed a shave kit and dress shirt from a White House aide, and we went to the Knesset for the viewing of Prime Minister Rabin's body.

In front of me in the viewing line at the Knesset were Senator Robert Dole and Speaker of the House, Newt Gingrich. President and Mrs. Clinton entered and stood quietly before Rabin's flag draped coffin. The president was red-faced, puffy-eyed, and very somber. Former Presidents Jimmy Carter and George H. W. Bush also paid their respects. The crowd was very quiet. People were looking on from the upper floors of the Knesset. The clicking of cameras sounded like rainfall. Thousands of candles and trinkets surrounded the casket. Two Israeli military rabbis stood and read from the Psalms and the Torah for the entire time.

We filed by the simple casket and then adjourned to the cafeteria at the Knesset where a "who's who" was gathering. I made it a point to shake as many hands as I could: Presidents Jimmy Carter and George Bush, Cyrus Vance (Carter's secretary of state), Senator Bob Dole of Kansas, Senator Tom Daschle of South Dakota, Senator Ted Kennedy of Massachusetts, Senator Frank Lautenberg of Maryland, Senator Dianne Feinstein of California, Senator Jesse Helms of North Carolina, Congressman John Lewis of Georgia, and General John Shalikashvili (Chairman of the Joint Chiefs of Staff). Everyone was kind, but preoccupied with the funeral, paying their respects, and eating. As we were leaving, I saw a grief-stricken Mrs. Rabin, whose countenance was so different than when I saw her a year earlier at the Hilton Hotel reception.

The next hours were surreal in many ways. Our bus was filled with preachers and politicians. Democrats sat in the front and Republicans in the back with pastors and religious leaders in the middle. I guess we were a kind of peace-keeping presence in no-man's land. Later, as our bus moved toward the Herzl cemetery, Dr. Schuller asked me if I had ever officiated at a funeral for someone who had been murdered. He had not. Nor had I. Between the two of us, we had nearly eighty-five years of pastoring, but had been spared that awful duty.

As our funeral procession moved through the streets which had been cleared for the motorcade, I saw many people, as well as police officers and soldiers standing side-by-side, six to seven deep, on both sides of the street. The enormous crowd was quiet, many holding flowers and weeping openly. Yet, all was eerily silent. It was like looking at a photograph—a snapshot of grief and shock. At the cemetery, I sat about 75 to 100 feet from the coffin, which had been carried in by six Israeli military generals. By my side was Congressman Dick Gephardt of Missouri (the House Majority Leader at the time, who later ran unsuccessfully for the Democratic nomination for president). As we talked, he told me his greatest challenge was getting "his people" (Democrats, who had lost majority status in 1994 elections) to believe in themselves and not give up.

About five thousand people were present for the memorial service, including seventy-two heads of state. Noteworthy was the presence of King Hussein of Jordan, who had worked with Rabin for many years, and President Hosni Mubarak of Egypt, who were in Jerusalem for the first time. The service began with the wailing of air raid sirens that sliced through the air like machetes. For two minutes no one spoke or moved, as the sound cut the air and pierced our hearts. Then, the sirens began to wind down, one at a time, until all was silent and the last one moaned its tribute.

There were tributes from nine or ten leaders. I was most impressed with King Hussein's eloquent words. He said he "hoped he would die like his grandfather and Rabin," who were both assassinated. I hoped he did not mean what he said. (Thankfully, he died of complications related to non-Hodgkin's lymphoma in 1999, and was not assassinated.)

The Secretary-General of the United Nations, Boutros Boutros-Ghali of Egypt spoke, followed by President Clinton. The president did an excellent job and quoted a number of Scriptures. Speaking in Hebrew and English, Rabin's eighteen-year-old granddaughter was eloquent and very emotional. All of us were deeply moved with her obvious love for her grandfather, and many wept openly as she spoke of the loss of their "pillar of fire," an Old Testament analogy she used to describe her grandfather's legacy as a national leader.

I had the privilege of being a part of a few hundred invited to the burial. The grave site was very simple as was the wooden box in which his body lay. I processed to the grave just behind Queen Beatrix of Holland. John Major, the Prime Minister of England, and Prince Charles walked within two feet of me, as did the Prime Minister of Russia. The crowd crushed in exceptionally close to the family and open grave, so much so I was concerned for their welfare.

The graveside ceremony was simple. There was a prayer, the Jewish national anthem, and a twenty-one gun salute. Then dirt was thrown on the coffin—much like our practice, particularly in rural church committal services. Senator Ted Kennedy did something unusual. Holding a bag with some dirt from his brother, John Kennedy's burial site at Arlington, he got on his knees beside the grave and mixed the dirt of these two assassinated world leaders. I tried to approach Mrs. Rabin to pass on condolences. However, when I got within three feet of her, Mrs. Rabin's body guards removed her and the children far from the growing pressure of people.

That night we had a buffet dinner at the Ambassador Room in the King David Hotel. Newt Gingrich and his then wife, Marianne, were at my table. She was very personable and talkative. I asked Newt how I could pray for him and he said, "…for wisdom and strength to get changes through Congress. It's most important that we do this." (Apparently the prayers of many prevailed, for many positive changes were made by that Congress.)

A few minutes later, President Clinton entered the banquet room. Newt leaned over and said, "Watch him. He will go to every table. He's a master at this."

And he did. He made his way to our table, and thanked me for coming. "It's important for you to be here to represent us," he said. "Our friend Rex [Horne] was elected President of Arkansas Baptists. I'm glad about that."

I told the President he did a good job with his tribute, to which he replied, "It was the most difficult thing for me… very hard."

On the way to the airport, Linda Kamm, a Jewish woman very involved in the Democratic Party and politics, told me that a friend of hers in Israel said that the Palestinian leader Yasser Arafat had called three times, because he could not believe that Rabin was dead. Then he broke into tears. He called Leah Rabin, and together they wept. Former enemies were friends in death. Linda asked me why Southern Baptists were so pro-Israel. I told her our position was based and God's promise in the Bible to *"bless those who bless you [Israel] and whoever curses you, I will curse"* (Genesis 12:3). It was interesting to me that she was cognizant of our position on Israel: one, I pray, we will never forsake.

At the memorial service, Rabin's longtime friend and aide read the lyrics of "A Song of Peace,"[52] a hymn that Rabin had read and put in his breast pocket shortly before his assassination. It was blood-soaked, a powerful symbol. The first stanza well expresses the universal yearning for peace:

This is my song, O God of all nations,
A song of peace for lands afar and mine;
This is my home, a country where my heart is;
Here are my hopes, my dreams, my holy shrine:
But other hearts in other lands are beating
With hopes and dreams as true and high as mine.

That is a message for which we all pray and hope. It will be realized when the Prince of Peace, Jesus Christ, returns to usher in peace for all eternity.

With All My Heart

To Those Who Struggle with What to Say in Difficult Times:

Scripture tells us: "There is a time for everything: a time to be silent and a time to speak; a time to weep and a time to laugh; a time to kill and a time to heal; a time to mourn and a time to dance."[53] Silence can be eloquent, especially when words do not adequately express your thoughts. There will be those moments and experiences in your life when silence can be the greatest voice. In the stillness, you become

---

[52] The first two stanzas were written by Lloyd Stone when he was 22 years old in the interval between WWI and WWII (1934). Additional stanzas were added later by other authors.

[53] Ecclesiastes 3:1-7.

more sensitive to His Voice. That is good. Don't run from the quiet. Listen. God probably won't shout; instead He will speak to you in a quiet whisper. However, that whisper can seem louder than a thunderbolt in your heart.

CHAPTER NINETEEN

A DALLAS PARADE AND "BUSH 43"

ONE OF THE RESPONSIBILITIES of being the president of the Southern Baptist Convention was to represent our people at the functions of other denominations. One such opportunity was when Robert Schuller invited me to preach at the Crystal Cathedral. I will never forget being escorted to their preparation room, where they seated me in something that looked like an old-fashioned barber's chair and proceeded to cover up my blemishes for my on-air appearance. Huge and well-appointed, this room was a far cry from my study where our church's makeup ladies dusted me up to help me look more presentable. It was rather surreal to stand at the pulpit from which I had watched Dr. Schuller preach many times. The pulpit towers above the pews. I missed the intimacy of First Baptist where the pulpit was built in a way that allows an easier connection with the people.

On another occasion, I was delighted when the invitation came to bring greetings at a celebration for one of my heroes in the faith, Dr. W.

A. Criswell.[54] The service honored the fiftieth anniversary of Dr. Criswell's serving as pastor of First Baptist Church, Dallas, one of the great churches of America.

The church had gone all out in making this a memorable event for Dr. Criswell; his family and friends; the congregation and the city; as well as those of us who were invited to participate in this special occasion.

Prior to the public festivities, I was privileged to join Dr. Criswell, Dr. Hobbs, Dr. Jack Graham (the pastor of Prestonwood Baptist Church in Dallas), Dr. O. S. Hawkins, and Jack Pogue (a close friend of Dr. Criswell's and faithful member of First Dallas) for lunch at the Petroleum Club. We feasted on good food; however, above all, we feasted on listening to these giants of the faith share some of their rich ministry adventures. I asked about difficult situations they had faced in their ministries.

Dr. Criswell told about two deacons who had opposed him early on in his ministry at First. The men spoke for one hour to the deacons at First about why they should remove Dr. Criswell. Instead, the deacons voted to oust them! Dr. Criswell also shared that the widow of his predecessor, Dr. Truett, had not been fond of Dr. Criswell. Dr. Truett had been buried by an old friend, Robert Coleman, who also supported Dr. Criswell.

When the time came for big events to honor Dr. Criswell, Jeanette and I enjoyed the privilege of participating in a parade to kick off the big day. The church housed us at the Fairmont Hotel, the location from which a parade down the major thoroughfares of Dallas was to launch and then wind its way to the church. Jeanette and I rode in a Pontiac Firebird with Dr. Herschel Hobbs—noted Southern Baptist pastor, author, close friend of Dr. Criswell's,

---

[54] Dr. Wallie Amos "W.A." Criswell (1909-2002) served as the president of the Southern Baptist Convention, 1968-1970.

and the oldest living former Southern Baptist Convention President. Dr. O.S. Hawkins—president of GuideStone Financial Resources—and his wife were transported in a vintage car. Dr. and Mrs. Criswell rode in a 1948 Cadillac convertible. It was an amazing sight to see the people crowding the parade route all the way to the church. I nudged Jeanette and told her to enjoy this once-in-a-lifetime ride down the main streets of Dallas.

The impressive service at First Baptist Church of Dallas was filled with excitement, appreciation, joy, tears, and laughter especially when Dr. Hobbs called Dr. Criswell "lad," although he was also in his eighties. "Lad" was a favorite term of Dr. Criswell's. Whenever he placed his hand on your shoulder, looked at you with those twinkling eyes, broad grin, and called you "lad," you never forgot it.[55]

My tribute to Dr. Criswell lasted about five minutes. On the platform with me were Ray Hutchison, husband of Senator Kay Bailey Hutchison, and George W. Bush ('43). When I sat down, he leaned over and said, "I see why you were elected president." I'm not sure what I said. It had to be of the Holy Spirit, because they hadn't told me I was to speak for five-minutes until after I got there. To God be all praise and glory!

Later, at the reception, the affable, one-day-to-be-president of the United States, asked if he could join me and Jeanette for a few minutes. He pulled up a chair, grabbed a Coke, and began to talk. I made note that he said, "Whether I win or lose my bid for the upcoming election for governor of

---

[55] Along those lines, I recall another occasion when Dr. Criswell invited me into his beautiful home, gave me a tour, and described the antiques and memorabilia he had assembled. When it was time for me to leave, he had me kneel, put his hand on my shoulder, and, in his inimitable way, prayed for me with a line I will never forget: "And, Lord, bless that dear church in Orlando, where there's a Disney World, a Sea World, and, Lord, that Baptist World."

Texas, the Lord has given me a peace and calm. I trust in God's sovereignty." In that happy setting, none of us could imagine that in a few short years, he would not only be elected governor of Texas but president of the United States, and lead us through the biggest crisis since WW II—the terrorist attacks of September 11, 2001.

Dr. Criswell was saluted by President Reagan, Billy Graham, and a representative of the Jewish community, who thanked him for his support of Israel and reminded us that he knew all the Israeli prime ministers. City and county officials also lauded him. Dr. Criswell's response was awesome. He quoted a long poem and a hymn. Jeanette and many others were in tears.

There were two other cameo moments I took away from those cherished hours. The first was when we saw Dr. Hobbs, who had a room next to ours, in the hall as we were headed into our room. Jeanette hugged him goodnight. A widower, he smiled and said, "I don't get much of that now."

Dr. Hobbs told me he had written 160 books. He went on to explain one of the reasons: "I write because I want to live after I die."

The second vignette was at the luncheon. For dessert, Dr. Criswell ordered two dishes of ice cream and then covered the ice cream with cream and several spoons of caramel sauce. He then asked for the caramel sauce pitcher, and drained it! Since he lived to the ripe old age of 93, I may need to eat more ice cream and caramel sauce.

With All My Heart

To Those Who Wonder If Their Life Has Had a Significant Impact on Others:

As I participated in the events of that weekend in Dallas and observed the people—the great, the soon-to-be-great, the not-so great, and the never-will-be-great—I wondered if their teachers, schoolmates, parents, and colleagues realized they may have been influencing a life that would impact millions of lives from the religious to the political realm. Whomever God puts in front of you, treat them well, encourage them, and be an example of Christ's holiness to them. Your being in their life may not seem noteworthy, but is a part of God's plan.

CHAPTER TWENTY

AL GORE AND THE BURNING OF BLACK CHURCHES

O N THE NATIONAL SCENE things were not good in several areas, especially in race relations. As a denomination we had demonstrated reconciliation and repentance. Our churches were perhaps more open to people of all races than we had ever been.[56] However, in 1996 hatemongers were on the prowl. A large number of black churches were being torched all across the South.

At our Southern Baptist Convention, I approached some of our leaders about demonstrating our concerns, not only with words and prayer but by giving a love offering to help rebuild the churches. All thought it was a great idea; however, one of our by-laws stated that we could not take offerings for outside groups (or something to that effect). I huddled with Dr. John Sullivan, one of our exceptional parliamentarians, to see if we could work

---

[56] Years later, the fruit of our actions in Atlanta and by courageous pastors and churches was being seen. This culminated in the election of Fred Luter, a dynamic African-American pastor in New Orleans as our president, by acclamation, in 2012.

out something. I do not remember how they did it. They found a loophole so we could take this love offering. John led the way by pledging $50,000 from Florida Baptists. Alabama and Georgia joined in. Adrian Rogers pledged $10,000 from Bellevue Baptist Church in Memphis, Tennessee. Tom Elliff pledged $15,000 from First Baptist Church, Del City, Oklahoma. I committed $10,000 from First Baptist Orlando. By the end of the morning, we had $281,000 in money and pledges.

Within the week, Alexis called me and said the White House was lining up a conference call with President Clinton and Vice-President Gore about the church fires. The day of the call, the vice-president welcomed us to the noonday conversation, and the president joined us ten minutes later. On the call were three black pastors whose churches had been burned, as well as one rabbi, a representative from the Jewish Anti-Defamation League, Cardinal Keillor, Joan Campbell of the National Council of Churches, and I. When the president joined us, he greeted us and asked for suggestions.

I offered a few suggestions, and was somewhat surprised when the others were basically silent. The vice-president said he liked my suggestions which included combined worship services, prayer vigil, calling the nation to prayer, extra security for targeted churches for a season, and meetings with mayors, law enforcement and religious leaders at the local level. A few days later, Flo called from the White House again. She said the president took several of my recommendations and passed them on to Southern governors, who said some of the suggestions would be implemented. (I pray they did.)

In late August, I was coming in from a Saturday night prayer walk when Jeanette met me at the door and said, "You've either got a challenge or an opportunity. The White House called."

Alexis called to say the president was looking over the Democratic Convention program. He wanted me to do the benediction on Tuesday night in Chicago. I raised the question about our Southern Baptist Convention resolution on Jewish evangelism,[57] as I knew my doing so could cause some flak. I also asked if I could pray in the name of Jesus. Alexis said she would raise these issues with the committee, but did not think they would be problematic. She suggested I just consider myself a chaplain, not a pastor, with no agenda but for the nation, families, et cetera. Flo called back on Sunday afternoon to say there were no problems with any of the concerns I raised.

I shared the opportunity with our church and asked them to pray. Many applauded. As soon as I arrived at home, I received an irate call from a faithful member, who said I was making a terrible mistake. If I did this I would be "endorsing Clinton," abortion, and gays in the military. I told him Billy Graham had prayed at the president's inauguration to which he replied, "Billy Graham and you are too kind."

I did some more thinking and praying. Two things came to my mind. I had previously refused to pray at several Republican and Democratic rallies and meetings, as I did not want to appear favorable toward any one political party. To accept this invitation could violate what I had previously refused. Secondly, the theme on Tuesday night was the family. I would be praying after the First Lady's speech. Also, I would be praying with the knowledge of the president's veto of the Partial-Birth Abortion Ban Act, which I had joined with eleven other Southern Baptist Convention presidents in sending a letter to him urging him not to do so. I knew I would have to hedge my prayer or publicly embarrass the president. After much thought and prayer, I decided I could not offer the prayer.

---

[57] The Southern Baptist Convention supports the view that we, as followers of Christ, are to bear witness to all people. This includes our Jewish friends.

I called Flo and left word to get someone else. In my journal I wrote, "I regretted it in some ways, because it was an opportunity to intercede for families with nationwide television coverage. However, I could not compromise. These kinds of decisions are tough for me to navigate. How much do you engage the world and when do you disengage?"

Shortly thereafter, I received word that Jack Kemp and Senator Bob Dole were having a conference call on the Partial-Birth Abortion Ban Act. The Senate was going to vote on September 26 to override the President's veto. On that conference call were Chuck Colson, Senator Lott of Mississippi, Senator Nickles of Oklahoma, Cardinal O'Connor of New York, Bill Bennett, former Secretary of Education under President Reagan, some other participants, and I. Nickles said that in allowing these abortions, our nation would "be no better than the Nazis."

"It was the defining moral issue of our day," Colson insisted.

Both were prophetic. Reading about the selling of aborted babies body parts by greedy, calloused, cold-hearted merchants of death in Planned Parenthood clinics, has become the sad fulfillment of those words I heard nearly twenty years ago.

The Senate failed to override the threatened veto: 41-57. Colson said this was the first of three tipping points to bring God's judgment on the United States. The other two were the legalization of homosexual marriage and the legalization of euthanasia. If those occurred, he said that Christians must recognize we are truly aliens here and should no longer pledge allegiance to the United States.

I have observed the downward spiral in which we currently find our nation. What was considered unthinkable three decades ago has become a tragic reality in our lifetime. I believe we must contemplate: *How long will God have mercy on us? Has His hand of judgment already fallen upon us? The* unravelling of society seems to say that we are now reaping what we have sown. We must prepare to live as the early church did. Nearly two thousand years ago, Peter exhorted believers: "I urge you, as aliens and strangers in the world… to live good lives among the pagans… that they may see your good deeds and glorify God on the day He visits us" (1 Peter 2:11-12).

I have seen President Clinton a couple of times recently. He always calls my name, and is affable and cordial. When I was interim pastor of Biltmore Baptist Church in Asheville, North Carolina, Hillary Clinton was campaigning in the state. Congressman Heath Shuler, a member of the church, called to ask if it was okay for former President Clinton to worship with us. Of course, it was.

When Clinton arrived at the church and saw me, he immediately called my name and gave me a big hug. After greeting him, I said, "We've both turned grayer since the last time we met," which made him laugh.

When we had talked for several minutes, one of Hillary's operatives—a Southern Baptist who had been in Hong Kong as one of our denomination's journeymen with the International Mission Board—asked me to pray for the former President. I had everyone join hands, and I prayed. Several times I heard Clinton whisper "amen" as I prayed. I am not sure if he was wanting the prayer to end or agreeing in spirit; however, I believe it was the latter!

I think that if President Clinton had been a faithful believer, lived a morally pure life, and had come down on God's side on the sanctity of life and the sacredness of traditional marriage, he would have been one of our greatest presidents. If life gave mulligans, I think deep in his heart, he would like a "do-over." He and Mrs. Clinton are still prayed for by me and countless others: that God will turn their hearts toward Him and the things He has made good, sacred, and forever right.

With All My Heart

To All Who Walk the Tightrope of Being Salt and Light in a Secular World:

Throughout my ministry I had to struggle with being a prophet in confronting a lost world with God's truth while trying to be compassionate so as to build bridges that would help the lost cross over to having their spiritually blind eyes opened. I am not sure I totally succeeded; however, I constantly prayed I would. Speaking the truth in love is not easy, but necessary.

CHAPTER TWENTY-ONE

MADELEINE ALBRIGHT AND RELIGIOUS PERSECUTION

O N MY 59ᵀᴴ BIRTHDAY (1996), I received a letter from Secretary of State Warren Christopher, asking me to be on the Presidential Advisory Council on Religious Persecution Against Christians.[58] When I called to inquire about what this would entail, an advisor to President Clinton said that the president wanted to do something substantial about the issue. I was also concerned about the makeup of the committee. I was assured there would be a representative group of evangelicals present.

Before I committed to serving, I asked my men's Bible study group and other prayer warriors to pray with me about it. When the press released the story about the committee and its makeup, I received a lot of response: some urging me to accept and others urging me to decline. After much prayer,

---

[58] By the time our advisory group convened at the State Department, the official name of our committee had been changed to the Advisory Committee on Religious Freedom Abroad, which reflected a more positive tone.

I chose to serve. I felt it better to have some input regarding the plight of Christian brothers and sisters than none at all.

We convened for our first meeting in February, 1997. My hotel was the Wyndham Bristol, a twelve-minute walk to the state department, which was made more brisk by the cold weather! About twenty of us were then taken to the White House to meet with the First Lady. We had some pictures taken, and afterward, Mrs. Clinton chose to spend a lengthy amount of time with me. I told her that I prayed for her and for Chelsea. I prayed that Chelsea would find a Christian husband. She laughed and said, "Me, too, but not for ten years!"

Dressed in a dark blue suit and a necklace of interwoven pearls, Mrs. Clinton spoke to our group for seven or eight minutes without notes—never repeating herself—to assure us that the president and she were strongly supportive of our work. She said they wanted more "balance" in foreign policy, which some of us interpreted as more interest in human rights and religious freedom. At the close of her time with us, Mrs. Clinton thanked us and turned our group time over to a Secret Service agent, who gave us an extensive tour of the White House.

On this fascinating tour, I saw areas I had never seen before, including the chairs President Roosevelt and Winston Churchill sat in during their World War II meetings. Later, Don Argue, the president of the National Association of Evangelicals (NAE), told me the president told him he had made three mistakes during his first term. The first was appointing a staff that was too young. The second was misunderstanding Washington and "the system." And the third? Reportedly, the President said, "I can't mention the third until I am out of office." I still wonder what that was that bothered him. Could it have been the Lewinsky situation?

The president told Tony Campolo—sociologist, pastor, author, spiritual advisor, and one of the most influential leaders in the "evangelical left"—that President Lincoln was not a Christian until after Gettysburg's awful carnage. The pressure and the burden turned Lincoln to Jesus. Clinton pointed Tony to a place on the floor where, he said, Lincoln knelt often in prayer for mercy and guidance. Then the president added, "And so do I."

Interesting in its diversity and composition, our committee included one of the sons of Elijah Muhammad—the leader of the Nation of Islam, who was with Martin Luther King, Jr., near the time of his assassination in Memphis. Assistant Secretary of State for Democracy, Human Rights, and Labor John Shattuck seemed to be balanced and committed to action, led us in our inaugural meeting. Secretary of State Madeleine Albright[59] also addressed us. Quite personable, she spoke of recent meetings that included one with Benjamin Netanyahu, who later became prime minister of Israel.

Later, we heard fifteen speakers in what was called "public access time." Some of these speakers were very emotional. Several urged us to speak out about the persecution of Christians. Another spoke of the persecution of Muslims in Bosnia, and also referred to an incident at the Al-Aqsa Mosque in Jerusalem, a city that "should be a free city for three faiths."

In my opening remarks, I shared Psalm 142:5-7:

> *I cry to you, Lord;*
> *I say, "You are my refuge,*
> *my portion in the land of the living."*

---

[59] Later, when I had the opportunity to meet Madeleine Albright, I told her I was praying for her. She replied, "I need it… lots of it."

Listen to my cry,
  for I am in desperate need;
rescue me from those who pursue me,
  for they are too strong for me.
Set me free from my prison,
  that I may praise your name.
Then the righteous will gather about me
  because of your goodness to me.

I am not sure what I said after that; however, several individuals of many faiths—Jewish, a Greek Orthodox, and Bahá'í—approached me afterwards and thanked me.

In our next meeting, we had a panel discussion. The consensus seemed to be that the state department was becoming more "flexible." One observer noted that there was a "sea of change" in attitude. It was pointed out that religion had a tremendous input in human affairs—good and bad—and that the state was beginning to teach new ambassadors to become more knowledgeable in this area and to press for religious freedom. Sanctions and boycotts were discussed. Their effectiveness seemed to be a mixed bag. Conflict resolution and mediation were also topics of discussion and debate.

On my taxi trips to and from the meetings, two drivers made an impression on me. One driver was a Sunni Muslim, who was not fond of Shiite Muslims. The other taxi driver was from the Punjab state in North India and was a Sikh, who had a strong belief in reincarnation, the transmigration of the soul from one body to the next. He told me that if he did not make it to heaven the first go-around, he could be reincarnated 844,000 times and came back a human being. As I listened to these two drivers discuss their faiths, I thanked God for revealing His love for me through a personal relationship with Jesus Christ. I was—and remain—grateful for my Lord and

Savior who has a plan for my life. I also had a renewed thankfulness for others who trust in Jesus Christ, repent of sins, trust in Jesus' completed work on the cross to cover our sin debt, and know the guarantee of being in God's presence immediately after our last breath. Just as Jesus promised the repentant thief who turned to Him on the cross and asked for mercy: "*Truly I tell you, today you will be with me in paradise*" (Luke 23:43). So it is for all of us who turn our hearts to Christ!

By November of 1997, the advisory council had begun the draft of a report to be presented to President Clinton and Secretary of State Albright. We heard an interesting piece of news from John Shattuck, the assistant secretary of state. The president had met President Jiang Zemin of the People's Republic of China and the general secretary of the central committee of the Communist Party of China—at a summit the day before our meeting. President Clinton had come down hard on President Zemin concerning religious and human rights. Interestingly, Wei Jingsheng—Chinese human rights activist and dissident writer, who had been imprisoned a total of eighteen years for his involvement in the Chinese democracy movement—was released "for medical reasons" that day and promptly deported to the United States.

When the time came to present our report to the president and secretary of state in January, 1998, the media was ablaze with allegations about President Clinton's having an immoral relationship with White House intern Monica Lewinsky. Madeleine Albright received our report and spoke to our committee for the last time.

Our report's first recommendation was that a person be put in place at the state department whose assignment would be to give special attention to only religious freedom issues. After receiving our entire report, our committee had a picture made with Madam Secretary. I was placed next to her as I, like her, was short in stature. I guess being short does have some perks!

In retrospect, I am not sure what happened to our diligent work. With the uproar over the Lewinsky affair, I feel that the report was buried under bureaucracy. As I write this nearly twenty years later, it is apparent that the eradication of religious freedom and the systematic persecution of religious groups—particularly of Christians—are at their highest levels since the days of the Roman Empire. Do I think things will improve? Probably not. The Bible warns us that as the coming of Jesus for His church comes closer, the pace of attacks on believers will increase. I find myself with other Christians praying like the early church: *"Even so, come, Lord Jesus"* (Revelation 22:20*b*).

The Lord certainly hears the prayers of His children. Over my lifetime, my prayers have been answered in amazing ways. As I have prayed *"Thy kingdom come...,"*[60] and if it pleased Him, that God would use me in any way that suited His purposes to expand His Kingdom on earth. I would have never imagined that my Lord would give me the amazing opportunities to counsel world leaders that He has. This has definitely kept me humbled and on my knees as I know that apart from His power and wisdom, I am inadequate for the Kingdom tasks He has brought my way during the course of my ministry.

Another opportunity revolved around peanut butter. I have always loved peanut butter. From childhood, I loved the delicious taste of peanut butter and jelly, peanut butter and banana sandwiches, Reese's peanut butter cups,™ and peanut butter ice cream. And so it seemed fitting that God would bring the peanut farmer who became president into my life through another one of those Kingdom opportunities.

---

[60] See "The Lord's Prayer," Matthew 6:10*a*.

With All My Heart

To All Who Love Those Who Are Persecuted for Righteousness' Sake:

When you observe the enormity of worldwide events—especially the increasing persecution of Christians—you want to do something, yet you feel practically helpless, unable to achieve any meaningful results. You resolve it is better to aim at something and fail than to aim at nothing and succeed.

We all must try our best to make a difference in the world. We cannot forget our suffering brothers and sisters in Christ. We must do what we can, when we can, where we can, and leave the results in God's sovereign care.

CHAPTER TWENTY-TWO

BORN-AGAIN PEANUT FARMER AND PEACE MAKER

WAS SOMEWHAT STARTLED WHEN I received a telephone call from the assistant to former President Jimmy Carter. I was told he would call me at 4:45 p.m. on October 23, 1997. At exactly 4:45 p.m. the phone rang, and it was President Carter. Very cordial, he immediately put me at ease as he told me how much he liked Orlando, and had taken his family—twenty-two members—to our city to see the sights. President Carter said that taking a vacation with his family—skiing, cruising to the Caribbean, et cetera—was something he did every year. He said it was important to him; however, it was expensive. He said he saved all year to be able to do it as he did not get "big honorariums like Reagan and Bush." I told him he needed to start taking love offerings, which made him laugh.

President Carter explained the reason for his calling was to inform me of, as well as invite me to, a meeting he was going to convene of Baptist leaders, including pastors and leaders of predominantly black denominations and congregations; members of the Cooperative Baptist Fellowship (CBF); Dr.

Timothy George, dean of Beeson Divinity School of Samford University in Birmingham; and Senator Mark Hatfield of Oregon. The president went on to explain that although he was a Southern Baptist, he felt left out of the denomination. The church at Plains, where he has faithfully taught Sunday Bible classes for decades, was Southern Baptist. He said his church "would split in two if we tried to pull out [of the Southern Baptist Convention], but we also give to the CBF."

As I listened to President Carter's explanation of why he desired to convene this meeting, I thought it would be helpful to the discussion to include some conservative leaders. I suggested Adrian Rogers, Jimmy Draper, John Bisagno, Tom Elliff, Ed Young, Jack Graham, and others. I accepted his invitation, and immediately began praying and thinking about our forthcoming meeting.

In mid-November, I headed to the Carter Center, two miles from downtown Atlanta, Georgia. In partnership with Emory University, the non-for-profit center works to advance human rights and alleviate human suffering. Located next to the Jimmy Carter Library and Museum on thirty-seven beautiful, well-kept acres, the Carter Center has helped to improve the quality of life for people in more than eighty countries.

Upon my arrival at the center, President Carter's assistant said the president wanted to see me. After greeting me, he thanked me profusely for coming and wanted a briefing on (Southern Baptist) "Convention things." He told me that none of the conservatives I had suggested to him accepted his invitation. He wondered if a meeting with mostly conservatives would help, and asked if I would be willing to set up such a meeting. I assured him I would. I do not know which conservatives he asked; however, I could sense how disappointed he was. Frankly, I was, too.

Though his term as our president (1977-1981) does not receive high ratings, I respect him for his heart for seeking peace and reconciliation on a global scale, as well as in denominational struggles. In fact, in 2002 President Carter received the Nobel Peace Prize for his work "to find peaceful solutions to international conflicts, to advance democracy and human rights, and to promote economic and social development" through the Carter Center.[61] This former president followed the words of our Lord Jesus, "*Blessed are the peacemakers: for they shall be called the sons of God*" (Matthew 5:9, ESV).

When the group was convened, we met in an office filled with mementos, art, sculptures, letters, and gifts of appreciation for Carter's work as a peacemaker and humanitarian. The president asked me to lead the opening prayer. After which, we met for three hours. President Carter spoke extemporaneously. Later, he gave us a copy of the words he had prepared that morning.

The meeting was cordial. All there expressed hope that in some way in the future, we could present a united front on the things on which we agreed. Dr. George and Denton Lotz both said to me, "I think we are the token conservatives." I agreed we were, as far as those in attendance; however, I did not think it was President Carter's intention, as he had invited other conservatives who chose not to attend.

In the course of our meeting, Dr. Herbert Reynolds, the former president of Baylor University, presented the president with an honorary doctorate, which he had been unable to receive previously.

Throughout the course of our meeting, the president thanked me several times for coming. I was, and am, glad I attended.

---

[61] Norwegian Nobel Committee, 2002 Nobel Peace Prize announcement, October 11, 2002.

When I returned home, I composed a letter—which I ran by Dr. George, who affirmed its contents—that I (with Dr. George) sent to ten Southern Baptist leaders to invite them to meet with President Carter. I also forwarded my observations of our previous meeting to President Carter. Within five days, the president called and said he liked the letter Dr. George and I had sent. He wondered if we should include any moderates. I suggested that we should not at this meeting, but at a later meeting. He asked with whom he should talk about the meeting. I suggested Richard Land—then president of the Ethics and Religious Liberty Commission, the public policy arm of the Southern Baptist Convention, and now president of Southern Evangelical Seminary; Paige Patterson—then president of Southeastern Baptist Theological Seminary, and now president of Southwestern Baptist Theological Seminary; and some others. The president also asked me to attend.

We chatted informally for a few minutes. He told me about bringing his family to the Key West area the previous year, using his frequent flyer miles to fly them in. Then he mentioned that he had caught me the previous Sunday night on an interview on "60 Minutes" (CBS) with Leslie Stahl in which she and I dialogued about the Disney boycott, genetics, and homosexuals.[62] We closed our phone conversation with best wishes for the upcoming Thanksgiving holiday and Godspeed until our next meeting.

The next time I spoke with the president was in February, 1998. We talked by phone about our upcoming meeting with my conservative brethren. The president felt like the Southern Baptist Convention and the Cooperative Baptist Fellowship could agree on racial healing, which would

---

[62] Following our taping, I asked Leslie Stahl who were her most fascinating interview. She mentioned two: Yitzhak Shamir, the former Prime Minister of Israel, and Margaret Thatcher, the former Prime Minister of the United Kingdom. I asked Leslie why these individuals? She responded, "Because they had passion."

be an important focus in our discussion. He was also open to my suggestions for other topics of discussion.

I told him that we would probably bring up his statement about Mormons, which gave the distinct impression that he felt they were similar to evangelicals. His view of salvation seemed to be on shaky ground. While President Carter professed that salvation is by grace through faith in Jesus Christ, his statements of embracing Mormons as part of the Christian community and not being concerned about converting them are far from the beliefs of Southern Baptists.

The president said that Tom Elliff—president of the Southern Baptist Convention (1996-1998) and, at that time, pastor of First Southern Baptist Church, Del City, Oklahoma—had written him about this. I suggested he listen to our concerns, and then we would go from there. He assured me that his purpose in meeting was not to try to get any of us to change sides; however, he was concerned that he was not considered a Southern Baptist, when his Baptist church in Plains[63] gave ten percent to the cooperative program of the SBC (Southern Baptist Convention) and generously to its special mission offerings.

The group the president had invited gathered at the Carter Center in late February. President Carter warmly greeted our group, which was composed of Dr. Timothy George; Dr. David Dockery—the former president of Union University and now president of Trinity International University; Dr. Mark Corts—the pastor of Calvary Baptist Church in Winston-Salem, North Carolina; Dr. Jimmy Draper—the president of Lifeway Christian Resources; Dr. Morris Chapman—the president of the Executive Committee of the

---

[63] President Carter continues to teach his Sunday school class at Maranatha Baptist Church in Plains, Georgia.

SBC; Dr. Paige Patterson; Dr. Tom Elliff; and me. The group was privileged to be given a tour of his study. President Carter seemed to enjoy explaining some of the things we saw and the work he was doing.

After lunch, we assembled in a conference room. The president opened with a prayer, and then made some comments before our discussion began. When the matter of his statement regarding the similarity of Mormon and evangelical beliefs came up, the president flashed the familiar Carter smile and said, "I've received lots of letters, books, and tracts, and I understand better!"

The president wanted to clarify his position on abortion. He said that while he personally was against abortion, as president, he had to uphold the Constitution and the laws, which he had sworn to God to uphold.

President Carter then presented a statement that had six points he wondered if we as Baptist brothers could sign. With some adjustments, we all agreed we, as individuals, could sign the statement; however, we could not do so as representatives of our denomination as the CBF was not a denomination. He agreed. President Carter and Dr. George would redraft the document prior to its publicly being released.[64]

---

[64] Based on our discussion in Atlanta, Dr. Timothy George redrafted the following statement (February 27, 1998):

"Acknowledging that there are unresolved issues among us, we Baptists wish to overcome differences that may impede spiritual awakening in our nation and around the world. Therefore, in the Name of Jesus Christ, our Lord and Savior:

a) We call all believers to a common prayer effort in a spirit of forgiveness and Christian love. We will pray for one another and adhere to Paul's admonition to the Ephesians, "Be kind to one another, tenderhearted, forgiving one another, even as God for Christ's sake hath forgiven you" (Ephesians 4:32).

b) We pledge to forgo any public criticism of each other's motives. In response to the love of God which has been shed abroad in our hearts by the Holy Spirit, we will treat one another with mutual respect as brothers and sisters in Christ. We will cultivate holiness and purity of life in our personal devotions and public acts.

As our time together was coming to a close, I asked the president what were the most difficult and the best times of his presidency. He said the worst time was "the hostage situation.[65] I prayed a lot." The best time was "getting Prime Minister Begin of Israel and President Sadat of Egypt to agree to the peace pact between the two ancient enemies." He noted both leaders were deeply religious. As a side note, he added, "Menachem Begin was the first religious prime minister of Israel. The rest of them were quite secular in their attitudes, particularly Golda Meir, who laughed when I brought that up when I met with her when I was governor. A devout Muslim, Anwar Sadat had a mark on his forehead where he had knelt to pray for many years." When I asked if there was another best moment in his presidency, President Carter said, "It was when we were at Reagan's inaugural parade, and an aide whispered in my ear that our hostages were on a plane headed home."

For all the shortcomings attributed to him as our national leader, President Carter has earned my respect for the bold witness of his personal faith in Jesus Christ; his unashamed testimony to leaders of other nations of his Christian faith; his example of servanthood in the Habitat for Humanity project; his multiple efforts as an ambassador for peace at every level of

---

c) We will reach out to all of our neighbors in a spirit of racial reconciliation. We call on every Baptist church to form a partnership with a church of a different culture or ethnic group.

d) We covenant to exert our maximal efforts to end religious persecution in all nations and to encourage unfettered religious liberty for all peoples.

e) We will seek other ways to cooperate to achieve common goals, without breaching Baptist polity or theological integrity, in order that lost souls may be saved for eternity, and God be glorified in ever-increasing measure.

[65] The President was referring to the Iran hostage crisis, in which more than sixty American diplomats and citizens were held hostage for 444 days.

strife from denominational struggles to international crises; and his spirit of humility. He is a good brother.

With All My Heart

To Any Who Wonder What You Can Possibly Accomplish Next:

I was keenly disappointed in President Carter in his service as our president. However, my opinion of him as a man who has served mankind after leaving office is quite different. Jimmy Carter did not retire from service after holding the most powerful position a person can hold in the world. I believe what he has accomplished in serving God after his presidency has had more eternal impact than what he did while in political office. It is a good lesson for each of us. We must keep on doing our best wherever God has placed us until the clock runs out in the game of life.

CHAPTER TWENTY-THREE

WE'RE NOT GOING TO DISNEY WORLD

O NE OF MY LAST sessions as president of the Southern Baptist Convention was winding down when a messenger from California, Wiley Drake, made a motion that we put the word "boycott" in our resolution of concern about Disney World's retreating from family values. It passed overwhelmingly. I had expressed my concern in private conversations when I heard the word *boycott* coming from several sources. It had problems that were threefold in my mind. Number one: *What was our exit strategy? How could you measure its effectiveness? Did that mean our people should not watch television programs that Disney was producing or attend Disney movies?* Number two: *What about other entertainment industries that were doing some of the same things as Disney? Were they also to be boycotted?* Number three: *Our church had a large number of Disney employees, some in executive positions. They were having Bible studies with fellow employees; bringing them to church; caring and sharing with many of their lost and unchurched friends. What would this do to our witness?* My voice was lost in the stampede to vocalize our disdain over Disney's direction.

The press jumped all over it. I was rushed to the media room and a press conference. ABC, CNN, local TV, press from the New York Times, papers in Dallas, Houston, Shreveport, and others were there. Tough questions were asked. We were grilled for forty-five minutes. I was also asked about our offering for the black churches that were burned and about our resolution on evangelizing the Jews. I felt a kinship with a steak being grilled at a backyard picnic!

Mark Pinsky, the religion editor for our local paper, the *Orlando Sentinel*, who was always fair and objective in his reporting, asked if I would serve as a mediator between Disney and the Southern Baptist Convention. I said, "Yes, I would, if asked."

We closed the convention with a rousing message by Coach Bill McCartney, founder of Promise Keepers. Then I handed the gavel over to my good friend, Tom Elliff, my successor. Three bangs of the gavel and my eventful two years as Southern Baptist Convention president were over, but the Disney resolution followed me home.

We had raised a firestorm in Orlando. I knew I had to speak to our people about it. I drafted a statement about the Disney situation and read it in the Sunday service. It was well received by our people. Letters and calls—some for and some against—poured in from every direction. A few days later, Disney announced that the homosexual community event was going to be expanded to a three-day weekend. Our Disney employees said that there were many gays in their offices, who were giving them, Baptists, and the church a tough time.

The threat of a boycott lingered for the next year. Rumors flew. I met with some of our godly laymen for input. All were against the boycott. After much prayer and thought, I decided I needed to be upfront about my opposition to a boycott before we convened in Dallas. A member of the resolutions committee called and said the committee had three resolutions before them: one to boycott, one to monitor the situation, and one to widen the boycott; however, they were going to try to remove the word "boycott" from the resolution.

On arriving in Dallas, I had a call from Pinsky of the *Orlando Sentinel* saying the resolutions committee planned to come out with a strong resolution to boycott all Disney entities. I felt we were backing ourselves in a Vietnam-type quagmire. I knew I had to speak against the resolution, so I arrived early to get a seat near microphone 11. Once in session, a young lady messenger said, "We need to demonstrate we love Jesus more than entertainment." Wiley Drake, the original instigator of the resolution, took off on a harangue. A couple of men gave thoughtful concerns against the resolution. The emotional stampede was on!

Someone jumped in front of me before I could speak and called for the question. The vote was taken. The resolution passed by about a two-thirds majority. I was immediately besieged by the press, radio, and television for comments. My fellow Orlando pastor, Mark Matheson, worked up a statement about our concerns over the resolution. It was a full-page ad that several of us signed, declaring that we were here to minister to sinners of all kinds.

I decided to address the issue head-on the Sunday following our convention. On Saturday, I disguised myself in sunglasses, a baseball hat, and clipboard and headed to a local mall. I told shoppers I was doing a survey to find out what they thought about the Baptists and the Disney boycott. I surveyed fourteen shoppers. Thirteen said they thought it was wrong. I included that in my message on Sunday morning. The people listened to the message intently, and interrupted several times with applause, followed by a standing ovation at the conclusion. Many called for a copy of my message. I believe the Holy Spirit helped me articulate the truth so that it resonated with the people. I, in no way, wanted to dilute the gospel or retreat from biblical standards on the homosexual issue; however, I did not I want to close the door on those the Good News was meant to reach. I pray that we succeeded in that.

In the ensuing years, the issue was in and out of the news. Baptist people were divided. No one could measure the effect of the boycott decision. Paige Patterson, who wanted to reach out to Disney executives, approached me in December of 1999 about arranging a meeting with the Disney leadership to see if we could talk over our concerns. We were able to arrange such a meeting in April of 2000.

The Boardwalk at Disney was our meeting place—a huge meeting room overlooking a lake and hotels. Our hosts were most gracious and had a lavish buffet laid out for us. Michael Eisner was not there; however, Bob Iger, former president of ABC, and Al Weiss, president of communications for WDW, were some of the Disney people present. We immediately got down to business. Paige said he wanted the meeting to assure them there was no personal animosity. We were seeking to raise our people to holiness and higher standards. He expressed concerns over the seeming drift away from family values at Disney.

Bob Iger talked about their challenge with "creative" people and a diverse culture. He said they were considering adding a second religious reporter at ABC. Paige and I discussed a way to encourage them to issue a statement saying they would be more sensitive to the concerns we had raised. Iger said that would leave them vulnerable to more criticism if they did not live up to it in the same area. We asked them to continue to think about it, and we would try to bring closure at our end. There was no commitment from them.

Paige presented each of the Disney team with a leather-bound copy of the *Criswell Study Bible*, and, again, expressed love for them and their children.

Having done all we knew to do, we closed in prayer. Paige maintained some contact with Michael Eisner for some time thereafter.

Morris Chapman tried to get some of the main architects of the boycott to do something to bring closure the next year, but was unsuccessful in doing so. My earlier concerns about no-exit strategy, no way of measuring effect, and the negative witness it would bear on an unbelieving world had come to pass. Eventually, the issue drifted off the radar for most people.

I could see some silver lining in that it did cause us to think more deeply about our own value systems. It caused us to explore how or how not to impact a secular business model. It provided us the opportunity to share Christ's love with the leadership team of Disney. Only eternity will reveal the impact of these things.

On a lighter side, our church came up with scores of disguises for Baptist Disney visitors to rent while in our area so as not to reveal their identity if their church or pastor had come out for the Disney boycott, and made lots of money. (Just kidding!)

With All My Heart

To Those Considering What's The Wisest Course of Action:

It is said that all good strategies include an exit plan should it ever be needed. It is so easy to be moved passionately about issues and events, and then wade into the fray. Jesus reminded us that before a man built a house or a king went to war, he figured out his resources so as to best assure a successful outcome. If it's building a house, buying a car, choosing a mate, changing jobs, relocating or investing money, time, and talents, it is wise to pray, seek counsel, and evaluate the situation with the best information available. Ultimately, only God knows the end result. Yes, "the battle is the Lord's" (1 Samuel 14:47b). However, more wars are won when we consult with the Wisdom of the universe instead of launching out on our own.

CHAPTER TWENTY-FOUR

WHEN TIGER CAME TO CHURCH

THE MONDAY OF OCTOBER 25, 1999 was like most Mondays: full of calls, staff meetings, correspondence, and the debris from a busy Sunday. It had been a powerful Lord's Day. I did something I had only done once before: I invited those battling cancer or who knew someone close to them who was facing that fight to come to the altar and pray. I did not know what to expect. God moved in unexpected ways. In both Sunday morning services the people flocked to the altar—four or five deep—and some just knelt in the aisles. Tears were shed; petitions made. It was an unforgettable day!

The next day on that particular Monday, I had lunch with Randall James—a cherished friend, staff aide to three Orlando mayors, and fervent witness, who was a part of our pastoral staff team. Five minutes after returning from our lunch, he burst into my office and said, "We've got an emergency! We need to pray! I just heard that Payne Stewart is on a plane that is flying out of control over South Dakota… seventeen minutes of fuel left…with no sign of life." We hit our knees and prayed. We were in shock. I had a sinking feeling that they were doomed.

Payne Stewart had become a part of my walk when his children—Chelsea and Aaron—became students at our school, The First Academy. Payne's golf prowess was known worldwide. There was another side of his life that was not as well known. His life had taken another direction when he met Jesus Christ.

J.B. Collingsworth, an assistant pastor at our church, was close to Payne and shared the following about Payne's embracing a relationship with Jesus Christ: "Payne was surrounded on all sides by people who lived out their faith. Dixie Fraley Keller and her late husband Robert Fraley lived life full and abundantly in front of him for many years. They gave such great guidance and encouragement to Payne, Tracey, and their kids in every way possible. Van Ardan and others at Robert's business, Leader Enterprises, were vital to him and they too lived out the Christian life before him. Those who worked for Ronald Blue and Company were consistently pouring in encouragement and help. Godly guys on the PGA tour—Paul Azinger, Tom Lehman, Bernhard Langer, Corey Pavin, as well as many others—were great influences on his life. Scores of people from many walks of life did the same. Payne was easy to encourage."[66]

J.B. got to know Payne after he and Tracey enrolled their children at The First Academy. It was in those days that Payne began to be exposed more and more to people at the school—other parents, coaches, and teachers. Payne told J.B. that when he was home he worked with Chelsea and Aaron on their Bible verses. He shared how this really helped him to understand the Bible more. He asked good and sincere questions. God's Word is for real

---

[66] Joe B. "J.B." Collingsworth.

and does not return void. That is for sure. God was planting seeds in Payne's heart and life.

Along life's way J.B. would chat with Payne when he was home or away on PGA tours. J.B. recalled enjoying "the questions Payne asked. When he was at home he was in the Sunday school class I [J.B.] had invited Tracey and Payne to attend. If he missed the cut there, he was bounding up the stairs with a hug, and a huge smile. One day he looked at me [J.B.] and said, 'Knowing the Lord is like the most awesome thing.'"[67]

J.B. shared: "We talked over breakfast one day and he shared more about his love for Christ. I asked him this: 'So, Payne, you know that you know Jesus is in your life and you have been forgiven?' His words were a resounding, "There's no doubt!'"

Collingsworth recalled, "My wife, Shugie, and I walked into the lobby next to the room where Payne's Open[68] celebration party was being held. As soon as he saw us walking in, he began to hold up his WWJD[69] bracelet and started pointing to it. He gave us both big hugs. People were in the room eating and visiting and some were watching a video of the last couple of holes at Pinehurst. We made our way into the room and enjoyed some food and fellowship with other friends. Payne was watching the video as were others, and soon I saw him getting teary eyed. A couple of the guys laughed and said, 'It's okay, Payne; you already won.'"

---

[67] Joe B. "J.B." Collingsworth.

[68] Reference to the U.S. Open at Pinehurst.

[69] Reference to the popular "What Would Jesus Do" bracelets. At that time, many believers were wearing these bracelets as a witness and a reminder of the lifestyle we, as Christians, are to exhibit.

J.B. went on to describe what happened: "Payne, kind of walked to the side. I understood something deeper was going on. I went over and put my arm around him and said, 'Payne, I just want you to know I appreciate what God's doing with your heart.' He looked at me as hard as he could, and now tears were streaming down his face, and said, 'J.B., I'm not going to be a Bible-thumper. I'm not going to stand up on some stump. But I want everyone to know: It's Jesus! I just want everyone to know!'"

I distinctly remember Payne's putt on Number 18 at Pinehurst, which won him the U.S. Open. I was on vacation and watched the dramatic finish with a young Phil Mickelson. When the putt dropped, I leaped off the couch in celebration. I noticed he had something on his wrist and said to Jeanette, "I believe he is wearing a WWJD bracelet."

Payne and Tracey became active not only in worship attendance but also in Bible study, the life of our church, and our school. They even sponsored a cookout at their home to raise money for athletic fields for our young school. Thousands of dollars came in, with a large amount of it coming from Payne's generous heart.

On the Monday of the fatal plane crash, the headmaster of our school, Ed Gamble, and I started for the Stewart home as soon as we heard the news. We were met at their driveway by Tracey, who was weeping profusely. She fell in our arms as she desperately asked, "Why? It just can't be." We had no answers. Still don't.

Soon thereafter Chelsea and Aaron came home from school. We embraced. Tracey hugged them and took them into their bedroom to be alone with them. I closed the door and waited prayerfully. We could hear their cries. Our hearts ached as this beautiful family had their lives shattered in such an inexplicable event. After several minutes, I went in the room, hugged the kids, prayed, read Psalm 91, and recited John 11:25: *"I am the resurrection and the life. The one who believes in me will live, even though they die"*

In their home and around the house, friends quickly gathered. The Orel Hershishers, the Lee Janzens, Bill Curry, Jr., Mrs. Mark O'Meara, as well as Scott and Sally Hoch quickly came to be with the family. Scott said, "Payne could have been playing a charity match with me at Bay Hill. Instead, now he's gone."

Ed and I then drove to the Van Arden home. Their father, Robert, had also been on the plane. They too had children at our school. We gathered Debbie and their four children together, prayed, and read the Bible. By then, the school community and other friends were converging, bringing food and comfort.

The next days were a blur. I did a radio interview on Pat Robertson's *The 700 Club*. J.B. Collingsworth and I spoke on *CNN Live*. ESPN carried our interview with our local ABC affiliate. The Associated Press and other media outlets were flooding us with requests for anything you could imagine. The CBS local affiliate asked for an interview. Their reporter shared some intriguing information with me. He said their board had met earlier and decided to do a story on "what these people have that enables them to respond like this? We could not do that. Go find out what they have." Truly, the response of Tracey, Debbie, and the others was remarkable.

Tracey wanted our pastors and church to have a major part of the celebration of Payne's life. She wanted to have the service at the church. Through all of her grief, she did a stunning job in selecting who was to speak, as well as many of the arrangements. I was deeply honored that she wanted me to be a part of the service. The realization of the responsibility and opportunity overwhelmed me. I would have eight-to-ten minutes to comfort and offer testimony to an international audience. I prayed about what to say.

My friend, Pastor Ike Reighard, called from Atlanta with some ideas. I decided to go with a golf theme. Here again, I saw the providence of God. Just a few months earlier, Jeanette and I had begun to take golf lessons. Golf had been on my bucket list of things to do when I hit sixty.[70] Church member, Patti McGowan—an instructor at the David Ledbetter Golf Academy—had heard me say that when I reached sixty, I wanted to play golf. She remembered that, and one day she said, "I'll make a deal with you. You answer my Bible questions and I'll teach you to play golf."

Jeanette and I took her up on her offer. When Payne left us, I had learned some golf language and enough about the nuances of the game that I could frame my eulogy in golf terminology.

I wrote it in my study. It rolled out as fast as I could write. (I felt akin to George Frideric Handel when he wrote *The Messiah,* writing swiftly to produce that awesome music in only twenty-four days.) While I am no Handel, I did feel "caught up." When I forgot something, the Holy Spirit brought it back to me.

Payne's memorial was on a Friday. When I arrived at the church, the place was buzzing with thirty to forty mobile TV units, photographers, journalists: media everywhere. I met in one of our offices with Paul Azinger, Michael W. Smith, J.B. Collingsworth, and others to pray and walk through the order of service. J.B. had placed me earlier on the program, but I prevailed on him as I believed the Holy Spirit had given me a message and I needed to follow Him.

---

[70] Snow skiing was another that I tried out at Breckenridge, Colorado, with our family and my brother, Joe's family. But after going to the "Bunny Slope"—which appeared to be Mt. Everest to me—getting off the chair lift at the black slopes, taking two hours to scoot down on my rear end, having my grandchildren roar by me, and hearing their laughter at my pitiful attempt to ski, I went with golf!

The service that followed was one of the most powerful worship experiences in which I have ever been. Tracey's words were deeply moving. Azinger had us laughing and crying as he related personal events that he had shared with his fishing buddy. J.B. spoke and gave out WWJD wrist bands, which even the media reps wanted. The video of Payne's life flashed before our eyes as we watched and listened to the words of *If You Could See Me Now*. I watched the children. Aaron was more outwardly emotional than Chelsea. When I stood to speak, I was looking into the faces of many of golf's greatest: Jack Nicklaus, Ernie Els, David Duval, Tiger Woods, Hal Sutton, Greg Norman, Mark O'Meara, Fred Couples and Davis Love, III. I noted that Norman was deeply moved, and Fred Couples began to weep.

With my own heart and emotions galloping at full tilt, I shared my eulogy:

Where's Payne? Payne's in the Gallery

How do I remember Payne? That's a question I've been asked many times in the last few days. I'm sorry I didn't get to know him sooner. Although my time with Payne has been brief, it was a great relationship. I'm a new golfer, picking up the game when I was sixty years old. I can tell you one thing: Payne sure got me excited about golf!

I thought many times about how I could remember Payne. While I have a quiver full of memories about him, I have filtered my thoughts in these tumultuous days and have come up with one word that I think best describes Payne: cheerleader. The last time I saw Payne was at The First Academy football game on my birthday a few weeks ago. Jeanette and I were a little bit late, and we had to go to the top of the stands to find a seat. As we were sitting up there in the nearly packed stadium, all of a sudden I heard someone singing "Happy Birthday" and looked down ten rows or so below us, and there was a bunch of guys, sitting down singing—and right in the middle of them was Payne. He had his hat off and he was singing, "Happy birthday, Brother Jim." I thought, "I can't believe it! Here is a guy—with a bunch of other guys—at a football game, singing, 'Happy Birthday.' What a cheerleader!" Now, as I think about the events in the last couple of years of Payne's life, I think describing him as an enthusiastic cheerleader best sums it up.

It's been said that adulthood begins when a man begins to think about how he wants to be remembered. Payne first looked around and then finally he looked inside. He had everything, but there was a missing link—a void that nothing, no honor, no person could fill. And then something happened. A change took place. What happened? Payne described this dramatic change in his life by saying, "I'm proud of the fact that my faith in God is so much stronger, and I'm so much more at peace with myself than I've ever been in my life. Where I was with my faith last year and where I am now is leaps and bounds [apart]."

Using parable form, I believe this is what happened to make Payne's life so unique, beyond even the uniqueness of Payne that we already knew. Payne received an invitation to the World Open Invitational. Being the competitor, he jumped at the opportunity. With clubs in hand, he appeared at the gate of the most magnificent golf course he had ever seen. It was surrounded by soaring mountains, sparkling lakes, and clear creeks. The fairways were immaculate and very forgiving with every blade of grass perfectly tailored and each grain of sand in every bunker carefully raked in place. The clubhouse, even from a distance, was the most palatial he had ever seen. He thought it strange, however, that he could see no spectators, yet he could hear the faint sounds of a crowd's roar and, amazingly, the sound of the most unearthly music he had ever heard.

As he prepared to enter the gate, a strong-looking man with an imposing presence stood at the gate. "Where are your credentials, your money clip?"

"Is this some kind of joke?" Payne asked. "Listen, I've won three majors, been on the Ryder's Cup team several years, and am the third leading money winner. I'm not on the qualifying tour, you know."

"I'm impressed, Mr. Stewart, but it takes more than that."

"Hey, I'm a devoted family man. I love Tracey with all my heart. And Chelsea and Aaron are the best kids in the world. They love me and I love them dearly. I have a great family. Tracey's done a lot of the work, but I get a little credit on that, too, don't I? And I love my parents and my in-laws. I cherish my family."

"That's the way it's supposed to be. When the Master Designer planned all of this, He intended for the man to be committed to his wife and to train, provide for, and guide his children. You've done a good job, Payne, but there's more to it than that."

"Do you realize that I've given a fairly good hunk of my winnings to charities, especially to benefit children and schools? I have a huge place in my heart for children. They really touch me."

"Oh, Mr. Stewart, that's most admirable. The One I work for, once said, 'Let the little children come to me. For that's the kind of spirit that gets you into the Kingdom of God.'"

"Well, how about this? I go to church sometimes. Of course, unless I miss the cut, (which is rare). I can't make it often. Even though I can't always be there, I am definitely for the church."

"That's good. The Builder of this course also owns the church, and it's very special to Him, but you're still missing the mark. Payne, you have done so much so well, but that won't get you to the championship. I know you really want to get in on this, but there's only one way."

"Tell me what it is. I'll do whatever it takes."

"Oh, there is really nothing you can do. It's already been done for you by Someone who loves you incredibly. You need to check in with Him. He is over there by the gate."

"What gate?"

"There's only one gate, and you will recognize the Gatekeeper. He will be the only one there."

About that time a friend stepped forward and said, "Payne, let me help you towards the gate." And with this friend and some other friends, Payne was taken to the gate and introduced to the Gatekeeper. As they approached the gate, Payne noticed that it was a narrow gate, yet over the entrance it said, "Whosoever will, may come." Sure enough, there was a Gatekeeper there. He looked at Payne and said, "Payne, I've been looking for you."

"How long?" Payne asked.

The Gatekeeper responded, "From all eternity."

"You sound like God. Are you God?" Payne asked.

To this the Gatekeeper proclaimed, "I am! My Father and I are one. We designed this place for all who accept our invitation."

"Here I am. I'm ready to play! What's the fee?"

"Payne, it's been paid for you."

"Who paid it?"

"I did."

"What did it cost you?"

"Everything."

"What do you mean, Sir?"

"I mean, Payne, it cost Me my life. I died for you." With that He held out His hands, and Payne saw the scars of nails where they had been driven into a cross.

Bewildered, Payne asked, "Sir, why did you do that?"

Then the Gatekeeper explained, "Payne, because this is a perfect place, only perfect people can get here. And, Payne, we both know that you are not perfect. You have some moral hooks, slices, and missed putts that we don't need to discuss now. You have an inborn flaw in the swing of your soul, and there's only one way to correct it. I want to be your Life Coach—for the rest of your life. Will you let me?"

"Yes, Sir, I will. But what must I do?"

"Only one thing. You've got to trust Me. You've got to put faith in Me. You trusted your earthly coach to correct your golf flaws. You must trust

Me to correct your spiritual flaws. I'm the One who can make you perfect by forgiving you. Payne, I love you. Do you invite Me into your life?"

Payne thought about it briefly. He, with his trademark knickers, knelt, removed his tam o'shanter cap, and said, "Sir, I want to invite You into my life. Will You forgive me of my sins? Please take control of my life. Thank You for dying for me. I want to do what the Master would have me do for the rest of my life."

In an instant Payne stood up and found himself in the warm embrace of the Gatekeeper. After a few moments he caught his breath. It seemed like a heavy load had been lifted from his soul—like the release that is felt after dropping a pressure putt on the 18th to win the Open—except this had a much more enduring effect. Payne gathered his wits and heard the Gatekeeper say, "Come in, Payne."

"Thank You, Sir. Wow! What a course! Can I play now? Oh, I forgot. You're in control. What can I do for You, Master?" Payne asked.

"I want you to be my cheerleader, Payne. There's a crowd gathering on the 18th and I think you'll fit right in."

Together they approached the 18th with its spectacular clubhouse. The roar of the crowd sounded like a thousand Niagara Falls. As he approached the gallery, Payne began to pick out some faces he recognized. He pointed and exclaimed, "There's Abraham, David, and Moses! There's Paul, John, Peter, James! Over there is Augustine, Calvin, Lincoln! Oh! Is it? Yes! There's Dad!"

There were millions upon millions of faces of every color from every nation there, as well as a myriad of angels packed in the bleachers. Payne could hold back no longer. He raced toward the crowd and joined the gallery as he heard the angels proclaiming, "You are worthy, our Lord and God, to receive glory and honor and power."

To that Payne exclaimed, "Yes!"

The angels continued proclaiming, "For You created all things, and by Your will they are created and have their being."

Swinging his cap in the air, Payne shouted, "Yes!"

The angels declared, "With Your blood You purchased men for God from every tribe and language and people and nation."

Payne exclaimed, "Yes!"

The angels lifted their voices in louder praise, saying, "Worthy is the Lamb, Jesus Christ, who was slain."

With that Payne threw his hands in the air and in loudest adoration shouted, "Yes!"

The heavenly crowd finished their tribute by proclaiming, "He is King of Kings and Lord of Lords."

And Payne cheered even more loudly, exclaiming, "Yes! Yes! Yes!"

You may ask, "Where's Payne now?" I am confident that Payne is in the gallery—the gallery of God's children who are forever joined in cheering on Payne's Coach and Payne's Savior. That's where Payne is. And that is where Payne delights in being.

It is important for those of us who appreciate golf to remember that there are two ways to spell golf. The choice is every person's.

First, golf may be spelled:

G*-Go* **O***-Out* **L***-Lost* **F***-Forever.*

Or, golf may be spelled:

G*-God* **O***-Offers* **L***-Love,* **F***-Forgiveness.*

You make the choice on how you choose to spell golf in your life. I am positive Payne would want you to join him with his friends in the gallery. As there were for Payne, there are friends who can take you to the gate and introduce you to the Gatekeeper. Do you want to join this gallery? Where's Payne? He's in the gallery. He'd like you to join him there some day.

Would you pray with me? "Thank You, Lord Jesus, that Payne and his fellow travelers accepted Your offer of love and forgiveness. We now rejoice that we, too, can have the blessed assurance of seeing Payne and, above all, You one day. For we understand and believe that all who accept Your offer of love and forgiveness will join in the heavenly gallery.

We ask that You help us make the same wise choice that Payne made. In Jesus' Name. Amen."[71]

The service was nearly two hours long. CNN broadcast it live, no commercials. Four local TV stations did the same. Golf Channel and others also aired the memorial. As the last notes of the music ended, the calls began. Letters, calls, and e-mails flooded our offices. Reports of numerous conversions and rededications were reported. To this day, I still meet people who watched the service and were profoundly affected. In retrospect, it dawned on me that I had the opportunity to share the gospel in that ten minute eulogy to millions of people—more than I would ever preach to in all my years of ministry. Payne's death and the mysterious malfunction of his aircraft remain a mystery. It is difficult to see God's hand in this, but one thing is undeniable: Payne's death resulted in untold numbers of people coming to personal faith in Jesus Christ or renewing their walk with Him. Payne Stewart won many trophies in his golf career; however, his eternal trophy lies in the reality that heaven's population was enlarged enormously by his life and his death. "If We Could See Payne Now,"[72] I think we would see that matchless smile and a host of golfers and others—now and yet to come—who are walking golden streets where there are no bunkers, no shanks, no out-of-bounds, and no three putts! Thank You, Lord, for that Missouri golfer, Payne Stewart.

---

[71] Henry, Jim. *Eulogy for Payne Stewart Memorial Service.* (First Baptist Church: Orlando, Florida). October 29, 1999.

[72] Reference to the Christian song "If You Could See Me Now" by Don Moen.

With All My Heart

To All Who Ask Why in the Shadow of Unexplainable Events:

Even Jesus on the cross threw out the haunting word of a searching heart: "Why?"[73] *Walking down the road with God's children, those who are not God's children, and those who are in our family, that question has been posed to me more times than I can remember. When faced with the incomprehensible and our finiteness, I have learned to respond, "I don't know." When a pastor colleague whose wife was dying from a terrible illness was asked, "Why?" the Holy Spirit whispered in his hear, "Trust Me." That is all we can do. "For now we know in part; then we shall know fully, even as we are fully known" (1 Corinthians 13:12).*

---

[73] Matthew 27:46.

CHAPTER TWENTY-FIVE

BACK-ROOM POLITICS, ROSE GARDEN, AND NATIONAL TREASURE

WAS SURPRISED WHEN A call came from Don Argue, the president of the National Association of Evangelicals, who, at the president's behest, asked me to come to Washington, D.C. to participate in a ceremony with a focus on children held in the Rose Garden the next day. Dr. Argue said that the president was also inviting Tom Trask, the general superintendent of the Assemblies of God. Scrambling to catch a flight on such short notice, I managed to arrive at Dulles Airport around midnight.

Early the next morning, prior to the Rose Garden ceremony, I joined a gathering that included James Dobson, founder of Focus on the Family; Adrian Rogers, senior pastor of Bellevue Baptist Church in Memphis, Tennessee and former president of the Southern Baptist Convention; Bill Bright, founder of Campus Crusade for Christ; Bob Dugan, the Director of the Office of Public Affairs of the National Association of Evangelicals; Senator John Ashcroft from Missouri; and several others. The focus of our group's discussion was centered on the evangelical vote in the forthcoming election. The consensus was that Dole could not defeat the president unless he generated more passion, as well as captured the evangelical vote. Adrian

Rogers said that someone needed to tell Senator Dole he could not expect the evangelical vote if he did not speak more clearly on moral issues.

Senator Ashcroft said he told Dole, "People aren't looking at your voting record on the moral issues. They want to hear you say it."

Adrian Rogers added, "You can't win with our vote, but you sure cannot win without it."

It was decided a small group—perhaps Bright, Dobson, and Rogers—would try to get Senator Dole's ear with our concerns, as well as the possibility of Senator Ashcroft's being the vice-presidential running mate. At the close of the meeting, we joined hands, and Dr. Bright asked me to lead in prayer.

I do not know if they ever got to Senator Dole or not. When I think of that meeting, I am reminded of Ashcroft's prior observation.

Following the meeting, we flagged a cab and dashed to the White House. Once there, Flo and Alexis—great aides to the president, who had become personal friends—met us at the door and ushered us past the Oval Office and to the Rose Garden for the ceremony.

Over one hundred beautiful children of all races and their chaperones had gathered. The president was about twenty minutes late in arriving; however, he took the time to greet the children and their chaperones, as well as to thank group for coming. While he gripped my hand with much strength, he appeared to be tired. The toll of the office and personal challenges were making their mark on him.

That weekend was highlighted by the presentation of the Congressional Gold Medal[74] to Billy and Ruth Graham, the first couple and first spiritual

---

[74] The Congressional Gold Medal and the Presidential Medal of Freedom are the highest civilian awards in the United States. George Washington was the first recipient of the Congressional Gold Medal. At the time of the Graham's receiving of this medal, only 263 others had been so honored.

leaders to ever receive this honor. We had heard that the president had not been invited, which I believe was a mistake. Though far apart on many issues, he still occupied the office of president and consistently had given evangelicals access to that office. Don Argue had mentioned this to the president in the Rose Garden. The president's countenance reddened as he responded, "That's all right. I understand. I had an hour with him yesterday."

After the Rose Garden ceremony, I went to Senator Dole's office for a reception for Billy and Ruth Graham. While I did not have an invitation, I walked in with the rest of the group with no problem. Senator Dole worked the crowd, but he was not very personable while doing so. He did not look us in the eye when he talked to us. Bob Clement—my old friend and Democratic Congressman from Tennessee—told Dole that I was "the president of all the Baptists in the world," (a little, political stretch there!).

"Yes," Dole said, "I see him all over the planet" (another political stretch!).

In that reception, I had the privilege of meeting Tricia Nixon Cox and her husband, Ed; Lynda Bird Robb (President Lyndon Johnson's daughter); and the iconic newscaster Paul Harvey and his wife, Angel. I enjoyed seeing NFL champion, Pro Football Hall of Fame and College Football Hall of Fame inductee, and sportscaster, Frank Gifford and his wife, talk show host, Kathie Lee—both of whom were known for being strong Christians.[75] I was pleased when I had my picture taken with Senator Jesse Helms of North Carolina, Franklin Graham, Senator Mark Hatfield of Oregon, and United States Senate Chaplain Dr. Lloyd John Ogilvie. What an eclectic group!

Following the reception, our group proceeded to the magnificent United States Capitol Rotunda, where the statues and portraits of past political

---

[75] Kathie Lee became a Christian at the age of twelve after watching the Billy Graham film, *The Restless Ones*.

luminaries stared down on us, for the Congregational Gold Medal ceremony. At this momentous affair, I was seated six rows from the front, where I
had the good fortune of sitting by James and Shirley Dobson, both of whom
were engaging conversationalists. I enjoyed getting to know this team, who,
for decades, have been the spokespeople for prayer and moral issues facing
our nation.

Once the ceremony commenced, Senator Dole, Newt Gingrich, and
Vice-President Al Gore gave speeches to honor the Graham ministry and its
enduring, worldwide impact. While Ruth Graham had to sit down after a few
minutes of all the festivities, Billy received the Congregational Gold Medal
with his usual humility amidst a thunderous and standing ovation. Calling
America to repentance and to stop its self-destruction, Billy proceeded to
preach as if we were in a stadium at one of his crusades. Packed with people
and its back wall jammed with media personnel and cameras, the rotunda
probably had never heard such a message proclaimed. It was all I could do to
keep from shouting "Amen!" and "Hallelujah!" as I heard the truth of God
proclaimed in such a powerful way. It was God, not Billy, who received all
the glory on this historic occasion. Truly, it was an unforgettable day.

With All My Heart

To All Living in Caesar's World:

*I heard well-known pastor Adrian Rogers says that all of life is poli-
tics. There are two kinds of politics: good politics and bad politics. I think all of us want to see good government made stronger
with good politics and good politicians. I think there was a period
when we worked hard at making government work better, often to*

be disappointed by people who said one thing and did another. We should continue making a positive alternative where we can. We cannot be isolationists. Until the righteous King comes to rule, the reality is the Kingdom of God has not yet arrived in its full perfection. That keeps me grounded when I want to scream at the foolish stupidity of the world system.

CHAPTER TWENTY-SIX

NEXT

READ SOMEWHERE THAT THE moment you succeed, you must start preparing for your successor to succeed. As I hit my sixties that weighed more heavily on me. *When do I leave? How do I leave?* I had watched some monumental failures in transition. I certainly did not want that to happen to our church, nor did I want to see a good part of my life's work go south. We were having some of our best years. No one mentioned anything about retiring, except for an occasional "you're not going to leave us" or something like that. Yet, I knew that there was the realization by some that I was becoming eligible to receive Social Security.

I observed coaches like Bobby Bowden of Florida State and Joe Paterno of Penn State successfully coach into their late seventies. One of my heroes, Dr. Criswell of First, Dallas, went into his eighties. My health was good, but it was taking more energy to maintain the pace; and my recovery time, after a demanding week of ministry and preaching, was taking longer, too. I made it a matter of continued prayer to seek God's wisdom and guidance in the course I should follow in wrapping up my ministry at First Orlando.

A game plan began to form in my mind. Knowing God's Word says *"plans fail for lack of counsel"* (Proverbs 15:22), I asked seven godly men to come to our house. All were businessmen. All loved our church and me. All would speak truth to me. The game plan was this: sometime in the future, at the nudging of the Holy Spirit, I would set a succession plan in motion. It would allow me to appoint a search team. They would bring God's man to the church. The church would call him to come alongside me in a copastor arrangement for a season. As he grew familiar with the people, staff, and the city, I would gradually back away from leading the staff and preaching. When he was solid in the saddle, I would move on. How long would this arrangement last? I privately told the men, (and, in time, my future successor, Dr. David Uth), the actual transition would all occur in two years or less. I felt if I set a deadline, I would be a lame duck and lose some effectiveness as pastor. The men promised to keep it in confidence—not even "pillow talk." I asked them to pray about what I had shared with them. Then, in one week, either give me a thumbs up or a thumbs down. One week later, I received a unanimous thumbs up from my group of confidants.

As the years went by it became increasingly evident that we needed to do at least two things: add a worship service—probably a Saturday night venue—and build more facilities. My concern was if I still had the energy to lead the people in another large building effort and another worship service. I had overseen about fourteen building programs and land purchase efforts during my ministry. Each took a toll on my energy, time, and resources. There was something else that was on my heart. I desired to be an encourager to churches and pastors. Some years before, the Lord had spoken a promise from His Word that leaped off the page into my heart: "*The righteous will flourish like a palm tree, they will grow like a cedar of Lebanon; planted in the house of the Lord, they will flourish in the courts of our God. They will still bear fruit in old age, they will stay fresh and green, proclaiming the Lord is upright; He is my Rock, and there is no wickedness in Him*" (Psalm 92:12-15).

Jeanette and I prayed about the plan I had shared with the men. In time, the "nudge" came. I shared the plan with our people. It was warmly received. Afterwards, I received numerous calls, letters, and e-mails, thanking me for the plan.

In May of 2005, I appointed a search team. This was no easy task. Our church was, and is, filled with some of the godliest, most mature men and women I have ever met. I made a long list of potential team members and prayed over the list. God led me in narrowing it to a final group. I chose John Bozard, greatly loved and respected in the church and in the business community, to be the spokesperson for the team. A letter was sent to each nominee asking them to pray about serving. All accepted.

We met for our orientation and instruction meeting. Several had never met each other, so we had a great time getting acquainted. Some of the counsel I gave them included:

- Choose a meal or a day each week to fast and pray.

- Encourage other church members—in fact, the entire church membership—to join them in doing so.

- Keep the church informed.

- Keep their discussions and choices to themselves. (Any leak, in Baptist circles, would soon spread like wildfire. The Baptist grapevine is faster than any computer!)

- I would serve as consultant to them, and may give them some names. However, the choice was to be theirs, not mine.

- Visit the top prospects in a worship service unannounced. Observe the little things: the atmosphere of the service, how the pastor walks away from the people, how he communicates the Word of God, and so on.

- Make notes. Compare notes with each other on the search team.

- When you get to the top three, meet with them and their spouses.

- Then choose God's man. Each person was to write his or her choice on paper, and turn it in to the chairman after much prayer.

- Their choice must be unanimous. They were not go to our people with even one negative vote.

They prayed. They cast their ballots. Every ballot had the name of David Uth, the greatly loved pastor of First Baptist Church, West Monroe, Louisiana. One member was torn between David and one other excellent candidate they were considering. However, when he saw the other results, he said, "Count me in. Let's be unanimous."

At that point, I was in touch with David. We spent the most part of a day in the Atlanta airport discussing everything we could possibly think of. I had compiled a page full of things about which I wanted to know. He, too, had his concerns. By the end of the day, I felt comfortable with everything I heard. My intense interest was born out of a passage of Scripture a seminary president, who was retiring after a long, successful tenure, quoted to me: "*I hated all the things I had toiled for under the sun, because I must leave them to one who comes after me. And who knows whether he will be a wise man or fool?*" (Ecclesiastes 2:18-19). While I did not hate, but rather loved that for which I had toiled, the rest of the passage resonated with me.

We made plans for David to come. The search team's work was fabulous. A week-long round of introductions and meetings was planned. We wanted as many as possible to meet David and Rachel before the Sunday he was coming to preach in view of a call. A beautiful brochure that introduced the Uth family was mailed to everyone in our church. The Friday night before David was to preach on Sunday, we had a Bible study teachers' and leaders' meeting at a hotel in Daytona Beach. This meeting had been planned months prior; however, it worked out perfectly for the Uths to meet the backbone of our church body.

While all of this was transpiring, something else was happening in the Henry household. Jeanette had gone in for her yearly physical and mammogram. While all was clear on her mammogram, Dr. Yonfa, her gynecologist—whom we had had the joy of visiting in his home and seeing him and his lovely wife, Estelle, nail down their relationship to Jesus as Savior and Lord—did something that I can only observe was a "holy hunch." As cancer ran in Jeanette's family, he sent her for a more diagnostic test of breast tissue. A spot no larger than the tip of the nail on your index finger was discovered. A surgery was performed. What we believed would be a benign spot, turned out to be malignant. Our world changed in a moment.

Jeanette had difficult, life-altering choices to make: lumpectomy, chemo, and/or mastectomy. We received wonderful counsel from doctors, nurses, and knowledgeable friends. We prayed, and Jeanette chose a double mastectomy. The word of the diagnosis came the Thursday before our call to the Uths. We told them but no one else beyond family, because we did not want any diversion from the historic moment before us. On Sunday, David preached magnificently to two worship services packed with excited First Family members. He was called unanimously and with a rousing standing ovation.

Plans for Jeanette's surgery were set for June. By this time, David would be on the scene. The surgery and reconstruction process would involve an eight-to-nine hour surgery. Recovery would take several weeks. With David at the church, he could jump in with our good staff and lay leaders to give me the opportunity to assist Jeanette in her recovery. This removed a tremendous amount of pressure from me and allowed me the privilege to look after my lady. The surgery was successful. No chemo or radiation were necessary—just a pill every day for five years. She was declared cancer free in 2011, and remains so as of this writing.

In retrospect, I saw the hand of God working from eternity. Each step we took fit into the gracious providence of God. Providence is a word that means "to see beforehand." Our Father saw! The timing was impeccable. Later, I wrote and preached a sermon I entitled "The God Upstream," taken from Joshua 3 and 4. God commanded the priests, who bore the Ark of the Covenant, to step into the flooding Jordan River to lead two million people into the Promised Land. The moment their feet hit those swirling waters, the river and ground dried up. That is mentioned four times in those chapters. They dried up beginning at a place called Adam, twelve miles upstream! We saw our God step into the swirling Jordan of our lives, and take us across on dry ground. What an awesome God and Father!

David and I sat down and mapped out a game plan. We would team-preach through the book of Philippians. When I was preaching, he could visit Bible study classes and schmooze with the people. This sped up the get-acquainted period. Our people quickly came to love David, Rachel, Joshua, Andrew, and Hannah. By January of 2006, I realized we would not need a two-year transition. I told my faithful assistant, Sandi, first. She cried, and so did I. Then I told David. It seemed that the last Sunday in March would be good.

The church gave us an unbelievable send-off. It was a long and sweet good-bye. They hosted dinners and receptions. Our daughter, Kitty, sang and played the song "Jesus is the Way Home." Family, church, and community leaders came to toast and, occasionally, roast us. On our last Sunday, we were overcome with the love and care they lavished on us: a golf outing to Scotland, a golf cart with cart fees paid for several years, a generous financial gift, the naming of an auditorium at Ridgecrest Conference Center in our honor, and the title of pastor emeritus. (I looked up the word *emeritus*. It is composed of two Latin words that in Tennessee vernacular means, "stick a fork in him, he's done"!)

Prior to that last worship service, I wanted to do something special for David. I decided to wash his feet as a part of passing the baton. When I told David my plans, he said, "No, the Holy Spirit told me to wash yours."

I protested, but how could I prevail against this six-foot-six, gentle giant? I decided to have a garment designed as similar as possible to what an Old Testament prophet would wear. On leather bands on the front would be emblazoned the names and tenure of our pastors dating back to our founding in 1871. The seamstresses in our church did a magnificent job. Today, it is still on display in our Faith Hall.

When David finished washing my feet, I read the passage from 2 Kings 2, where Elijah placed his cloak on Elisha, symbolizing the passing of leadership. I placed the mantle on David. He knelt, and I laid my hands on his head and prayed for the "double blessing" to be on David.

That service was one of the most powerful worship experiences in which I have ever taken part. We had prayed that our transition would be a positive example for other churches facing similar dynamics. We have been able to give counsel to a number of churches about transitioning, which God is using to His glory.

David Uth has completed eleven excellent years as our pastor. He has led the church to new heights in missions and ministry. He has been most thoughtful and kind to us. He has had me back to preach on several occasions. He is our pastor and greatly loved.

On my last Sunday as the senior pastor of First Baptist Orlando, I walked out the door and waved good-bye to a great and generous people. I bid the fondest farewell to nearly twenty-nine years of a walk with God and His people. During these years I had prayed about some other opportunities and offers that had come our way: president of my beloved alma mater New Orleans Baptist Theological Seminary; dean of the Pledger School of Practical Theology at Palm Beach University: and president of GuideStone Financial Services. I was humbled to be considered by these wonderful institutions. We prayed and sought God's face in these opportunities; however, we never got the green light to leave. I concluded that I needed to stay. God had given me a shepherd's heart for the local church. While walking away from these beloved people when our tenure was over was gut-wrenching, we were confident it was our time to leave. As we walked out to our cars, I looked around and saw my family, and was reminded of something I heard Ed Dobson say on one of Maurice Templeton's January Bible cruises. Ed, a prolific writer and significant pastor of a large Midwestern church, spoke to nearly a hundred pastors in an afternoon gathering. Ed was battling Lou Gehrig's disease for which there is no cure and results in a gradual loss of bodily function. His voice was still strong and clear as he talked for nearly an hour. He told our group, "When I realized I was terminal, I immediately refocused my spiritual roots, talking to Jewish and Christian coaches."

Ed then concluded his talk with three things for each of us to hang on to:

(1)   "Cherish every day. Make the most of it."

(2) "Wear your church lightly. Someone else's name will replace yours someday."

(3) "Your real family is your real family. Make them your priority."

Ed explained his last point by saying, "As I left my church on my last Sunday, I looked around me and I saw my wife, my children, my parents; and realized as much as the church loved me and as many cherished friends we had there; as I walked this road of struggle with my disease, my real family was my real family."

Then he looked at a room full of moved and attentive pastors, and said, "Don't forget, your real family is your real family." As I looked around me as I walked away from my tenure at First Baptist, I realized afresh, "my real family is my real family."

I was blessed to have a close group of men who were like brothers that were my Bible study and prayer group and with whom I have met every Friday morning for nearly fifty years of ministry at Two Rivers and First Baptist. They were men who had my back in prayer, counsel, and encouragement. (Every pastor should be blessed by such a group.) One who had been a part of my "band of brothers," Tom Gurney said, "Leave the woodpile bigger than you found it." I pray I did.

On my last day, I folded a large piece of paper and placed it on the desk behind which I had sat for nearly thirty years—the one Pastor David would now inherit. On the paper I had written four words: "THE BEST IS YET."

With All My Heart

To All Who Face Transitioning to the Brave New World of Retirement:

When you walk away from what you have done most of your life, it can rise up and smack you pretty hard. I was reminded that your job or calling is not who you are. It pays the freight for you to do what God has purposed for your life. It does not define you. God's not through with you when the last pay check comes. He simply redeploys you for a new mission to use your skill sets and wisdom in even greater measure. Retirement provides the time to draw closer to Him with whom you will be spending eternity. Plus, you get the added bonus of more time for the grandchildren!

CHAPTER TWENTY-SEVEN

I FORGOT TO REMEMBER

SOME YEARS AGO, JEANETTE and I went to see the movie *The Notebook*. It was the story of a couple who had been happily married for years when the wife was stricken with Alzheimer's. The story was powerful and emotionally charged. I had no idea at that time we would be walking down the same road with Jeanette a few years later.

It crept in quietly. I remember finding a pair of my socks in the dishwasher and teasing her about it. She denied it. So I joked, "A little elf did it," and we laughed it off.

A few other things began to show up: forgetting the names of longtime friends and church members; taking a long time to make menu choices; trouble keeping bills paid—sometimes duplicating checks.

She had a different gait when she walked. Something just was not right. I decided to meet with my daughter Betsy to see if she had noticed anything unusual about her mother. Before I had a chance to contact Betsy, I received a text message from her that read, "Dad, could you meet me at Panera's? We need to talk about Mom."

Betsy and I met. When we compared notes, she said she had seen some of the same things. A couple of Jeanette's close friends had asked Betsy if everything was okay with her mother as Jeanette seemed "a little different." As we talked, tears welled up in her eyes and mine. With an unspoken grief about what we were sensing might be a new and different world for all of us, we gripped each other's hands.

Jeanette and I visited our doctor for her regular checkup. In the course of our visit, he gave Jeanette three objects to remember. A few minutes later, he asked her what those three things were. She could not remember. He advised we see some specialists in the field of neurology. Then he turned to me and said, "Buckle up. You may be in for a wild ride." It shocked me that he said it in her presence. The sheer rawness of his statement temporarily numbed me.

We got in our car and drove away. Jeanette did not mention it. However, every time I looked at her and we talked about the routine things of life, I could not picture this brilliant, cum laude college grad losing the ability to do the simple things of life.

Jeanette and I began a series of visits and tests with some of the best neurologists in the state. One recommended that she not drive for a while. He also placed her on two medications. When I googled these medications, I discovered they were supposed to slow the effects of dementia, but not cure it. The new meds were not effective. In fact, they made her worse so we stopped using them.

In the beginning, she seemed to recognize that something was wrong. She would say: "Something isn't right." "My mind isn't working." "Am I losing my mind?" We would assure her that it was just a part of aging, and explain that we were giving her medicines to alleviate some of these challenges. That seemed to calm her. She seemed to be most troubled that she could not drive and had lost her independence.

Things at which she never blinked now became mountains to climb. She got nervous about having family or guests in the home. Selecting clothes became an ordeal. She was fearful and insecure. She did not want me out of her sight. Preparing meals became difficult. She forgot which buttons turned on which part of the stove. Forgetfulness began to affect her in many ways. Knowing our grandchildren's names, even our sons-in-law, became difficult. I began to hear her call the names of people she knew as a child: her childhood friends, neighbors in their farm community, school teachers, and principals.

One day when our son, Jim, his wife, Tammy, and our grandson visited us, she came into the bathroom and asked, "Who are those people in our house?" The list could go on, but the reality of a "new normal" settled into my mind and our family's lives.

Though I knew people, including family members who had dealt with dementia, I only knew about it at an arm's length. Now, it had walked right into the middle of our existence. I read all I could on the disease. Kind people who had walked that road with loved ones gave good counsel. I learned to do things around the house that she usually handled. My job description grew. I was business administrator, chauffer, pharmacist, dishwasher, day-planner, grocery-shopper, menu-planner, appointment-maker, and decision-maker.

One of the most difficult challenges I faced was having to learn to lie to my beloved wife, which I found tremendously difficult as I had spent most of my life speaking the truth and not lying! Nearly every day, she asks, "Where is Mom?" At first, I told her she was in heaven, (where she has been since 1985). She would insist, "No, she isn't. I talked to her this morning." Soon I learned to respond in a way that would not cause Jeanette any more distress, such as: "She went to the Bible conference," or "She is shopping with her friends." To this day that seems to satisfy her.

I am still learning to live in Alzheimer's world! I never say, "Do you remember?" as, for the most part, she does not. A maxim I have learned about Alzheimer's world is "First in; last out. Last in; first out." While she does recall people, places, and events from years gone by, she cannot remember the name of the restaurant in which we are dining, even though I have told her a half-dozen times in the last few minutes.

One day as she was talking, Jeanette said, "I guess I forgot to remember." That is her world now. However, there are some things she still regularly practices—things drilled into her mind from childhood and in her spiritual journey. She reads her Bible every night, which had been her lifelong practice. She still, by memory, sings the hymns of faith, which she has sung for decades. She still kisses me goodnight every night, sometimes twice! Sometimes I am her husband, Jim, to her. Other times, I am her dad. Occasionally, I am her old boyfriend!

On several occasions when we have been traveling to our condo in North Carolina or back to our Orlando home, she will say, "Where are you going to spend the night?" I respond, "In our house." She promptly (and firmly) says, "No! You will have to find a room somewhere else. We are not married yet. If you say overnight, what will people think? It would ruin everything we have stood for. Our Christian witness would be gone. What would our parents and friends say?" Upon hearing her response, my heart smiles with gratitude that even Alzheimer's cannot drive away the deep things of God planted early in life. I also pray she will soon forget her adamant demand that I find a motel room to stay in until we get married!

There is so much I miss because of her illness. I miss her keen mind and intelligent insights. I miss conversations about our past, our friends, and events that no longer register and that we are unable to discuss. I miss her great sense of humor, her wise counsel, and godly insight. I miss being her husband for a good part of most of our waking hours. I miss playing golf with her and doing things together. I miss discussing the news of the day and theological issues. Yet, in all of this, I remain grateful to God for the privilege of being her caregiver as long as I can; for family, friends and volunteer caregivers; for prayers and encouragement that frequent my e-mail, text, and mailbox; and for the promise that one day "now she knows in part, then she shall know fully, even as she is fully known" (1 Corinthians 13:12 paraphrase).

One night after she had gone to bed, the reality that the Jeanette I had known and loved for fifty-six years, was not the same Jeanette, hit me. It was one of the stages of grief with which I have had to deal in this heartbreaking process of losing the Jeanette I have always known and loved. I was forced to come to the sober realization that I would now have to feast on the multiple blessings and experiences the Lord had given us. I would have to go fishing in my memory well. Out of my deep hurt, I cried. In my desperate need for solace and courage, I cried out to my Lord Jesus and asked Him to help me be whomever I needed to be to her as long as I could. I threw myself on the only One who could carry me through these uncharted waters, and asked Him to help me trust Him to carry us through whatever might lay ahead of us. I rejoice to share that He has, He does, and He will!

I have learned to cherish the small things more than I ever did. For example, when she says, "I love you, Daddy. You are the best daddy in the whole world." I have come to look deeper at the message she is trying to convey. So, the best way I can share my love and appreciation of her is to respond, "Jeanette, you are the best daughter a daddy could ever have. And I love you." There is a sweetness and a new dimension of love between us I have never before experienced. Jeanette, the caregiver, is now the one being cared for.

I read that the Chinese have a saying that we are not born fully human and that we only become so as we practice caregiving—much as a parent does for a child. The vows we exchanged on December 27, 1959—"...in sickness and in health, for better, for worse..."—are being fleshed out in real time. I pray I am not only becoming more fully human, but more fully engaged and like Christ, who is in me. I have learned to praise Him daily, allowing Him to conform me to His likeness through the hardest challenge I have ever faced: the prolonged process of losing my partner, my best friend, my comforter, my beloved Jeanette.

Life is a journey... a journey with open roads and dead ends; twists and turns; the predictable and the surprises; joys and sorrows; the familiar and the mysterious. I have been wonderfully blessed to journey nearly six decades with a truly remarkable lady, whom I love with all my heart.

The Journey I Well Remember

The journey began on a fall afternoon in Georgetown, Kentucky, when I spotted a lovely, black-headed, Kentucky belle walking with a guy totally undeserving of such beauty. I moved quickly to relieve her of this burden. Thus, began the journey.

The journey began with two years of dating that produced a relationship that had some starts and misses.

The journey got serious when I gave her my fraternity pin after she told me to make up my mind or hit the road! I decided if I hit the road I wanted to hit it with this lassie from Bear Wallow Road in Cave City, Kentucky.

The journey escalated when I took her to Nashville to meet my dad and mom. I knew I was in the trap when Dad asked her why she went to college, and Jeanette replied, "To get a husband." Dad's quick response was, "Son, you've had it."

The journey nearly train wrecked when I showed up at her house for the first time, and a gentleman showed up at the door. Being the outgoing conversationalist that I am, I instigated the first remarks with the words, "You must be Jeanette's grandfather." He said nothing, left the room, only to come back and be introduced as Jeanette's father. It took about fifteen years for Papaw to forgive me!

The journey almost abruptly ended when I surprised her at the county fair and saw her walking around with an old boyfriend! It took a while for me to cool off, be convinced it was a chance meeting, and I was number one.

The journey was tested when I graduated and went off to Panama City to teach while Jeanette was still in school. That summer, she took her first flight on the old Republic Airlines to Knoxville; and I drove over the mountains from Ridgecrest to see her.

The journey was headed toward marriage; however, the one thing we had to settle completely in our hearts was whether or not Jeanette was willing to serve with me in ministry. The Lord was so good to have gone before us in leading Jeanette in making that commitment. We were able to settle that important decision that same fall night in October of 1959.

The journey reached a most important destination on December 27, 1959, when we tied the knot at Salem Baptist Church, which was filled with family and friends. We enjoyed a brief honeymoon as Jeanette had to return to college and I had to get back to my teaching position in Panama City.

The journey took an interesting turn when Jeanette graduated and joined me in Panama City. As I drove her to the little house I had rented and painted canary yellow, I asked her to guess which one was ours to which she responded, "I sure hope it is any one, except that ugly, yellow one. Who in the world would paint something that color? What were they thinking?!"

The journey reached a new level of testing when we bought a German shepherd puppy we named Rommel. His presence in our home lasted about a week as he ate not only his food, but our chairs, tables, and carpet as well!

The journey wound through summer staff at Ridgecrest then off to New Orleans Seminary. Jeanette taught school in a tough section of New Orleans—the experience included several stare-downs with hard-nosed Cajun children—and then a stint at Charity Hospital in a government position.

The journey added a fresh look when our first baby, Jamae Kathryn Henry, entered the picture at Baptist Hospital in New Orleans on Halloween night, October 31, 1981. While Jeanette was delivering, I was studying for a Hebrew and Greek test.

The journey found us at our first church, Mt. Pisgah, in the piney woods of Mississippi. There we survived a firing attempt as we learned a lot about people, culture, and tradition. That trial-by-fire toughened us for other faith-stretching experiences down the road.

The journey next took us to the cotton fields of North Mississippi and Hollywood Baptist Church, where we had no air conditioning in our home. After purchasing a window air conditioning unit and opening a window to put it in place, there were so many mosquitos that came in the window that Jeanette used a vacuum cleaner to suck them off the walls and ceiling.

The journey enlarged when Jane Elizabeth joined us on a bright July day at Baptist Hospital in Memphis, Tennessee in 1963. We were now a happy family of four!

The journey took a new direction when Nashville came calling in February of 1965 for us to head back home to pastor a young, three-year-old church in a pastoral setting of horses, cows, a dairy, and an eight-car ferry to move us from one side of town to the other.

The journey expanded our family size and budget on June 7, 1967, when James Bascom Henry II, came into our world at Baptist Hospital in Nashville. He had a little problem at birth that put a scare into our lives. Through this stormy experience, Philippians 4:19[76] came alive for us.

The journey allowed us to enjoy twelve-and-a-half momentous years, close to home and watched God's power and miracles take place. While we could have spent a life there, our Lord had another mountain for us to climb.

The journey called for us to leave family, friends, and a great ministry to jump into a historic First Baptist Church, Orlando. Jeanette was praying there was no Baptist Hospital in Orlando!

The journey for twenty-nine years was a magnificent odyssey in a booming city and a faith-filled church. During those years, Caleb became our first grandchild. Danny, Stan, and Tammy joined our family circle. Then came Seth, Trey, Asa, and Will—all of whom added a ton of joy to our journey. And then came Cali, and soon our first great-grandson, Shiloh, and great-granddaughter, Belle.

The journey of fifty years has had the usual tears and laughter. Grandparents and parents have left us. While their absence has left large holes in our hearts, we rejoice in the knowledge we will rejoin them one day.

The journey has given Jeanette and me three lifetimes of blessings and privileges. We have met presidents and governors; All-Americans, coaches and spiritual leaders; the humble and the ordinary; the giants and the extraordinary. We have had little and had much. We have traveled from

---

[76] "And my God will meet all your needs according to the riches of His glory in Christ Jesus" (Philippians 4:19).

Oslo to Oregon; Cairo to Copenhagen; Bethlehem to Boston; Gettysburg to Glasgow; Normandy to New York; Amazon to Anaheim; Paris to Prague. We have cruised, flown and walked oceans and rivers and mountains and deserts. We have listened to the distant howl of dogs from our porch at Wolf Laurel; the ocean waves at New Smyrna and Maui; the pounding waters of Iguazu Falls; and the gentle rains of Scotland.

Through the journey my companion and lover, confidant and prayer partner has been the steady hand at the wheel of our home and mission. Jeanette has courageously gone through the valley of the shadow in bringing our children into the world, suffering the darkness of depression, and dealing with the scourge of cancer. She has devotedly stood by my side through receptions and meetings. She has graciously reached out to the unsung, the unloved, and the ungodly. She has skillfully been seamstress and decorator; chef and engineer. She has lovingly encouraged women and pastor's wives. She has faithfully taught the Word of God and lived it. Her life is one of integrity and truth. Her greatest love: our Savior; her greatest joy: her family. She can be as tough as hardwood, yet as tender as a snowflake. She has tenaciously been the glue—the powerful adhesive—in our family and ministry.

The journey continues. The road before us shorter than the one behind us. We will walk that road hand and heart together so long as our Father grants us the privilege. If I had the opportunity of a thousand lifetimes, I would choose Jeanette to be my journey partner. She has given me her lifetime along with the time of my life.

With All My Heart

To Those Whose Loved One Is Journeying with the Long Good-bye of Alzheimer's Disease, Dementia, and Other Mental or Emotional Illnesses:

I had to go back to school when the reality of Jeanette's illness sank in. It was an education of unlearning, relearning, and new learning. I don't know if you have ever graduated from that university. If you have, you pray that you will pass the many tests! With long, required research sessions in the library, the challenging field of forgetfulness has more pop quizzes than I ever imagined. All of this is necessary to prepare you for the new, higher-level courses that are a part of tackling the rigors of this disease. Although I have tried my best, I do not know how well I have done in all of my preparation. However, I do know my new life studies have given me a greater compassion for all who deal with these illnesses every day of their lives. I have gained a very deep appreciation for caregivers who help me and others shoulder the burden of lovingly and compassionately embracing the opportunity to demonstrate Christ's loving care to our loved ones who can no longer care for themselves in the way they formerly were able to do. I have begun to better embrace the promise that there will be the day when "we shall see Him and be like Him."[77] I am at the point where I am feeling no self-pity, just learning on the everlasting arms of Him who promised, "My Presence shall go with you, and I will give you rest" (Exodus 33:14). His grace is truly sufficient. It is enough. In fact, it is more than enough to get me and others like me through this course of life.

---

[77] 1 John 3:2.

CHAPTER TWENTY-EIGHT

THE BEST IS YET

Always true to His Word, the Lord has kept me busy "teaching this generation."[78] My days and years have been wonderfully challenging and filled with opportunities. I am privileged to serve as an adjunct professor at New Orleans and Golden Gate Baptist Theological Seminaries. I have been interim pastor at Green Street Baptist in High Point, North Carolina; Biltmore in Asheville, North Carolina; Mt. Vernon in Boone, North Carolina; First Baptist in Ocala, Florida; First Baptist in Plant City, Florida; First Baptist in Bradfordville, Florida; First Baptist in Charlotte, North Carolina; Germantown Baptist in Memphis, Tennessee;[79] and Downtown Baptist in Orlando, Florida.

I have enjoyed each one of these opportunities. I have met some tremendous men and women on the staffs and in the congregations, as well as built friendships that continue to this day. Being interim allows me the privilege to encourage churches; assist in making changes before the next pastor arrives; consult with staff, deacons, elders and leaders; speak the truth in

---

[78] Reference to "The Great Commission," Matthew 28:18-20.

[79] This was my shortest term as interim pastor. It only lasted a few months as their search team found their next pastor. I told the church I lasted about as long as one of Elizabeth Taylor's husbands!

love; and make helpful observations as a pair of fresh eyes on the scene. Since I have no dog in the hunt (apart from the advancement of the Kingdom of God), most churches receive the counsel with gratitude. They do not always follow through; however, at least, they are aware of needed adjustments. After I have done that, the ball is in their court.

One of my most rewarding endeavors is my continuing to take groups to Israel. I never tire of going. I learn new things every time. To see the joy of pilgrims walking in the footsteps of Jesus, the apostles, and patriarchs is worth the long trip. Through the years we have seen many come to faith in Jesus, and many have been deeply encouraged in their faith; had the accuracy and inerrancy of the Bible verified; and developed a new interest in history and prophecy. One of my greatest joys has been to take my parents, our children, grandchildren, and in-laws on this journey. I have baptized all our grandsons in the Jordan River as it flows out of the Sea of Galilee.

I have not retired since leaving First Baptist Orlando. Rather, I have been "redeployed." Some of the other ministries that have occupied these years of redeployment have included addressing deacon conferences at the church, association, and state level; helping conduct staff and leadership retreats; speaking at marriage conferences; challenging at mission and generous giving meetings; entertaining through sharing stories at senior adult gatherings; mediating conflicts with troubled churches and personnel; preaching at evangelism and state convention meetings, church revitalization conferences; and serving as a trustee at GuideStone, as well as Southern Baptist Theological Seminary.

How long this continues will be dependent on the sovereignty of God, Jeanette's well-being, my health, and the opportunities my Lord provides. Of this I am sure: The road before me in this world is much shorter than the walk behind me. I know when the time comes for my exit, I am not going to be like Enoch who "*faithfully walked with God; then he was no more, because God took him away*" (Genesis 5:24)—unless the rapture occurs. Nor will I be like Elijah, who was "walking along... [when] suddenly a chariot of fire and horses of fire appeared... and Elijah went up to heaven in a *whirlwind*" (2 Kings 2:11). But what an exit that would be!

It could be like my first pastor—Dr. W. F. Powell, First Baptist Nashville—who, after retiring, stayed busy preaching and so on. One evening, while being driven to a nearby city to preach, he and his driver passed the Tennessee Highway Patrol headquarters. Dr. Powell, a chaplain for the THP, commented, "I've just been promoted" (speaking of a recent upgrade he had been given as an honorary patrol member). A few minutes later, the driver turned and asked Dr. Powell, who was riding in the back seat: "Would you like to stop for something to eat?" There was no answer. Dr. Powell had just been promoted!

Pray that I finish well and finish strong. But at the end of the walk, when I go home and see my Lord Jesus in whatever manner He chooses, I imagine a scenario that occurred with my experience with Jeanette when she was being rolled out of the recovery room after her long cancer surgery. The nurses stopped long enough for me to hold her hand and kiss her. Still groggy from the anesthesia, she said, "Did I do okay? Did I do okay?"

"Honey, you did great," I lovingly assured her.

A faint smile spread across her face and she said, "Thank You, Jesus. Thank You, Jesus. Thank You, Jesus."

So when my footsteps halt, and I kneel before my magnificent Lord and Savior, I might well ask, "Lord Jesus, did I do okay?" My heart's greatest desire to hear Him say, "*Well done, good and faithful servant*" (Matthew 25:21). To which my humble response will forever be: "Thank You, Jesus! Thank You, Jesus! Thank You, Jesus!"

In the depths of my heart, I long to hear my Lord welcome me to my eternal home that has been prepared for each of His children after they have made their way in the world: "Come, walk with Me. 'No eye has seen, no ear has heard, and no mind has conceived, the things God has prepared for those who love Him" (1 Corinthians 2:9).

Let's walk!

The Best Is Yet!

With All My Heart

To All My Fellow Travelers Who Have Yet to See Our Father's House:

A brother in Christ went to see his dad, who was in his last stages of a war with cancer. A bus driver for many years, his father said to the son, "When I am gone, don't cry for me. I am going to experience the most exciting trip of my life." Sooner or later, we all arrive at the departure gate. Until that day, we should look at life's end as one of my pastor friends who is also battling illness. He said, "Even though I know I am going to see Jesus, I want to live as long as I can. I am greedy for life."

Only two men never died: Enoch[80] and Elijah.[81] Lazarus died and was resurrected;[82] however, his personal account of what happened

---

[80] Hebrews 5:11.

[81] 2 Kings 2:1.

[82] John 11:1-45.

after death is not recorded in Scripture. Because death is a road we have never walked and an experience we have never had, there is a measure of uncertainty in our minds about the mystery of that great unknown. While we, as believers in Jesus Christ, do not fear eternal separation from God, we do receive great comfort from God's promise: "I am with you always, even to the end of the age."[83] Jesus: He truly is all we need.

[83] Matthew 28:20.

IF YOU'RE A FAN OF THIS BOOK, PLEASE TELL OTHERS...

✔ Write about Jim Henry's **Son of a Gunn** on your blog, Facebook and Twitter.

✔ Suggest the book to your friends, neighbors and family.

✔ When you're in a bookstore, ask them if they carry the book.

✔ This book is available through all major distrib-utors, so any bookstore that does not have this book can easily stock it!

✔ Write a positive review of **Son of a Gunn** on www.amazon.com.

✔ Purchase additional copies to give away as gifts.

CONNECT WITH US...

To order another copy and or learn more about Jim Henry, go to **www.jimhenry.today**.